Study skills

Bill Kirton

Prentice Hall
is an imprint of

PEARSON

Harlow, England • London • New York • Boston • San Francisco • Toronto • Sydney • Singapore • Hong Kong
Tokyo • Seoul • Taipei • New Delhi • Cape Town • Madrid • Mexico City • Amsterdam • Munich • Paris • Milan

PEARSON EDUCATION LIMITED
Edinburgh Gate
Harlow CM20 2JE
Tel: +44 (0)1279 623623
Fax: +44 (0)1279 431059
Website: www.pearsoned.co.uk

First Published in Great Britain in 2010

© Pearson Education 2010

The right of Bill Kirton to be identified as author of this work has been asserted by
him in accordance with the Copyright, Designs and Patents Act 1988.

ISBN: 978-0-273-73437-6

British Library Cataloguing-in-Publication Data
A catalogue record for this book is available from the British Library

Library of Congress Cataloging-in-Publication Data
Kirton, Bill.
    Brilliant study skills / Bill Kirton.
        p. cm.
    Includes bibliographical references.
    ISBN 978-0-273-73437-6 (pbk.)
  1. Study skills. 2. Report writing. 3. Education, Higher. I. Title.
    LB2395.K378 2011
    371.3028'1--dc22

                                                2010010956

10 9 8 7 6 5 4 3 2 1
14 13 12 11 10

Typeset in 10.5/14.5 Plantin by 30
Printed and bound in Great Britain by Ashford Colour Press Ltd, Gosport, Hants

About the author

Before taking early retirement to become a full-time writer, **Bill Kirton** was a lecturer in French at the University of Aberdeen. He has also been a Royal Literary Fund Writing Fellow at the RGU in Aberdeen, and the universities of Dundee and St Andrews. His radio plays have been broadcast by the BBC and on the Australian BC. His crime novels and a historical novel have been published in the UK and the USA and his short stories have appeared in several anthologies. He lives in Aberdeen with his wife, Carolyn.

His website is **www.bill-kirton.co.uk** and his blog is at **http://livingwritingandotherstuff.blogspot.com/**

Contents

part 4 Developing the necessary writing skills 169

part 5 Developing the necessary research and dissertation skills 249

part 6 Developing the necessary examination skills 313

Publisher's acknowledgements

*B*rilliant Study Skills draws on the researches and writings of Kathleen McMillan and Jonathan Weyers as published in *The Smarter Study Skills Companion*; *How to Write Essays and Assignments*; *How to Write Dissertations and Project Reports*; and *How to Succeed in Exams and Assessments*.

Introduction: You are here

The title we've chosen for this introduction is the solid bit of information you need whenever you're consulting a map on a notice board in an unfamiliar town or in a shopping centre. And that's exactly where you're standing at the moment in terms of your university career. You know you have a place, you may have a more or less clear idea of where you want to end up, so you'll want help finding how to get there. That, in brief, is what this book is for.

So, first, what's wrong with these two sentences (both of which you'll find in this book)? 'This opens up possibilities for every student, whatever their personality or preferences' and 'Ask a member if you can go along with them.'

Well, in case you didn't spot it, they're examples of the same grammatical 'error' (note the quote marks). In the first part of each sentence, we've mentioned something that's singular – 'student' and 'member' – but in the second part, they've become plural – 'their' and 'them'. The reason we put quote marks around 'error' is that usage is making those 'errors' acceptable and so all but the purists see nothing wrong with what we've written.

And then there's the whole problem of political correctness and gender-specific language. When we give examples involving an individual student or lecturer, do we say he or she? Or do we stay correct, use the either/or form and write sentences such as 'The student must ensure that he or she writes his or her essays in a style that suits himself or herself?' We hope the answer to that one is self-evident.

The reason we're starting with these questions is to warn you against copying the style of this book in your academic writing; it breaks lots of the rules which you'll need to respect. Our aim here isn't to be academic or formal; we want our style to be personal, conversational, direct and easy to read. So we don't mind starting sentences with 'And' and 'But' and we'll be using the sort of contractions familiar in everyday speech, such as 'you'll', 'we've' and 'doesn't'. We don't want the writing to be sloppy or to give you examples of 'bad' English, but nor do we want to be constrained by the formality of conventional academic style.

So that's why we've used the 'incorrect' formulae in the sentences we quoted. And the way we'll overcome the gender-specific issue is by using 'he' or 'she' at random. Students and lecturers alike will sometimes be male, sometimes female. There'll be no attempt to make sure there's a fifty–fifty split to guarantee political correctness either.

Here's another example taken from the book: 'Tell participants how you'll be storing their data and when you'll delete or destroy it.' What's wrong with that? Well, 'data' is plural, although common usage rarely acknowledges that. If we'd insisted on academic 'correctness' there, the sentence would have read: 'Tell participants how you'll be storing their data and when you'll delete or destroy them', which is highly ambiguous.

So our main intention is to communicate.

As the book's title shows, our stress is on study skills – not just those which apply directly to your reading and attendance at lectures, but to the whole range of things at which you need to become proficient to make your university life more fulfilling. We want to help you focus on essentials, encourage you to do things which enable you to get the most out of your social life as well as your studying. We want to help you to get organised, manage your time properly and feel more confident about your work. University is just about the only place you'll get time to read all you want and be free to explore both the world and yourself.

The book is organised in six parts. Part 1 deals with all the preparations you need to make before you get there – administrative and personal things such as accommodation, finding your way around, and opening bank accounts. Part 2 aims to start getting you organised, help you to find out who you are, what type of learning suits you and what you want to get out of it all. In Part 3 we move to academic skills such as getting the most from lectures and tutorials, and Part 4 concentrates specifically on writing. Part 5 deals with what you need to consider when you have to research a longer piece of work such as a dissertation or report. And the last part focuses on exams and how to prepare for and cope with them.

You'll find that some points, such as those concerning plagiarism, value judgements and note-making formats, are repeated in different places. We've done this deliberately whenever we feel it's worth stressing or re-stressing something. With tricky areas such as plagiarism, we need to reinforce our message.

If, when you've read the book, it's helped you to feel more confident about things, we've achieved our goal. University is a great opportunity for self-discovery and a great foundation for your future. It's also a place where you can enjoy things to the full. We hope this book will help you to get the most out of all its aspects.

PART 1

Getting
yourself ready

1 Getting ahead of the game

This book is about the many different aspects of university life that might affect you. It'll obviously focus on the specific skills you'll need to get the most out of your studies, but there are things you can organise at the outset to make life easier for yourself.

Before you start

Before you even get to sit in a lecture, write an essay or open a course book, you'll need to ask yourself a few questions about things such as study techniques, how you're going to pay for it all, where you're going to be living and what sort of social and personal life you'll be leading.

Going to university is a big step. It's challenging but it's exciting and opens up possibilities for every student, whatever their personality or preferences. The education you'll get there will come from books, lectures and chats with fellow students, but also from learning to handle the mundane aspects of daily living and from the new social situations in which you'll find yourself.

If you're just starting out, there may be some things about it which seem slightly scary, but it'll give you plenty of opportunities to do new things, some of them quite surprising. For many, it turns out to be a life-changing experience. Make the most of it because, before you realise it, it'll all be over.

At this stage, it makes sense to ask yourself some questions. What do you want to get out of it? And how can you set about achieving that? Well, first let's work through the basics that you need to get right before you even get there. There are the academic aspects, of course, but there's also finance, accommodation, and the day-to-day business of looking after yourself and making your life as full and satisfying as possible.

There's no single rule that covers everyone. You may have just left school or college or you may have left some years ago and be coming back to study after doing other things. People have different interests, different priorities, and some have more resources (financial and otherwise) to indulge themselves. But the basic environment and challenges of university life are much the same for everyone. It's how you react to them that matters.

So, you know who and where you are now, but what about in five or ten years' time? Do you have any particular goals in life? What sort of career do you want? If you're not sure yet, do you think going to university will help you to choose one? The sort of answers you give to these questions will help you to make the necessary choices. If you've decided what job you want, you'll have a better idea of the subjects you need to study. And if you haven't, you can choose combinations to keep your options open.

brilliant tip

It's early days – you don't need to make definitive choices yet. Circumstances may change, things may happen which shift your priorities. Keep an open mind, but think positively about why you're at university at all. It needn't commit you irrevocably to a single course of action, but it'll help to ground you. Take time out. Get your mindset right.

The academic you

In general terms, university gives you more freedom to seek out information and use it in your own individual way. The academic skills you need may be quite different from those you used at school or college. So, rather than be surprised by it, do a quick inventory of what you think your skills are. That way you'll know your strengths and also where you need to improve.

Try to work out the kind of learner you are. Do you already have an idea of what's involved in studying at university? Will it be all work and no play? Is it the type of work you've done before? And, as you ask yourself these things, think of the implications of your answers. Are you ready to put in the necessary effort to be successful? Can you do it alone or will you need help from others? And exactly what skills do you think you're going to need?

Know the game

The first step towards making things go your way is to understand the game. Think about it all, work out what's needed, play to your strengths. Once you get going, you'll see more clearly what's available in terms of support. There'll be skills-related courses and workshops, such as those for working with IT or improving your writing. You'll have access to textbooks, self-help books such as the one you're reading now, and web-based resources. Your tutors and other support staff will be there to offer free, confidential advice on all aspects of study. And, as you get more involved in written work and classes, you'll get feedback in many forms – written, verbal, continuous assessments and more – which you can think about and use to keep on improving.

You're not on your own; the system's been designed to help and support students at all levels.

Money, money, money

Unless you live like a hermit or have a secret bank account in an offshore tax haven, money will play an important part in your calculations about what university will be like. So wherever you are on the pauper/plutocrat scale, it's a good idea to think about how much your education's going to cost.

You need to get an idea of overall expenses and how much help you'll be getting from your family or similar sources. If you need loans, think about how much debt you're prepared to take on. If you decide you need to take a part-time job and/or work in the holidays, you'll need to balance your time and energy to make sure that the work doesn't have negative effects on your studying. Basically, to avoid trouble in future, you need to think hard about what you spend and how you spend it.

The extent of your financial commitments will depend on the type of accommodation you choose and the complications of the various fees and loan systems, which differ according to your nationality and the location of your university. If you live at home, it might cost less, but then transport costs may be higher. And what you spend on the other aspects of day-to-day living and your social life is, of course, up to you.

brilliant example

To give you an approximate idea of the various things that will eat into your finances, we've got figures from 2008–2009 which suggest that, depending on your location, the total cost of being a student is around £6000–£9000 a year. About half of that goes on food, accommodation and other necessities such as toiletries, deposits, insurance and utilities. Socialising, clubs and societies take about 20 per cent, clothes and laundry 10 per cent, and the rest is for books, stationery, the telephone, computing and other miscellaneous recurring expenses.

Fees

There are two types of fees: tuition and university accommodation (halls of residence). Your university may have people who can advise you on money matters and there's often a student hardship fund, which can help those who are having serious financial difficulties. On the plus side, as a student you may not have to pay council taxes and you'll get cheap travel and concessions in some stores and entertainment venues.

brilliant tip

The obvious accommodation costs are rent or mortgage, food and drink, but don't forget things such as insurance premiums and gas, electricity and phone bills.

Travel

Travel costs include fares, season tickets, car maintenance, fuel, parking and tolls and, naturally enough, they depend on how far you live from the campus. Living at home may be cheaper, but travelling to and from the university may then cost more.

Study

As with travel, specific study costs are self-evident. They include books, notepads, stationery, computing, photocopying, printing and, in certain subjects, lab deposits or field trips.

Personal

In a way, it would make more sense to leave this section blank because it'll depend entirely on your personal attitudes and preferences. But it's still worth thinking about before other issues become more pressing. Personal spending will include your mobile phone contract, laundry bills, toiletries, haircuts, clothes, shoes, presents and other incidentals from holidays to TV licences.

It all adds up, so check the literature that the university sent to you and make sure you send back all the necessary forms in good time. Look at your university's website to see whether you qualify for any grants or bursaries. Try to work out a realistic budget and assess the gap between what you'll be spending and what you've actually got. If you're planning on taking out a loan, it'll help you to get an idea of how much debt you might be incurring.

Accommodation

You have to live somewhere, preferably somewhere comfortable, warm and secure, and, since you spend more on accommodation than on anything else, it's worth looking at the available options and considering their advantages and disadvantages.

Living at home

It may be that, for financial or other reasons, you decide to stay at home. The attractions are obvious. It's a familiar, established environment where you're surrounded by people who care about you. It's probably cheaper than all the other options and you won't have to sign any contracts or come up with a deposit. You'll be able to keep on seeing your friends and doing the things you like doing. You'll get your laundry done, there's the home cooking and no one will be asking for insurance premiums or payments for other services.

Sounds pretty good. But it won't be just the same old same old. Your life will be different. There'll be other calls on your time, you'll develop new relationships, and so you and the rest of your family will need to make some adjustments.

You'll need time, space and peace to study. You really need a place that's exclusively yours, where you can connect to the internet, store books and files, and know where everything is. The demands on you will be different and you may find it hard to concentrate on your studies. It's even possible that the new freedom you sense as a student may cause conflicts and introduce stress into contacts with other family members.

Then there's the cost of travel and the time you might have to waste while commuting to and from the university. Perhaps most of all, there's the fact that you won't find it as easy to get involved in the all-important social life of the university and you won't have as much academic contact with fellow students. These are the sorts of things to consider when you're choosing to stay at home.

Living away from home

If your choice is to strike out on your own, there are two basic options: university accommodation or renting in the private sector.

Student halls and flats

University halls of residence are generally a safe option. They're not too expensive and they tend to provide most of the things you need, from meals to laundry facilities. They're clean, warm and safe and, since you're surrounded by other students, they represent a ready-made social network. There are usually student committees which organise social events, sports and games, and you have access to hall wardens to talk about anything which may be of concern, from issues relating to study to more personal matters.

As for the downside, you may have to commit to a long stay (for the whole academic year, for example), which can be a problem if you find the place is too noisy or offers too little privacy. You might not like the food and you won't have much choice, if any, of neighbours or flatmates. In some halls, you might have to share a room.

brilliant tip

It's all about becoming part of a different social structure. Live at home and you might miss out on some aspects of university life; live in a hall of residence and you might feel you're getting too much of it. Either way, be ready to adapt to new relationships and develop an awareness of others and their needs.

Private accommodation

You've probably heard tales from both ends of the spectrum when it comes to renting rooms or sharing a flat. Squalor makes for better headlines but there are also plenty of examples of high-end comfort and facilities. Private accommodation can vary a lot, but many universities have schemes through which they inspect properties and give them a stamp of approval.

It's up to you to decide on whether to go cheap or be prepared to spend a bit more to get more. The good thing is that you usually find a wide range of properties to select from. You can also choose who you live with. If you're with friends who have similar preferences, that means you'll get more privacy, there'll be less disturbance and noise (although that can become a bit of an issue when the party animals are unleashed) and overall you can choose when to eat, sleep and study. In general terms, living in private accommodation does give you more freedom.

However, it can be expensive and you always have to pay a biggish deposit up front. You may have to pay more for phone calls, gas and electricity and the contract may lock you into a lengthy stay. You may even have to pay rent during the holidays. On top of that, if you're not sharing with friends, you could feel isolated and lonely. And then there are the extra travel costs and commuting time and also the need to shop, cook and clean, few of which come naturally to a typical student.

Balance freedoms against inconveniences to decide whether this is really your best option. But make sure you know what you're letting yourself in for. There's lots of legislation involved in contracts concerning private renting. Check the details with the local Citizens' Advice Bureau and with the university's student services.

Think before you commit

How important the various points we've made about the different types of accommodation are to you will obviously depend on your priorities, but before you lock yourself into a contract, with either the university or a private landlord, use this checklist to make sure you've considered all the relevant factors.

- Is the room big enough and does it have the study facilities you need?
- How far is it from the campus and lecture halls?
- Are meals included or will you have to feed yourself?
- Will you have to share a room? If so, how much choice of co-tenant do you have?
- Who are your neighbours? Are there likely to be any issues or conflicts with them?
- Are the bathroom facilities en-suite or will you have to share?
- Is there an internet connection? If so, is it free or will you have to pay extra for it?

To get help making these decisions, use all the services and facilities the university offers. Talk to its support staff and also to other students who've already experienced what it's like living in the place you're looking at. Go and inspect the actual rooms and surroundings.

Whenever you're presented with an inventory of the equipment and furniture in a flat or room, check it carefully. If any of the contents are already damaged, make a note of them on the inventory, and sign and date it. You don't want to be charged for things which weren't your fault.

brilliant tip

Before you sign a contract, read the small print. It will spell out exactly what's required of you – if you don't fulfil your obligations, it could prove expensive and stressful. There'll certainly be details of what you'd have to pay for any damage you cause and there may even be penalties for failing to clean the place to a standard the landlord thinks is acceptable.

When you've made up your mind, reserve the accommodation right away. You've taken lots of trouble to choose a place so don't miss out on it because someone else has been quicker off the mark.

And, once you've taken up residence, try to make it yours. Personalise it with photos, posters and favourite objects. It's the base from which you'll be experiencing all these new things, so make it feel like your home.

Looking after yourself

Being independent is part of living. Even if you're staying at home, the new context in which you find yourself will be challenging at first. If you're leaving the family home to spend months away from it, that calls for some major adjustments. It can be liberating and exciting, but it can also be stressful and traumatic. It's a time when you'll have to take responsibility for yourself and live with the consequences of your decisions. Whatever you choose, there'll no doubt be compromises. But that's all part of the university experience and part of the education process.

So before we launch into more detailed considerations of the university system, it's worth pausing to think of where changes might occur. If you're staying at home, for example, it's not just you but everyone in your family who'll need to adjust to the new situation. If you're moving out, remember that you'll have to learn to live with other people who, at first anyway, may be strangers. Can you manage that? Will you get on with them? And do you think they'll get on with you? What exactly will it be like having to make compromises?

Surprising new skills

You won't be alone. You'll still have the support of your family and the university's services. But you'll cope better if you're prepared for change and you know the skills you'll need to cope with it. For example, how's your shopping technique? Do you make lists and shop carefully or do you need to ask someone where the shops actually are? And when you've bought food, do you know how to cook it? These may seem trivial questions, but they're part of becoming self-sufficient. You're looking after yourself now. You're in charge.

You may already know how a washing machine works. If not, you'd better learn. Not only that, you'd better remember to use it regularly. Hygiene is not just a health issue, it's a social issue too.

brilliant tip

Follow the instructions on the machines in the laundry. If you don't, your prized replica football strip may come out of the tumble drier in the form of a lump of tangled plastic.

There won't be people around reminding you of things, so you'll need to learn how to manage your schedules properly to meet deadlines. And you'll need to stay healthy. It all calls for particular skills, skills you may already have or which you need to develop. As well as those we've mentioned, there's the need to budget with care, open a bank account, deal with a landlord, register with a doctor. If you're not sure about some of these things, find out about them from family or friends. And do it before you get to university.

Also, before you move into shared accommodation, think of the skills you'll need to keep life pleasant. You'll need to negotiate to make sure that chores and the costs of communal living are shared equally. For the sake of harmony, you'll have to be prepared to tolerate things which may not be entirely to your liking, and you'll need to be considerate when others have to study or work on an assignment.

Even on the small scale of a shared flat, social interaction can be tricky. It's easy to form cliques and create an atmosphere which excludes one or more people and creates tensions. Whether you're the excluded or the excluder, it makes life more stressful.

You're in charge

This is the start of real independence. There'll still be people to turn to, but the onus is on you to make the decisions and make life easier for yourself and those around you. Nobody will be telling you what to do or when to study, or even what to study. It would be all too easy to lounge about having a great time and hoping that tomorrow will take care of itself. It won't unless you set yourself some rules and then obey them.

Whether you've come from school or college, a job or unemployment, there'll be major changes in what you do and where and how you do it. Don't just slide into things, plan for them. We mentioned at the outset the need to think a little about your goals and how university will help you to achieve them. Now's the time to decide what sort of study regime you're going to adopt. Which societies and sports clubs are you going to join? What sort of balance can you achieve between study, a part-time job (if you have one) and your social life? Think about these things now and you're not likely to find yourself under pressure later.

What next?

We've been talking about practical things ...

... and the skills you need to handle them. We've also been talking about what may seem like abstract things – time management, aspirations, awareness of others. It's time to put them into practice. One last thing, though: if you're leaving home, make a list of what you'll need to take with you. You're going to personalise your room and you'll want to take things that are important to you, but it's easy to forget even those when there's a wholesale upheaval such as this.

You'll obviously need the basics ...

... such as clothes for all weathers and for festivals, clubs, parties and all the other social events you favour. There'll also be sports gear and equipment and maybe a musical instrument.

Then there are the study essentials ...

... such as books, stationery, pens, computers and calculators. (And maybe a CD player, iPod and TV for those times when relaxing seems a better idea.)

If you use any medication regularly ...

... it'll probably be automatic for you to pack that, but you may not think about more official things. For example, you may need documents for purposes of identification such as your passport and driving licence, and it's best to make a note of your National Insurance number and details of your bank accounts. But make sure it's not written in such a way as to make it accessible to someone else.

We're now going to look in more detail ...

... at how the university system works, but if you get these preparations right, the whole process of integrating into university life will be much smoother.

🡕 brilliant recap

Going to university is potentially a life-changing experience.

You'll need skills other than academic ones.

Ask yourself what your goals are and make choices accordingly.

Organise your financial arrangements.

Research accommodation possibilities and choose with care.

Always read the small print.

Be sensitive to relationships with others.

Create a balance between work and relaxation. Both are important.

Develop self-sufficiency and the practical skills needed in everyday life.

Gearing up

Universities are large organisations. Many of them have been around for a very long time and have a distinct character. But their main element is people. Each one is a community made up not just of professors and lecturers but also administrators, cleaners, janitors, secretaries, technicians, specialist support staff and, of course, students. Each year, a new batch of students arrives and has to learn how to fit into structures that have been in place for generations. It's not always obvious what's required of you.

brilliant definitions

Discipline – a specific subject or field of study.

School – an academic unit in a university, usually covering the various approaches to a single discipline.

Faculty – an academic unit made up of a group of related disciplines (Social Sciences, Arts, Law, Medicine, etc.).

Matriculating – registering or enrolling for a course.

Virtual learning environment (VLE) – web- or internet-based software that gives you access to information about and support for courses. Sometimes, with distance learning, all teaching is done through a VLE.

Good communications

In every walk of life, we find out about things by communicating. So make sure that you maintain good two-way contact with your institution right from the start.

Professional communications

You've been given a date and time for matriculation, so be there at that time. If you change address or any other personal details, tell the university. The same applies if you're absent through illness. These are all simple, basic things, but if you don't attend to them, they could escalate into more serious omissions. Check your university email account regularly and reply quickly to communications from staff members.

You may be surprised at just how many notice boards there are everywhere, but they're there for a reason. Read notices regularly, and make a point of checking for announcements about courses that use the university's VLE.

There are all sorts of things which may be confusing or a source of anxiety in your early days – the way to deal with them is by communicating. You may feel that you've chosen the wrong course. If so, arrange to see your adviser or director of studies to discuss it. It may be possible to change, but it may also depend on how many weeks you've been following that course. Don't wait. If there's a problem, talk about it.

brilliant tip

Transfer all your mail to your university email account. It makes it easier to check messages from staff and receive news of possible changes in your courses or classes.

Personal communications

At first, the university can seem vast, unfriendly, anonymous. You arrive and you're just one of many hundreds, maybe thousands, who are simply being processed by its systems. That's a false perception. There's almost always help available when you come across a problem. So if ever you find yourself having to cope with something difficult in your life or you need time off for personal reasons such as a family bereavement, you don't have to deal with it alone. Ask for help. If it's personal, it'll stay confidential.

If you don't ask, the problem will probably just get worse. It's not weak to ask for help. On the contrary, it shows a maturity in problem-solving which is a basic part of life at university. And it's not just about crisis management, but all facets of student life. You'll get most out of it if you take the initiative. Whether it's contributing in a tutorial or complaining about some aspect of a course, you'll get more satisfaction and gain more benefits from speaking up than holding back.

Who can I talk to?

There's no standard setup for university support services, but most of them provide the same sort of help and it comes under recognisable categories:

- Academic skills/advice is self-explanatory. It handles issues and skills such as academic writing, learning strategies, exam techniques and anything relating to the whole academic process.

- More general advisory services deal with things such as finance, hardship, tenancy issues, leases and other matters relating to day-to-day life.

- The careers service offers advice not only on careers but also about how to find part-time work, placements, internships and holiday jobs.

- Chaplaincy centres are for people of all (or no) faiths to talk about anything from personal to public matters. And they don't necessarily have to have anything to do with religion.

- Counselling is there to help people cope with personal emotional problems such as stress, being homesick or feeling lonely.

- The health service does what it says on the tin.

- The international service is there to help and advise overseas students.

- Accommodation services deal mainly with university accommodation, but they may also be able to suggest other property available for rent.

- Finally, apart from the obvious fitness and sports remit, sports and well-being centres are also places where you meet people and generally de-stress.

Getting organised

Even if you've been there only a week, you'll be bewildered by just how much there is on offer at your university. As well as all the things you need to know about enrolling for your courses, there'll be sports, clubs, facilities, events, all clamouring for your involvement. Once again, the choice is yours. It's all part of the freedom that comes with being there.

Maybe one of the first real lessons you'll learn is the need to exercise that freedom with care. There's only so much you can do and, until some Stephen Hawking-type breakthrough occurs to make the time–space continuum more accommodating, each day still has just 24 hours.

So make the most of the leisure activities, but keep a balance. Organise your activities and time effectively so that you're not faced with constant clashes between what you have to do and what you want to do. You'll soon know what course and other work is expected of you, so plan your workload. Set your deadlines and make sure you meet them. If you have a part-time job, keep it realistic. If you do more than 15 hours a week, that's too much. Get your priorities right. Arrange your social life around your studies, not the other way round. As we keep repeating, maintain a sensible, workable balance between the various parts of your student life.

New skills to open your mind

University is not the same as school or work. It calls for new skills and also new ways of using those you already have. Be open and receptive to these new demands; be ready to change the ways you study, adopt new techniques. We all have our preconceptions about things; university gives us the time and space to reflect on them, maybe challenge them and consider alternative ways of thinking and seeing. Part of the pleasure of studying is to begin to think logically and see that there's more than one side to every argument. This requires powers of analysis, the skill of thinking critically about ideas. It makes all of experience richer.

Planning your studies

We can't predict what form your courses will take because they're taught differently depending on both the tutors and the subject itself. There may be lectures, tutorials, lab or other practical sessions, field trips, PowerPoint presentations – the list isn't quite endless, but it's long. Whatever elements are involved, you'll have to participate fully and also prepare for them. On top of that, you may be assessed on any aspect of the whole process. The basic guidelines will be given to you, but it'll be up to you to plan your studies effectively.

brilliant tip

To get the most out of your course, map out the things you need to do in a diary (paper or electronic) or a semester/term/monthly/weekly planner such as *The Smarter Student Planner*. Plan ahead.

How much work should I do?

How long is a piece of string? It would be comforting if we could give a straight answer, but there are too many variables, from your own abilities and inclinations to the nature of the course itself. The assumption is that in term time you'll do about 40 hours a week – that's lectures, tutorials, practicals and also reading, writing, working on assessments – but some do more, some do less. It's up to you to decide what you want to get out of your studies and what you're prepared to put into them. You'll find some students do as little as they can, others pretend not to be doing much but in fact study quite hard. The important thing is not to measure yourself against anyone else. Decide how much you need to do and organise your time so that you can do it.

These suggestions may help you with your planning:

Every day:

- Do some background reading for lectures or other activities. That can be anything from learning more about the wider context for the subject of the lecture to printing out lecture notes or PowerPoint handouts.

- Don't miss any lectures or other classes.

- Make sure you obey safety instructions and follow rules and regulations, especially for lab and field work and when you're using IT equipment.

Every week:

- Follow up lectures and other activities by reading over and making sure you understand your notes. Do some supplementary reading to reinforce the information.

- Be active in all forms of teaching and assessment. Ask questions, contribute to discussions, get involved. Don't hold back because you feel you might say something silly – nearly all the others in the class will be feeling the same way.

- Don't forget to look at teaching materials and other online facilities. Check your VLE modules several times a week, not only to read the latest announcements but also to get involved in discussions.

At other times:

- Go to class debates, year meetings, formal assessments and other events relating to your course.

- Meet with your tutor (and be on time for appointments).

- Hand work in on time.

- Take part in activities such as field trips. (And remember that you'll need to budget for such things.)

- Register for exams at the times you're supposed to.

- If necessary, give feedback on your course, online or in class.

- If there are any problems with the course or your studies, contact your course director, adviser of studies, personal tutor or whichever form of learning support your university offers.

You and the university system

Going to university is like moving to a new community with its own culture and conventions. It can be confusing, but you've earned your place there and it's up to you to get the answers to any questions you have. If you're not sure about something, start at the university's web pages. There'll be a search facility or an A–Z index.

Make the most of your freedom by deciding to think for yourself. At school, you were told what to do; at university, it's your call. But don't be afraid to ask for help. If you're not sure where to go, try the departmental secretary.

Another source of support is your fellow students. There may be others who are experiencing the same difficulties or have similar questions to ask. Chat with them. Even if you don't come up with an answer, the sharing and the discussion will be useful.

Finally, don't let problems escalate. Deal with them at an early stage.

What next?

Get into the habit of …

… using a diary or planner. It's useful for the day-to-day reminders of what you have to do and when and where you have to do it, and it's invaluable when you have to plan ahead for large-scale assignments which need a well-organised lead-up time.

Plan ahead for things such as …

… holiday jobs and next year's accommodation. In fact, you should try to keep in touch with the careers service and residence services to keep abreast of what's available.

Find out more about …

… the university's support services generally. They're not only there for crises; they also organise voluntary work, arrange social events and outings and may have information on things to do that you wouldn't otherwise come across.

brilliant recap

Keep good two-way communications.

Look after yourself and use support services.

Get yourself organised.

Learn new skills.

Plan ahead.

Coping with new learning demands

3

Higher education has different assumptions, different priorities, different educational aims. If you get a general grasp of the differences at the start it'll help you to recognise them and adapt your methods accordingly.

Teaching methods

Universities are big. There can be 250–300 students or more at lectures. So it's easy to think that, if you miss one, no one will notice. That may be true, but it's part of the whole learning process. In the end, it's up to you. The university trusts you to be responsible. This isn't passive learning, it's practical, active learning.

Some departments check attendance at lectures because they require certain conditions to be met by students seeking specific professional qualifications. But normally, there's no such check. However, if you're an international student, UK legislation requires institutions to monitor your attendance and if you miss a certain number of classes, you'll be reported to the UK Border Agency.

Then again, we shouldn't really be discussing missing lectures. The only person who loses out if you do that sort of thing is you.

Some of you may have experience of learning at other types of college or at work, but since for most of you the main teaching experience has been at school, we'll use the typical school model as a basis for comparison.

At school	At university
Lessons last about 40 minutes.	Lectures are around 50 minutes and most classes are scheduled to last multiples of one hour.
Communication is through daily bulletins and announcements, notice boards and some electronic media.	Communication is mainly electronic, using web pages, VLEs, electronic newsletters. But there are subject handbooks.
Classes are small and the teacher usually knows your name.	Classes are large, maybe in the hundreds, and you're one of the crowd.
You have to do homework or maybe finish off class work and hand it in.	You're expected to do some preliminary reading and researching around a topic, but there's no check on you. You decide what and how much you do.
The teacher controls the input into a lesson and gives feedback.	In lectures, it's controlled by the lecturer, but in tutorials, practicals and lab work, there's more interactive input. There's little direct feedback, but you learn from taking part in the discussions and activities.
The pace of learning is slow. There's lots of memorising of information, answers are usually short, even one-word, and the teacher says whether you're right or wrong.	Learning is very fast and you need to think for yourself.
In writing exercises, you're told to repeat what's been taught in class. You're acquiring knowledge and there's not much need for original thinking.	Your writing must prove that you know and understand the syllabus. You're expected to be original and show independent analytical thinking.
With presentations, there's often little emphasis on spelling, punctuation and grammar.	Presentations are expected to be carefully structured and correct in terms of spelling, grammar and punctuation. You may be required to hand in the work as a word-processed document.
Teaching materials are often colourful and visually explicit. They're less wordy and you're encouraged to reflect exactly what the materials say. Normally, access to library materials is limited.	You use traditional textbooks, academic journals, web-based resources, PowerPoint slides and class notes and there are extensive on-site library facilities.
Assessments often require just short or even one-word responses and the teacher gives feedback on them.	You submit work for assessment with little in the way of preliminary discussion. You get only the one chance to submit. It's marked and the mark's not negotiable.

Exams are at the national level and marked externally. The norm is for you to repeat what you've been taught in class. There's little need for original thinking. Coursework forms part of the assessment and, if you fail, you can't resit until the following year.

Exams are marked internally and checked by an external examiner. The results may help to determine your degree. Continuous assessment may be included and you can resit within a short period.

One of the main differences is in the notion of lectures. Lecturers have different styles and techniques. Some may expect you to absorb lots of new information, others may prefer to provoke or stimulate you to do your own research on a subject. You may, in the same module, get lectures from different members of staff. This is so different from the experience of school classrooms. With the huge numbers involved, tight schedules and different lecturers, opportunities for asking questions and discussing points are fewer. Most lecturers are happy to discuss coursework with you, but it's important to remember that it's up to you to make the approach. The assumption is that if you say nothing, you've understood everything. You'll get the chance to ask questions and put forward your ideas in tutorials and seminars, but if you want clarification about something a lecturer has said, you'll have to take the initiative.

Assessment

Another big difference concerns assessment. At university, there'll be deadlines; you'll be told a piece of work has got to be handed in by a certain time and date. In principle that means there are no second chances. And you won't be able to get a member of staff to have a quick look at it before you hand it in. If you're used to discussing work before you submit it, this may come as a shock. But it's all part of the process of being responsible for yourself, making and trusting your own choices.

As we said, it's a cultural change. Before, you depended on the staff; now there's only you and your fellow students. It's not cheating to read and comment on each other's work – quite the reverse, you can all learn from one another. And if there's a member of your family who's willing, ask them to read what you've written.

At university, marks are generally not negotiable. It's allowed in some places, but the risk then is that the second marker might give it an even lower mark. If you think your work's worth more than the mark suggests, the best thing to do is go and see the marker to find out where the weaknesses are. That way, you can make it better next time.

Learning to learn

It may seem a strange thing to say, but you need to learn how to learn. At school, there was a lot of passive absorbing of information, an acceptance that 'if it's in the book, it's true'. But now you need to think for yourself. Your sponge days are over. At university you'll have to think things through and not just take them for granted. As you acquire new information, you'll want to examine it, test it, suggest alternative interpretations.

It means adapting the way you learn, taking an active part in obtaining and processing information. It's rare to find an issue which is one-sided and straightforward; assessing new things calls for judgements, comparisons, decisions. The more you exercise these skills, the sharper they'll become. Ask questions, test materials and ideas, become an independent thinker.

brilliant tip

Lecturers will often argue for different cases or ideas to show how complex a problem is. They want you to reflect on these alternatives and decide their relative merits for yourself. In fact, they expect you to think for yourself.

Keep an open mind

You bring to university your own skills and talents, knowledge and experience. You'll be exposed to old ideas and values as well as encouraged to explore new areas and concepts. Approach it all with an open mind, an enquiring, critical attitude. Your present views and understanding may be challenged, but you'll come out of it stronger and more assured.

Keep up with the work

Ideas and information keep rushing relentlessly at you. Things won't be repeated and no one will be checking to see that you took it all in. Be careful not to fall behind. If something's not clear, ask about it earlier rather than later.

What next?

We've outlined the overall differences, but there'll be variations from one university to another. So, in the first few weeks of your course, think about how different the teaching is from what you're used to and decide how the way you study may need to change to make the most of it.

Find out how ...

... your work will be assessed. You may have been told about this in an introductory lecture and you'll certainly find details in your course handbook. Think about this, too. Ask yourself what study and revision methods will be best to get you the best possible marks.

Try to get into ...

... a study routine. There are lots of things you want to do, so work out a study rhythm which fits in with these other commitments.

brilliant recap

The differences between teaching methods at school and university.

New types of assessment and the importance of taking responsibility for submitting material on time.

You'll have to learn to learn.

PART 2

Who are you?

4

Who do you think you are?

You need to be active in your choices and you want them to be informed. In order to help you with this, your university may ask you to take part in personal development planning. It may not be called that but whatever the system, you'll have a personal development plan, or PDP. It will involve reflecting on your learning, performance and achievements and it will help you organise how you develop.

brilliant definitions

Personal development plan (PDP) – a reflective analysis of who you are, what you're doing and what you plan to do.

Reflecting – looking back over past events and analysing how you've learned and developed as a person, then using that information to think about who and where you are and what changes, if any, you're going to make.

Goals and achievements

Those definitions may sound a little abstract, but a PDP is a sound, practical way of organising how you live and study. It asks you to:

- think about who you are, what interests you have, your strengths and weaknesses and how you'd like to improve

- plan where you want to go, what skills and knowledge you need to get there and how you might acquire them

- act by setting yourself goals and checking your progress towards achieving them

- reflect on what you've achieved and decide which other activities and choices will help you to develop – personally, academically and in terms of your career.

It's not just a one-off exercise. Once you've started you should keep on checking progress and reassessing goals.

The general overview doesn't convey just how structured the process is. In fact, it breaks down into very specific elements:

- You record your personal qualities, achievements and skills and monitor how they develop.

- You state your personal and career goals in clear, specific terms.

- You examine and understand more fully what and how you're learning.

- You set yourself personal and academic targets and measure your progress towards them.

- You improve your chances of getting a job.

- You gather information for your CV and evidence to support job applications.

- And that process of professional development continues into your chosen career.

What it all adds up to is that you take personal responsibility for your development. The benefits are obvious and research suggests that students who do work on PDP activities perform better in their academic courses than those who don't.

Progress files

Your PDP will generally be held in a progress file along with other components which it's worth identifying.

Academic transcript

This is the university record of what you've learned and achieved. It'll normally have details of your modules and marks, and maybe record other activities and achievements such as the fact that you've attended a safety course or taken part in an IT induction session.

Portfolio

This is a collection – on paper or in electronic form – of evidence to support your PDP and CV. It might include examples of essays, literature surveys, posters, designs and artwork, reports on practicals, spreadsheets and more. It shows other people, including potential employers, the skills you have and the quality of your work. You can also use it yourself to measure and reflect on your achievements and goals.

Career planning component

There may also be a career planning component. The idea is to encourage you to think about your career options very early on and help you decide what qualities and qualifications you'll need to succeed with them.

Curriculum vitae (CV)

All of this feeds into the next component, your CV. This is the document you'll be sending out to potential employers. You'll be continually updating it as you progress. Focusing your thoughts on it will help you see how relevant your various courses and studies are and what may be missing from your schedules. Your CV is the first impression you give to a potential employer. It pays to get it right.

By the way, the CV we're describing here is a broad, general one. It's part of and results from your overall PDP. The CVs you send out to employers may be for different types of position so they should be targeted specifically to stress the qualities that particular job requires. Keeping a full, 'general' CV up to date will allow you to pick and choose the elements that will highlight your suitability for the post.

brilliant tip

You have the right to see your academic transcript. If you think there's something wrong with it or it's incomplete, ask for it to be corrected as soon as possible. It may be copied to employers so you want it to be up to date all the time.

If you're working with a paper-based scheme, keep the documents and materials in a portable filing system. If it's electronic, keep the files secure and make back-ups.

The first steps in your PDP

Before we move on, let's pause and try putting all this into practice. You need to decide where and who you are now and think about your short-, middle- and long-term goals and aspirations. So ask yourself these questions:

Your plan:

- Where do I want to be, career-wise, in ten years' time?
- What sort of degree will I need to get to start me on that path?
- What can I do this year to start working towards that degree?

Your motives:

- What are my personal interests?
- Are they just hobbies or could they be connected with my career choices?
- What do I want?
- What drives me?

Be honest with your answers. You may want to become rich and famous or to help others, to teach, to heal or to work with animals. You may want excitement or stability, adventure or predictability. It's not always easy to be specific, but getting a clearer, more honest idea of the forces that drive you will help you to choose a more satisfying and rewarding journey.

You and your learning:

- What are my personal traits, qualities and flaws?

- How do they relate to the potential careers I've chosen?

- What sort of learner am I?

- What skills am I learning from my academic studies and also from my extra-curricular activities?

You'll find information about the skills you're covering in your course handbook. There are also guidelines on subject benchmarking statements on the Quality Assurance Agency website (www.qaa.ac.uk/students/guides/understandcourses.asp). Websites such as www.prospects.ac.uk can help with questions about career choices.

There's a lot to think of here. It'll help if you make an actual note of your PDP planning at this point. You can then keep returning to it, adding things, changing things. The simplest way of doing so is by listing as headings the areas we've been looking at:

- Long-term aspirations and goals

- Medium-term aspirations and goals

- Short-term aspirations and goals

- Key interests and motivations

- Key skills – strengths and areas for development

- Important personality traits and personal qualities

- Preferred learning style.

Under each one you can note its present status, the actions you plan to take, any target dates you want to set and any general notes on your reflections.

 **brilliant** definition

Learning style – the way you acquire, process, remember and express information.

What next?

Talk to others ...

... about your plans. A friend or family member may have insights into your personality and personal qualities which are different from your own. Personal tutors, academic staff and fellow students may suggest things you hadn't thought of. And anyway, the whole business of having to explain your thinking to them will force you to think more clearly and with more precision.

Take great care ...

... when gathering and filing information for your CV. It's easy to mislay documents or forget important details. Create a file for paperwork, notes and other documents. Include coursework results, details of term-time and holi-day jobs you've had, club and society positions, awards and other certificates.

Visit your careers service ...

... even if you think it's too early to do so. The staff are always ready to discuss your plans, refine your career objectives and make suggestions for improving your chances of getting the job you want.

Revisit your PDP regularly ...

... try to check it after each section of your course and review and update what you've written.

At the start of each new teaching block ...

... think up fresh goals and plans. Take into account what you've achieved thus far and develop them. Be ambitious, but don't be afraid of failing. Even if you get only part of the way towards your goal, that'll be valuable. The real problem would be if you didn't have a goal at all.

brilliant recap

Personal development planning (PDP).

Progress files and their main components (PDP, academic transcript, portfolio, career planner, CV).

Starting the PDP process.

Planning ahead.

5 Ways to stop wasting time

As a student, you've probably got more freedom than many others to juggle the various needs of study, family, work and social activities, but you still need to manage your time with care. The trick is to focus on the right tasks at the right time, work quickly to meet your targets, and make sure you finish everything you start. Time management is a skill; it relies on being organised, setting priorities, and being a good timekeeper. You can learn and adapt it to fit your needs.

Some familiar excuses

Let's start with some 'typical' students and the ways they find to waste time and excuse themselves for it. Do you share any of their attitudes or techniques?

Luke ...

... is a night owl. He likes to work into the small hours. He's got an essay to hand in tomorrow morning, but couldn't face doing it earlier on. But now it's 2 a.m. and he's panicking. The library's shut, so he can't look up a reference he needs. He's tired and he won't have the time or energy to read over his work and correct any errors. In fact, he's so shattered that he'll probably sleep in and miss the deadline altogether. But this is Luke, so he thinks, 'Never mind. It was only worth 25 per cent. I'll make that up in the exam.'

Eleanor …

… is always asking her tutor for extensions of the time limit. Her assignments are always late, but she always finds good reasons for that and it's never her fault. Her tutors aren't amused; they're busy people. If it's not her printer packing up, it's tonsillitis or a visit to Granny in hospital. This time, Granny's ill again; Eleanor's asked for an extension, but she'll lose 10 per cent of the marks for every extra day she takes. Doesn't sound much, but she's a borderline pass in this subject. She needs all the marks she can get.

Shahid …

… always has difficulty getting started. He has to give a presentation to his tutorial group, but the idea of standing up in front of them stresses him out so much that he can't focus on writing the talk. He knows that if he had his PowerPoint slides and notes ready, he'd feel more confident, but his nerves have got to him. So he goes out for a walk. That'll settle him down and he'll feel better when he comes back. When he does, well, he'll maybe make another cup of coffee. And the procrastination goes on and on.

Lorna …

… does everything at the last minute. It's only when the pressure's on that she can get going. The adrenaline flows and she produces good work. The trouble this time is that she has a final-year dissertation to write. 10,000 words – that's a lot of writing and there's only a week to go. And now she's beginning to get nervous. It's not good for her.

Ken …

… has everything under control. No sweat. There are lecture notes on the web, so he doesn't need to go to the lectures. He'll catch up on sleep, maybe do some private study later on. Along comes the exam. He strolls in looking cool, starts writing right away, finishes in plenty of time and sits back, James Bond smile firmly in place. But there's a problem. In her first lecture, the prof handed out a sheet changing the focus of the course, eliminated one of the topics (the one which Ken had revised the most) and told the students that there would be two compulsory questions. Ken didn't know any of this.

Pat ...

... is a perfectionist. She wants to do really well. She knows the degree she wants and plans to get a great job in her chosen field and start climbing the promotion ladder. She's working on an essay and she's looking for the perfect sentence to start it off with a bang and grab the tutor's attention. But she can't quite get it right. So far she's had 15 tries at it, but none has been exactly right. Time's running out and she won't be able to meet the others at the club tonight. But hey, who needs a social life?

Jeff ...

... is a mature student. He's working part-time to make ends meet. At first it was just 10 hours a week, but now it's up to 25. He's juggling his shifts so that he can get to his lectures and tutorials and, as long as the staffroom's empty, he might be able to do a bit of coursework during his breaks. There's never time for him to go to the library to work on the short-loan material, so he'll have to leave that out. Every night, he's too shattered to read the core texts. He really does need to alter his priorities.

brilliant tip

Organising your time properly keeps you on schedule, reduces stress and makes deadlines easier to meet. It makes life simpler and increases your confidence. That's especially true for large or long-term tasks because, with them, deadlines seem so far away that it's easy to justify putting things off.

Diaries, timetables and planners

These stories and their variations are very familiar. They all demonstrate the clear need to get yourself organised and manage your time properly. And the most obvious tool to use is a diary, student planner or wall planner, which is useful for giving you a wide overview of everything you're doing or scheduled to do.

Universities and bookshops sell academic diaries. Like the academic year, they run from September to August. There are also academic planners, such as *The Smarter Student Planner*, which provide templates that help you to keep track of assignment dates and plan for exam revision. They also have reminders of important points of grammar, spelling, punctuation and maths.

The most obvious use for diaries and planners is for keeping track of your day-to-day schedules and noting when essays and other exercises are due to be handed in. But you can also use them to work your way back from key dates. If you know the deadline for an essay, for example, you can work back from that and note mini deadlines by which you should finish the preliminary reading, further research, first draft and final edit.

Get into the habit of looking at the next day's activities the night before and the next week's work at the end of the week. If you number the weeks, it'll show you how time is progressing (or, more likely, flying). And numbering the weeks in reverse gives you a countdown to important events such as exam dates and essay deadlines.

brilliant tip

If you have a big task looming. create a special detailed timetable of study. Try to schedule important activities for when you generally feel most alert and energetic. Break down the task into smaller parts and assign to each one the time it needs. If you cross out tasks as you finish them, it'll show the progress you're making.

Listing and prioritising

At times you may have several different tasks that need to be done. It's easy to forget some, so write them all down in a list each day and decide which should have priority. Number them accordingly, with the most important and/or urgent one first and the least important or urgent one last.

The list will change each day as you work through the tasks. Try to complete as many as possible every day. You'll get great satisfaction out of crossing them off as you do so. If the list has just about disappeared or if all the items have been crossed off, you'll know you've made real progress.

Important or urgent

Important tasks are those which can be graded by balancing the benefits you'll get from completing them against what you'll lose if they don't get done. Urgent tasks are those with a timescale.

brilliant example

Normally, doing your laundry is neither important nor urgent, but if you start to run out of clean underwear, the situation changes. Priorities don't stay the same. They need to be reassessed frequently.

Routines and good work habits

Sometimes it helps to do specific tasks at special periods of the day or times of the week. Such routines help with time management. Tuesday morning may be laundry time, Sunday afternoon means a visit to Granny, and so on. You can do the same thing with work-related activities. Set aside Monday evening for library study, for example, or for working on the next assignment on your list.

Most of us know instinctively when we're at our best for working. So it should be possible to do important work when you're at your most productive. Save the academic work for when you're 'most awake' and do the routine stuff when you're less alert.

Some of our time seems like wasted time, such as that spent commuting or just before going to sleep. Use it for thinking, jotting down ideas, editing work or making plans. Keep a notebook with you, even by your bed. You may think you'll remember a great idea in the morning, but most people don't. And organise your documents. If you know where to find things, you won't have to waste time looking.

Often, projects don't go well because they haven't been planned. Working out a detailed plan for a specific project helps you to identify how to structure it. It'll save you time in the long run.

> **brilliant tip**
>
> Think about making the working day longer. If you can bear the idea of getting up early, you may find that the extra minutes or hours you get from setting the alarm back a bit are very valuable, especially if it helps you to meet a short-term goal.

It's hard to start

Procrastination means putting off a task for another occasion. Sometimes it's hard to get started so we invent reasons for leaving things until later. We find something else which we decide is more important or easier, we switch from one task to another, not getting very far with any of them. Or we talk about working, take longer planning it rather than doing it. Perhaps we find some aspect more interesting than others, so we spend too long on that instead of getting on with it. And then there's writer's block, which is defined as an inability to structure your thoughts and start writing.

Displacement activities are activities which take the place of others which are more important or urgent. The classic examples are:

- checking and answering texts and emails
- watching TV programmes or playing computer games
- spending ages drawing a neat diagram when it's not necessary
- chatting to friends rather than going to the library
- shopping, making coffee, making phone calls, tidying your desk, washing the dog
- convincing yourself that studying in the sun or the pub will work.

Paradoxically, planning can also be a displacement activity. We keep stressing the need to plan, but it's possible to do too much. If you're planning all the time and not actually getting anything done, the balance is wrong. What's happening with all this is that your subconscious is telling you you're actually busy when, in fact, you're just avoiding doing things. So you need to make a conscious effort to overcome it. Think about what you're doing. Set yourself times or targets and reward yourself for meeting them. You could decide, for example, to write 500 words or the next part of your essay and then give yourself a break.

Use the list tactic to write down all the things you have to do and label them as 'immediate', 'soon' and 'later'. Then don't look at the 'soon' and 'later' categories until you've crossed off all the 'immediates'. And don't think that concentrating on the smaller things will free up your mind for the bigger things; you'll just find other smaller things to take their place.

It's hard to finish

Delaying finishing a piece of work is also procrastination. It's a particular problem for perfectionists. If you understand the importance of time management, you'll know that it's wasteful to keep trying to make something perfect before submitting it. The satisfaction and sense of achievement of finishing several competent tasks are greater than that of perfecting just one. And with multiple assignments it could mean a significant difference in your overall marks.

So what can we do to stop procrastinating and start managing our time better?

 **dos and don'ts**

DO ...

- ... improve your study environment. Tidying up can be a form of procrastination but if you create a tidy workplace from the start, it makes studying easier and there are fewer distractions. Cut down on noise; it's usually other people's noise that interrupts your train of thought, so consider studying in a quiet place like a library. Or indeed find a location where there won't be any interruptions, and to make sure your focus is entirely on the work to be done, take with you only the books and papers you need for it.

- ... work in short bursts when you're concentrating well, then give yourself a brief break and start again.

- ... find a way to get started that suits you. Students sometimes worry too much over finding an impressive high-impact opening sentence. There's nothing wrong with starting with a simple definition or restating the question or problem. If you just can't get going, think of the bigger picture – your degree, your career – and see the task to be done as a small but important part of the journey.

- ... cut up large tasks into manageable, achievable chunks. You'll feel better if you have a small task ahead rather than a massive one. And try to get one or more of these chunks finished every day. Completing lots of little jobs is easier than completing one huge one and, in the end, they come to the same thing.

- ... try working alongside others (unless you've opted for a quiet, solitary study location). It's comforting to have people doing the same sorts of things and you can cheer each other up, encourage each other and even stop for a chat over a drink or coffee after each study period.

DON'T ...

- ... let yourself be distracted. Learn to say 'No' (politely) to friends. Hang up a 'Do not disturb' sign and tell them why. Work somewhere else and don't tell them where to find you. Switch off your phone, TV or email program.

- ... be negative. If you get anxious about how your task may be received or assessed, you'll find it harder to get going. Don't let those negative things interfere. Focus on the things you do know, not those you don't. You have no idea how the task will be seen or received so don't waste nervous energy speculating about it. Remember your good results.

- ... always start at the beginning of a written task and work through. With word processing you can work out of sequence. So, if you're writing a long report, it might help to start with a more 'mechanical' part of it, such as a reference list or results section. You could also write out the summary, abstract or contents list. That'll get you going and also give you a plan to work to.

- ... be afraid to ask for help. If you feel that you don't know enough about, for example, maths, spelling, or how to use a software program, don't let it hold you back. Fellow students, lecturers, skills advisers, websites – there's help all around you.

- ... try to make everything perfect. This is all about managing time. It's precious and we must give each task its fair share. Perfection is very hard work and the nearer you get to it, the more time and energy it takes to achieve minor improvements. Use the time on the next task instead.

Serious time management

How do you really use your time? It's a difficult question to answer. So it might be an idea to keep a detailed record of what you do for a few days. You can make fancy spreadsheets and work out percentages if you like (as long as you're not doing so as a displacement activity). Whatever method you use, it'll help you see the things that are simply time-wasting and cut back on them. The same applies to the relative amounts of time you spend on useful activities and the balance you're achieving between them.

Create artificial deadlines

- Set a finishing date earlier than the official submission deadline for your assignment and stick to it. That'll give you time for the important process of reviewing your work, correcting errors and improving its presentation.

- Always expect the unexpected. If a timetable's got no flexibility, it won't be able to accommodate such things. So build in some gaps. Be flexible.

- It may be that you're committed to a single activity which takes up the bulk of your time – an outside job, socialising, looking after a partner or family member. If that's the case, you probably need to make some changes because you must find room for your studies. If you're uncertain where to start, make an appointment with a student counsellor.

- At a mundane but still important level, get the tools to help you manage your time – a diary, wall planner, personal digital assistant (PDA), mobile phone with diary facility, alarm clock. And don't just leave them lying in the drawer – use them.

What next?

Experiment with ...

... listing and prioritising. If you haven't used the technique before, test it out for a week or so. Write down all your current and future tasks, assignments, appointments and social events. If they're big, break them down into smaller tasks. Number and rearrange them in order of priority. Then work your way down the list. After the test you'll know whether it worked for you or not. Did it make you more efficient? Did things get done on time?

Declutter and reorganise ...

... your life. Start with your room and study environment. Tidy things away and leave out only what you need for current activities. It'll all help to make life much easier and less stressful.

 recap

Time-wasting activities.

Displacement activities.

Diaries, timetables and planners.

Listing and prioritising.

Routines and good work habits.

Avoid putting things off.

6 Stresses, pressures and how to respond to them

The word 'stress' has negative associations. But in reality it's part of the way we cope with difficult situations – adrenaline flows and our mind and body are alert, ready to act. If we recognise and understand stress better, we can use it to our advantage.

What is stress?

Most students feel degrees of stress at the beginning. You're leaving home, starting new relationships, having to budget carefully, facing deadlines and exams – and everything's happening all at once. But it's not all bad. In fact, you learn better under a certain amount of stress. Too much or too little means you perform less well. The secret, then, is finding out how much stress is the right amount.

We all have different ideas of what stress is and how it affects us. It's usually caused by some external pressure – we feel anxious, worried and, if it's extreme, it can even make us feel ill. But something that's stressful to one person may simply represent a stimulus or challenge for another. So, when you feel stressed, recognise it for what it is and either take steps to avoid it or use it.

Stress signals

As we've said, it affects different people in different ways and it's impossible to give an exhaustive list of the symptoms, but we can agree on some of them. Your general attitude changes and you become hostile and irritable and lose your sense of humour. It's hard to concentrate or motivate yourself so you look for displacement activities. You forget things, you can't sleep and you get depressed. So it's obvious that these things interfere with your ability to learn as well as making life miserable.

Some general causes

- You're under pressure from yourself and others to perform.
- There are too many calls on your time.
- You're afraid of failing.
- Things aren't how you'd like them to be.
- Events are out of your control, but you care a lot about how they might turn out.
- The pressure on you isn't strong, but it's been building up over a period.
- You've been told to do something, not given enough time to do it and it's now overdue.
- Your standards are high and you're afraid you won't meet them.

Student specials

It's possible to predict some of the stresses that students may experience and even create a sort of timetable for them:

- In the first weeks of term, especially for freshers, there's homesickness, unfamiliar teaching styles, the need to fit into a new context, anxieties about the choice of subjects, new relationships and the perennial feeling that everyone is academically smarter than you are.
- Mid-term or mid-semester, academic pressures are growing, the first assignments are due to be handed in and you're wondering whether you're up to the challenges. There may be financial problems, the balance between social life, studies and the need to work part-time may be difficult to maintain and you may not yet have made any 'real' friends.
- And even towards the end of the term or semester, fresh pressures intrude. Financial problems may have worsened because of

book-buying, partying, travel expenses or a combination of all of them. You may feel sad at having to give up some of your freedoms when you go home. And, of course, there are always exams to worry about.

So it seems that student life adds its own layer of possible causes of stress to those which we all face – unsatisfactory relationships, money worries, family troubles.

What to look for

We're going to list some fairly common student experiences. You may or may not share some or all of them, but it's useful to know that, if you do, you're not alone. That's the first step in being able to handle them and make them work for, not against you.

Everything's new

It can start right away. You can feel disorientated. Your accommodation may be unsatisfactory, the neighbours noisy, your study facilities poor and, with all the new things to remember, at times you have too much to do and at others not enough.

Domesticity

If you're leaving home for the first time, there's lots to absorb. You're used to your own home, so this is all strange. You have to work out travel arrangements and the many elements that are involved in the business of housekeeping, perhaps unfamiliar activities such as shopping, cooking, cleaning and doing your laundry. You need to sort out your finances, work out a budget, maybe get a job.

People

You'll meet new people and this may affect your old relationships. You'll start living a different sort of life and this may cause changes in the way you are with your family and old friends. You'll have less contact with them and this can lead to break-ups. It can be confusing and stressful, but it happens quite a lot.

Friends

At first, you may miss your old friends. The quicker you make new ones at university, the easier it'll be to settle there. Remember, most people are experiencing the same anxieties that you are and they may be shy about making contacts. Making new relationships takes energy and effort. Don't always expect others to make the first move. Joining a club or society will introduce you to other students with similar interests. It's a good start.

> **brilliant** tip
>
> Don't assume that other students are cleverer than you are. Most of them are thinking the same thing about you. They're all wondering whether they'll reach the required standard. You've all earned your places.

Academic concerns

When it comes to the academic side of university life, problems can multiply. Even the word 'academic' is scary. It suggests high intellects, long words, abstract arguments. On top of all this, you may think you've chosen the wrong degree programme; the new teaching methods – lectures and tutorials – may be confusing and demanding; the lecturers may assume you know more than you do. In turn that could make you afraid of embarrassing yourself in front of others in your class or group. There's also the need for you to take responsibility for your own learning, and there's always lots of work to be done.

It helps to talk

We're listing all these things in a seemingly dispassionate way, but if they combine and escalate, they can become serious issues. For some students, the pressure can become so intense that they feel like dropping out. In the most serious cases, they can even feel suicidal. So, whether it's trivial or serious, talk about it with someone. Friends, family or counsellors. There are well-known support services which deal with things anonymously and confidentially:

- The Samaritans (www.samaritans.org.uk)
- Nightline (www.nightline.niss.ac.uk)
- Your university's medical or counselling services (www.studentcounselling.org).

If you're stressed, don't sit back and accept it; that'll make it worse. It's important to do something. Be positive, talk about what's happening. Don't let it fester. Get it out of the way and get back to enjoying life.

⤴ brilliant dos and don'ts

DO ...

- ... share your problem. Talking about problems can help you to deal with them. Apart from getting a different perspective on them from the person you're speaking to, you'll have to look more closely at the problems yourself, articulate them so that the person can understand them. And, in the process, they'll become clearer and more understandable to you.

- ... find out more about it. Look for books or articles about your particular problem. If you Google it, you're almost bound to find a website which deals with it. If you understand it better, it may be easier to find a solution.

- ... join in. If you feel lonely or that you just don't belong, look for ways of getting involved. Join a club or society. Ask someone to join with you, or ask a member if you can go along with them.

- ... use lists. If you're stressed because you've got too much to do, make a list of tasks, arrange them in order of urgency and importance, and work through them systematically.

- ... change your perspective. Look around you and see how others are coping. There's always someone worse off than you are, some of them with unbelievable difficulties to overcome. If they can do it, so can you.

- ... face up to your problem. OK, there's an essay due in by the end of the week and you're worried about it. Stop worrying and just do it. Or a friend's being a pain in the neck. Tell them, let them know what they're doing that's upsetting you. If you keep running away from a problem, it's always there when you come back. So deal with it.

▶

- … something physical. Go for a jog or swim; join a fitness class; play five-a-side football. There's nothing like physical activity to help you burn off the adrenaline and nervous energy that's been building up to combat the stress.

- … learn how to meditate. Try yoga, taekwondo, TM or other relaxation methods.

- … change how you work. If the stress comes from the fact that you're skipping lectures, the remedy's obvious. If you're not doing enough work, do more by working longer hours or making your work methods more effective. And if there are activities that are getting in the way of your work, stop them.

- … manage your time better.

DON'T …

- … try to please everyone. At times, it may be necessary to be selfish. If accommodating the wishes of others is interfering with what you're doing, just tell them simply and apologise. You'll probably find they're more understanding than you thought they'd be.

- … focus on things you don't like. Instead of feeling that what you're doing is boring or hard or is taking too much of your time, take a break and do something you like doing. In other words, don't be afraid to give yourself a treat.

- … let the problem take over. Some problems certainly are serious, but there are others which just disappear as circumstances change. Friday morning's problem can disappear by Monday morning. Go to the cinema, watch a DVD, find some other way to occupy your attention. Get some sleep; the problem may just vanish overnight or you'll at least see it in a different way.

- … try to be a perfectionist. Get the balance between time spent and results achieved right.

- … worry about things over which you have no control. Stuff happens. You can't do everything so accept the fact. Yes, there'll be problems, but just try to find a way through them.

- … be afraid to have a good cry. Sometimes, for men and women, it's the natural way to relieve stress. It's not weak, it's human.

What next?

Be prepared to do something ...

... to change things. Just get rid of what's causing the problem. If noisy neighbours are causing you stress in halls, ask to move to a different room or floor. If they're in a private flat, discuss it with them. If you've got money problems, talk with someone at the bank. You'll need to be ready to make your case and be assertive, but that's better than sitting back and moaning that it's all someone else's fault. It's too easy to assume someone's being unfriendly, when in fact it's your unwillingness to make contact that's putting them off.

Use your university's ...

... counselling service. We've already mentioned this but it's important to realise that the staff are professionals, experts. They've seen it all and dealt with it all many times before. They'll listen, talk you through it, help you to find your own solution and, if necessary, put you in touch with others who can help.

If it's a health problem ...

... see a doctor or nurse. With some health issues, if you leave them too long, they get worse. Take responsibility for yourself. Look after yourself.

 **recap**

What is stress?

What particular aspects of student life cause problems?

What to do and what not to do about it.

7 Finding out the type of learning you prefer

There is such a thing as a learning personality and if you can get an idea of yours, it could help you to find out what learning style suits you best. For a long time, employers have been using tests for personality types to help them decide the best training methods for each individual. It's also a useful guide to how well they work in teams. There's such variety in university teaching that it's clear that the same process could have benefits for all concerned.

 brilliant definitions

Extrovert – someone who focuses on external things rather than on herself.

Introvert – someone who focuses on internal rather than external things.

Learning style – the way an individual takes in information, processes it, remembers it and expresses it.

MBTI – the Myers–Briggs Type Inventory (a way of categorising personality types).

Types of personality

There are many different learning styles and there's no one-fits-all solution. We've all got our own particular mix of elements and they may change as we acquire more knowledge and experience. So if we can work out what our mix is, we can identify our strengths and weaknesses, study more effectively, and be more flexible in our problem-solving, especially when we're working with others.

In fact, the research tells us that our natural learning style is already pretty well established by the time we're three years old. As we go through school, it's influenced by other types of behaviour. In normal classrooms, the tendency is to teach everyone the same way. It would be difficult, if not impossible, to do otherwise. So, even if you wanted to work in a different way, you weren't given a chance to. But now that you're at university, you're free to approach your studies to suit your own preferences. You can choose what you learn and how you learn it.

The MBTI

So how do you find out what your learning preferences are? What is your learning personality? Well, there isn't space in this book to conduct a full questionnaire or profiling exercise, but we can offer a simplified sketch of how the process works. Our terms and techniques are adapted from just one of several possible systems. It's called the Myers–Briggs Type Inventory (MBTI) and it's important to stress that this is a very generalised look at just some of its elements.

First, it asks you to identify four preferences: extroversion or introversion; sensing or intuition; thinking or feeling; judging or perceiving. The way you do this is by deciding which set of answers best represents your thinking. Let's just take one example. The first question is:

How do you focus your attention and energy?

Under Extroversion, the answers are:

- Like participation and socialisation; motivated by interaction with others.
- Act first and think second.
- Energised by outside world and people.
- Impatient of tedious jobs.

Under Introversion, they are:

- Prefer one-to-one communication and relationships; less comfortable in crowds.

- Think ideas through before speaking/acting.

- Want to understand the world.

- Need time to 'recharge batteries' regularly.

So you choose Extroversion or Introversion. Then there are three more questions and pairs of opposing statements under each. A shortened version of the questions and possible responses is:

How do you take in information, become aware of others and events?

- Sensing – focus on the here and now.

- Intuition – focus on the future.

How do you evaluate information, reach conclusions, make decisions?

- Thinking – analyse problem and logical impact of decisions objectively.

- Feeling – reach decisions on basis of personal feelings and impact on others.

How do you select your lifestyle, relate towards the outside world?

- Judging – plan in detail in advance.

- Perceiving – take things as they come, plan on the job.

By putting your choices together, you get an idea of your overall personality and learning preferences.

▶ brilliant example

Jack takes the quiz and his choices are Extrovert, Intuitive, Thinking and Perceiving. According to the MBTI, this means he's friendly and outgoing, has a good sense of humour and is flexible and unpredictable. He makes decisions based on logic and is an ingenious problem-solver. He doesn't enjoy routine tasks and likes to initiate change. Obstacles are challenges to be overcome, and he's good at debating and at 'reading' other people.

Where do you stand?

To find out your learning personality with more precision, you'd need to take the full test, but we can offer some general indicators which will help you to get some idea of where you stand.

Extroverts

Extroverts learn best by discussing things, engaging in physical activities and working with others. They're less happy when studying alone, reading, writing and researching, or doing any solo activity. They'd obviously benefit from a buddy system of studying or work as if they're preparing to teach someone else.

Introverts

Introverts learn best by quiet reflection, reading, listening carefully to lectures. They're shy in group discussions, need time to think things through, and don't like lectures that are delivered too quickly. In discussions, they'd benefit from writing down what they want to say.

Sensing

Those in the Sensing category learn best if they can memorise material, use step-by-step approaches and follow practical applications from real-life scenarios. They don't like complexities and lecturers covering topics too quickly and they're not good at finding out exactly what's required of them. They do better if they move from familiar facts to abstract concepts and use multimedia techniques for learning.

Intuitive

Intuitive people learn best if they're given theory. They focus on general concepts, use insight rather than observation and work from general outlines. They're less good at reading instructions thoroughly, they don't like what they consider slow lectures and they find repetition or practice boring. So they'd benefit most from using self-instruction techniques, such as multimedia presentations.

Thinking

Those choosing Thinking learn best by using objective material and when the course topics and objectives are clearly defined. They're less comfortable when lectures, textbooks and handouts seem to present things in illogical order. If a course seems incoherent or difficult, they should seek guidance and explanations from the lecturer.

Feeling

Those who choose Feeling learn best by relating ideas to their personal experience, working in small groups and helping others. They're not keen on abstract topics and lecturers who seem distant and detached. They should try to improve their contact with their lecturers by asking questions and seeking more explanations.

Judgement

Those who choose Judgement learn best by working on one thing at a time and knowing the marking criteria. They're not so good at handling last-minute changes in the syllabus or any timetable changes. They obviously need to build flexibility into their work plans to accommodate unexpected changes.

Perceiving

Finally, those choosing Perceiving learn best doing problem-based tasks and working under pressure. They don't like procrastination and impulsive reactions and they find it difficult completing tasks. They should find new ways to tackle assignments and break longer assignments into smaller sub-tasks.

As we said at the outset, each of us has bits of some of these tendencies in us. It's the mix that defines our individual personality and learning type. The way in which we've presented it is far from scientific, but it does show how particular attitudes affect the way in which we work and interact with others. There's no 'right' or 'wrong' way to learn, but looking at yourself honestly and identifying approaches can help you to make better choices.

What next?

Think about how …

… you learned at school. What did you like or dislike about it? How do those reactions support or undermine your idea of your learning personality?

Think, too, about …

… what your learning style means in terms of the different components of your studying. Should you change the way you take notes in lectures and from texts? Are you getting the most out of how you revise, study with others or express yourself in assessments? Is it worth rethinking the way you answer in exams?

Decide what your learning style is …

… and be ready to adapt it for different activities. Remember, too, that your lecturers also have different learning styles. Observe them, try to identify their style. It'll help you to understand why they take a particular approach and present information in particular ways. And that, in turn, may make it easier for you to get the most from their lectures and tutorials.

Now that you know that there are such things …

… as learning styles, talk about them with your friends. It's a good way of finding people with similar preferences and maybe collaborating with them in lectures, researching and learning. You don't have to be an extrovert to benefit from studying with someone else.

 recap

What are learning styles?

Why it helps to get an idea of your own.

Overview of learning personality tests.

8 Choosing how to study

We've made several mentions of the freedom you'll be having. The way you use it can make a huge difference to your performance. When you've started on your chosen course, it'll be up to you to organise how you handle your studying and getting together everything you need to support your learning, assignments and exam revision. With your freedom comes responsibility.

Getting organised

Good organisation is based on planning ahead, prioritising different study activities, and making sure that you meet deadlines. It also covers deciding what you want or need to learn and how deeply you need to understand it. So think about what you'll need and the best way to achieve it. Look at learning objectives and outcomes and make sure you understand them correctly. And use assessments and other forms of feedback to measure your progress and change things if necessary.

 brilliant definitions

Annotate – to expand notes that have been handed out or add notes to a text.

Learning outcomes, learning objectives – the knowledge and skills you should have acquired at the end of a specific course or part of that course.

brilliant tip

'Outcomes' has become a jargon word in these contexts and, as is the way with jargon, its meaning becomes corrupted. In simple terms it simply means 'something that happens as a result of something else'. You splay your fingers in a particular way on a guitar's fret board and the outcome is a particular chord. You swing a golf club and the outcome is that the ball flies up the fairway (or into the woods). You read about a particular period in history and the outcome is that you understand better what went on and can apply that understanding to other circumstances.

Where to get the information you need

Your starting point is all the information you get from the university and your department. Read it and file it away in the appropriate place. It's information you'll get through many different channels:

- The course handbook tells you what various lectures are about, where they're held and who's delivering them. It also gives reading lists, and dates and venues for practicals, labs and tutorials, and it outlines learning objectives and outcomes.

- Some offer guidance on writing and aspects of academic presentation and most give you an idea of marking systems.

- You'll find venues and times of classes and exam dates in timetables on the subject and departmental notice boards. Check these boards regularly for important announcements and any changes to the printed information you have.

- Information also comes through the usual electronic channels. Group and individual emails give the latest updates, reminders and special instructions. Make sure you check your university email account regularly. And the same applies to the virtual learning environment. It carries much of the information we've been talking about and you'll find the latest news on your course on the electronic notice board or announcements page.

brilliant tip

You may feel swamped by information, leaflets, timetables and all sorts of items, especially at the start. Check through it all, discard the gimmicks and file the rest, which is relevant to your studies, under the appropriate headings.

Your study space and notes

You need a place to study, preferably one that's exclusively yours. We don't all have that luxury though, so look around, ask if there are any study rooms in your department or special zones in the library. If you just want a place where you can be anonymous and won't be interrupted, try the public library or a different subject library on the campus. And make sure you find somewhere comfortable and well lit. But not an armchair or your bed – you might get too comfortable and just fall asleep.

We've already warned about information overload. Every one of your courses will generate a lot of paper. It may come as hard copy or through websites or your VLE, it may be notes you've taken yourself in lectures or from books. Keep it all where you can find it easily.

Day-to-day maintenance

- Do the general tidying up and other routine activities, such as writing up and filing notes, during your low-energy period. The high-energy time is for studying.

- Become a nerd. As you receive or create materials, put the date on them.

- Store everything in an organised way. Buy large ring-binder folders for each of your subjects, with coloured dividers to separate different elements of the course. You can arrange them alphabetically, chronologically or any way that suits you. The important thing is to be consistent.

- Whenever you get material from somewhere – books, websites, newspapers or any kind of source – always make a note of where you found it, the date, page number and anything else that'll help you to find it again if you need to. You'll also need all these identifiers if you ever quote it in work of your own. It'll save you lots of time if you find out right away what reference system your university prefers and learn how to use it.

Formulae

- Create a formula sheet for each of your subjects. Make a list of the formulae and another list to remind you what the symbols mean. Put each sheet in the relevant subject file in a place where you can find it easily.

- Make sure you copy formulae down correctly, with the right capital (upper case) or small (lower case) letters, subscripts and superscripts.

- You'll be consulting these formulae sheets a lot so keep them protected in a polythene pocket at the front of your file. Laminating them would be even better.

E-materials

- Use the same techniques for materials which you acquire or create electronically. Create separate folders for each topic in your course.

- Choose file names carefully. You may need to find something several months later so the label you're looking for needs to make sense. Dating file names helps too.

- Back up everything you do on a personal computer, including any electronic work you have to hand in. It's easy then to make extra copies if you need to.

- When you finish working on a document, note the page number and the date. That way, when you go back to it, you'll know you're working on the latest version.

- Find out how to print the file name and details in the footer section of your document.

Developing your skills

Once you know what you're studying and how the course will be delivered, you should take time out to think again about which learning and studying skills you need to develop. The main ones will probably relate to knowing how to get the most out of IT facilities and word-processing packages. When you search the internet, look for reliable source material and filter out what's irrelevant and misleading. Learn how to use any software packages specific to your subject, and familiarise yourself with the library's electronic catalogue and other electronic resources. With word-processing programs, the more you practise using their advanced features, the easier you'll find it to organise, structure and write essays and other types of presentation.

Being competent at all this will make life easier for you through your whole academic career, so it's worth going to the relevant service in your university to ask about courses or inductions that will help you develop these skills. The university home page usually has details of how to contact the various support services. Check out the IT support service for word processing, software packages and keyboard skills, the learning centre for advice on studying, and the library for familiarisation or induction programmes.

Getting down to the task

So, everything's ready. Now work out what you've got to do, how much time you've got, and how you're going to do it. It's hard at first, but once you get going, the ideas start to flow.

Deciding what needs to be done depends on your discipline and subject. So ask yourself what you need to do to learn within your particular field. Maybe looking over notes from lectures, expanding them, clarifying them is the best approach. You may need to find and read books or articles to add to your understanding of the topic. There may be more such material in a VLE or other web-based source. Or perhaps the task is to prepare or write reports or essays or even revise for exams. It's only when you've worked out what you need that you'll be able to decide how urgent and/or important each activity is and how much time you need to give it.

All this thinking about the subject material is as important as the actual study of it. It's getting you actively involved in your learning at a deeper level than the more passive processes of study and it helps you to identify the different types and 'levels' of thinking that tutors expect you to be doing.

Types of active study

It's easy to convince yourself you're working when you're copying out notes or reading a chapter right to the end. You are, of course, but it's a sort of mechanical, passive process, which you can do on auto-pilot. You need also to be thinking about what you're doing and why. Let's look at some typical learning activities and suggest the sorts of questions you should be asking yourself as you do them:

Rewriting lecture notes

- What are the key ideas?

- Would it help if I reorganised the notes into a sequence that reflects my understanding of the topic?

- Is this taking too long? If it is, try to be clearer and neater as you make notes during the lecture. If rewriting notes helps you to learn, structure them as bullet points, flow charts or diagrams rather than sentences.

Making notes from texts

- How is the information organised and how can I restructure it into short notes?

- How can I identify the key ideas quickly to get an overview?

- How much detail do I need? The answer there will vary according to whether you're learning about the topic, getting information for an assignment or revising for exams.

- What is the best way of organising my notes?

Thinking/reflecting

- What do I think about this topic? Your own thinking is a vital part of the learning process. Don't just accept someone else's approach to the topic as the only one, even if he's a respected academic. Think critically, question your own ideas. Be open to new approaches, information or evidence and ready to redefine your opinions.

- What should I be looking for – information or concepts? If it's information, is my source reliable? Can I cross-check with another resource? If it's concepts, what evidence is there for each viewpoint? How good is it? Is there any other evidence available? If so, where will I find it?

- Is there an obvious central thread of cause and effect? Are there other, similar threads leading off it?

- Are there any patterns, relationships or themes? There may be comparisons and similarities, contrasts and differences; arguments, supporting evidence and counter-arguments; problems and possible solutions.

Working through problems and examples

- Is the answer sensible and are the units correct?

- Have I done what I was asked to do?

- Is there anything else I was asked to do?

- Have I used the correct formula?

- Have I used all the information I was given in an appropriate way?

Asking questions

As we said, now you're at university, learning is up to you. But what if you've been to the lectures, read the set texts, discussed it with others on the course and you feel you still don't understand something? That's not an unusual feeling, so go to your department and ask to see someone who can help you. Departmental secretaries usually know when academic staff are available. Or you could email your lecturer to make an appointment or to just ask the question. It may well be something that can be sorted out quite quickly. It'll also let the member of staff know that he might need to go over the material for the whole class.

brilliant tip

Use your 'visual' brain. Coloured highlighters for headings and place tabs stuck on key sheets in your file will help you find things more quickly.

Building your confidence

Planning and organising your learning is a practical process which consists of a whole range of activities. The following list summarises them for you. Read through it now and use it to keep reminding yourself of what you need to do.

- Know your best time to study. Decide when you're at your most effective and focused and schedule your intensive learning activities for those times.

- Check out the opening and closing hours of places such as the library, study centre or computing facility. If that's where you like to work, plan your study periods around those times.

- Plan ahead. Keep a note of things to do over the next week and month. Manage your time so that you fulfil all your assignments, lab work and tutorial work on time.

- Create a personal filing system and be methodical in the way you use it to store notes, handouts and other printed material.

- If you're working on your own it's important to take breaks. It's also important to socialise; taking regular short breaks with friends helps you to keep a perspective on your work.

- Work with a buddy. Most of your work you do on your own, but getting together with someone else on your course to compare notes, see whether you understand the more difficult points in the same way and discuss a set assignment can help everyone involved. It'll help to consolidate your learning and identify any gaps in your knowledge.

- A good vocabulary is essential so try to develop both your normal and your professional vocabulary. It'll help you to remember words if you write them down with a simple definition. But don't just make long, indiscriminate lists; use a small, cheap address book with alphabetical sections and enter the words in alphabetical order.

- Reinforce your learning. Part of the learning outcomes of your subject will be that you should be able to use the appropriate terms and make sure they're spelled correctly. For some subjects you may need to master key formulae so that they become second nature to you. So check through your words, definitions and formulae lists frequently.

- Tackle tutorial questions. If you're handed a set of tutorial questions, do all the examples, even if you don't have to hand them in. If you find any particular solution difficult to work out, ask one of your lecturers or tutors to give you some guidance. When you've got the right answers, file them with the topic notes.

What next?

Go through your subject handbook ...

... and note down all your course's topic areas. Use these topics as headings for your file dividers to create spaces ready for the notes on them.

Go to your subject departments ...

... and find out where the notice board for your year is. Check the department's home pages to find out if there's any special area for updated student information and log on to your VLE to look at learning support sites in your subjects. It's all part of getting to know where to find relevant information. Do it now and it'll save you time later when the pressure may be on.

Think about your skills ...

... and learning patterns. If your word processing's not great or you're not quite sure how to search a database such as a library catalogue, do something about it right away. Ask about induction or training courses. Make the most of your independence and the many facilities on offer.

brilliant recap

Where to look for information for your subjects.

Organising your study space and your notes.

Developing your skills.

Types of study.

Taking responsibility for your studies.

PART 3

Developing the necessary academic skills

9 Getting full value from lectures

Lectures are a basic part of most university teaching and they vary in many of their aspects, from the demands of the subject to the idiosyncrasies of the lecturer. You may not have been to any before so you'll need to decide how to deal with different styles and approaches and how to make the best use of lecture time.

Understanding lectures

First, what exactly is a lecture? Well, originally they were readings and they still are today in many cases. Some lecturers do write out their lectures and read them to their classes, but many others prepare them in note form which they then use as the basis for a less formal delivery.

In general terms, a lecture usually follows certain conventions:

- It lasts for 50–60 minutes and is given by a specialist in the subject.

- It provides different approaches to learning, depending on the topic and discipline. It could contain factual information, ideas, analysis, argument, contrasting viewpoints, methods or examples.

- It's not complete in itself but more of a detailed guide for you in your study of a topic. You may have to do a lot of supplementary reading, work through examples or conduct experiments to add to your understanding and knowledge.

- The lecture may provide material that will be explored further in tutorials, laboratory practicals, field work or site visits.

More specifically, there are some key facts to remember when asking what lectures are for. For example, you won't necessarily find the information you get from the lecture in any textbooks. Again, it depends what lecturers want to achieve. They may present views which aren't necessarily their own or they may just be exploring or encouraging you to explore different attitudes and opinions. Approaches differ from one to another, even in the same subject area, and styles vary between individual subjects and disciplines.

Sometimes lectures are compulsory, especially in vocational subjects, such as law, medicine or nursing. But even if they're not, you should go to them. Listening to how a lecturer explains the topic will help you to understand and remember it.

Lectures aren't supposed to be a comprehensive treatment of any topic. They're more of an overview of the main points of the subject and a framework to help you with further study. Sometimes lecture notes are made available through VLEs, but you may find that they don't cover everything the lecturer said.

There's usually not much in the way of interaction between you and the lecturer. You may be asked to do something, perhaps in collaboration with someone sitting beside you. You certainly will have to take notes and also use the information you get from the lecture.

Sounds familiar

The subject of the lecture may sometimes be a repeat of something you've already studied, at school or somewhere else. But you'd be wrong to think you could skip it or not bother taking any notes. It'll probably be taught in a different way and with a different end in mind, and it'll come from a different perspective. In fact, it may help to look back over your previous studies of the topic because the lecturer may give you fresh insights to them and take you beyond the point you'd reached before. So don't make assumptions.

Some of the materials you'll need for note-taking, such as pens and paper, are obvious. But depending on your subject, it might be useful to have some high-lighters, a calculator and a dictionary.

Different lecture formats

Not all lectures involve listening and note-taking. Some lecturers prefer to stick to the same format, but others may alter their delivery depending on topic, class size or the stage you've reached.

A traditional lecture usually consists of a 50-minute non-stop monologue. It'll set out its aims and method of approach, cover the content in detail, then summarise the key points. A 'split' lecture may be divided into a 25-minute mini-lecture, a 5-minute break to let you discuss any points from it with fellow students, and a second 25-minute mini-lecture to take the topic further. An 'activity' lecture may start with about 20 minutes of content followed by 10 minutes of in-class activity, such as working with a partner or partners, 15 minutes' general discussion of that work, and a final 10-minute summary by the lecturer of key issues arising from all the activities.

How to get the most from lectures

Before

- Find out when and where your lectures are held, check the notice boards or VLE for any changes, then make sure you attend. If you miss lectures, you'll understand less as you go along. Be on time. If you're late, you'll miss something, but you'll also interrupt the lecturer's flow of thought and disrupt his delivery. You should aim to be sitting in your seat 5 minutes before the start of the lecture.

- Switch off your mobile phone.

- Do some basic reading about the topic.

- Check what the learning objectives or outcomes for the lecture are so that you can focus your attention on what's important.

- Note how many lectures there are for each topic. It'll help you decide how much work you need to do on each element when you're revising.

- It's not usual for students to record lectures so if that's what you want to do, you must get permission from the lecturer concerned before the start. If you're visually or aurally impaired, you can make special arrangements directly with the lecturer and the disability support service.

During

- At each lecture, write the name of the lecturer, the subject and the date on your notes. It'll help with your filing and your revision.

- If the lecturer gives handouts, highlight, underline or make additional notes on them as the lecture progresses. If there aren't any, choose a note-taking style that's right for the content and discipline. How you decide to take the notes may also be affected by the lecturer's style. In fact, be ready to adapt your style to the different types of delivery you'll hear.

- Invent your own abbreviations. This could include some contraction of words, texting tricks or standard abbreviations.

- In the next chapter we're going to outline a general structure for lectures. When you've read that, you'll know what to listen for. There'll be a statement at the beginning that outlines the aims and the way they'll be achieved, then 'signpost' words which mark transitions between points as the lecture progresses.

- If the lecturer puts any special emphasis on particular points, they may crop up later in assessment.

After

- Clear up any points you didn't understand by asking a fellow student, consulting a text or website. If you're still not sure about it, speak to the lecturer.

- Soon after the lecture, go over your notes. Some students rewrite all their lecture notes because they feel it's a way of consolidating the information and ideas. Others think it's a waste of time which could be better spent doing supplementary reading on the content of the lecture. The choice is yours.

● Follow up references and think about the ideas that were covered in the lecture. The more your course progresses, the more connections there'll be between the various topics and the theory behind them.

● There may be additional material and coursework to complete; make sure you do this because it'll almost certainly be part of some assessment.

● Think about the lecture content in terms of the learning objectives or outcomes. It'll help you understand why you're being taught these things and how they fit with all the other elements of your course.

● Add any ideas and questions of your own to your notes, but do it in a way that makes it obvious they're not from the lecture but are your reactions to what you heard. This is all part of critical thinking, which we'll deal with in Chapter 14.

Introductions and summaries

Most lectures begin with an outline of what they'll be covering. If you're late, you'll miss this and it might prevent you understanding fully what the lecture's aiming to do. You may also miss important announcements about tutorials or other course information, which are usually given before the lecture starts.

At the end of the lecture, the main issues, facts, theories or processes are summarised and there may be general information about the next lecture to show how one phase of the teaching relates to the next. If you leave early, it's not only rude – you may miss this crucial information.

Visual aids

There are many forms of visual aid available nowadays to help explain information and focus more precisely on some aspects of the presentation.

Overhead transparencies

Overheads which the lecturer prepares in advance can be particularly useful and some lecturers may be willing to provide copies before or after the lecture. Other lecturers prefer to write up their overheads as they deliver the lecture. In this case you need to pay particular attention to what they write and be ready to decode their handwriting.

Slides

Some disciplines need visual images that can be properly reproduced only on photographic slides, as in cases where the lecturer wants to show examples of micro-organisms or fine art. In your notes, you should write details of each slide as well as the comments the lecturer makes about it.

PowerPoint presentations

PowerPoint presentations are useful because you can listen, rather than having to write. But it's important not to let your attention wander. The points on the slides will be only the framework of the content or argument; if you have a printout, make notes on it as you go along to add more detail or set down your thoughts about it.

Your contribution

It may seem that lectures are primarily a one-way process, with you sitting there absorbing what's coming from the lecturer. But you can do a lot to make them much more effective. If you're motivated, positive and open-minded and have a real interest in the subject, the lecture is the springboard for acquiring and being able to use knowledge. So read and understand the learning objectives, read some background to familiarise yourself with the subject and, most important of all, use your critical thinking skills to make the experience deeper and more stimulating.

brilliant tip

Prepare for the lecture. Print out and study any published notes, read the textbook or try sample questions. You'll get more out of what you hear.

Go to every lecture. They're the basis of your course. If you miss one, it gets easier to miss others and in the end you hardly go at all. You may think you can catch up, but don't fool yourself. The material you get from the VLE will simply be printed notes, outlines of what was said.

Remember that the lecture content is only part of what you have to learn for assessment in assignments or exams. Lectures give you a framework for learning, but it's up to you to develop your understanding by further reading and critical thinking.

Listen intelligently. Recognise the lecturer's style, the structure of the lecture and the way the argument is developed. That way you'll be able to tailor your note-taking strategy accordingly.

Visual information is important. If there's something on a photographic slide, a PowerPoint slide, an overhead transparency or the board, write down the important details. It wouldn't be there if it weren't important.

Note down references, particularly those given by the lecturer. You may just get the author's name and maybe the date of publication, but more details should be in the course handbook. Look up the references as soon after the lecture as possible and add any notes you get from them to your lecture notes.

What next?

Find out about your set texts ...

... by looking at the relevant sections in your course handbook. If you familiarise yourselves with these, you'll know what they are when they're mentioned in the lectures, and you'll know where to find them in the library.

Practise 'intelligent listening' ...

... by watching and listening to discussions or current affairs programmes on television or radio. Listen for the introduction to the topic, the key points and the summary that brings them all together at the end of an interview or speech.

Make sure you know what's meant by ...

... critical thinking. We explain it in Chapter 14. It's a very important process and will help enormously with all aspects of understanding materials, evaluating information and applying it to other areas of study. Just because you're being taught by academics or getting information from books written by specialists, you don't have to accept blindly everything you're told. You're there to ask questions, to be curious, to look at the strengths and weaknesses of your own evidence or that of others. It's a fundamental part of university learning and it'll equip you to form your own opinions based on a genuine understanding of the issues.

 recap

What is a lecture?

Different formats.

Getting the most from lectures.

Visual aids.

What you can do to prepare.

10 Listening and learning

The idea of a lecture is to convey information, ideas and arguments. Different lecturers use different techniques and you need to be able to identify them and adapt your strategies to make sure you get the most out of them.

Understanding what lecturers say and how they say it

Lecturers, like every other group of individuals, vary greatly in their personalities and skills. Some are excellent, others are not, some are popular, others are hard to like. You'll probably come across examples of all sorts in the course of your studies. The important thing is to overcome any feelings you have about the topic, the lecturer or the style he uses because the most important thing is what the lecturer is saying. In other words, what interests you is the content and that's what should hold your focus.

Lecturing styles

Every lecturer is an individual with his own unique approach to the task. You'll get to know their mannerisms, idiosyncrasies, speech patterns and the whole set of behaviours they use as they deliver their pearls of wisdom. The challenge is to be aware of this and adapt your listening strategies and note-taking style accordingly. Whether the lecture is hilarious and entertaining or dull and depressing, your job is to listen to it carefully and take meaningful notes. The more you practise this, the more skilful you'll become and you'll soon know how to judge what's being said and decide what's important.

▶ brilliant example

Dr Millcroft is an entertainer. He's got great gags, ad libs his way through his lectures and seems to enjoy his job. Some students love his funny, relaxed style but others find it hard to take him seriously. The important thing is to separate the ideas from the jokes. When a lecturer uses this approach, he's not deliberately doing a stand-up routine but trying to use humour to keep your attention so that he can get his ideas across. So, in this case by all means enjoy the lectures, but listen for 'signpost' words and phrases. You'll find examples of them later in the chapter. They're words which tell you how the lecturer's going to deal with the topic and when there's a change of emphasis, a new development or a particularly important point. The jokes may help you remember the content afterwards, but they could also get in the way of your understanding.

Dr Sinclair is a drone. Everything he says is on the same note. He never speeds up or slows down, never changes the pitch of his voice. In fact, he's monotony in human form. Listening to him is boring and it's very difficult to absorb what he's saying and to separate the more and less important aspects of the content. Once again, note the sign-post words and also listen carefully to spot important points through the meaning of words rather than any stress he puts on them.

Dr Mostyn is a rambler. There's a certain eccentricity about her which is obvious in the way she delivers her lectures. She sets off in a particular direction, then seems to wander away from the point or get carried away by her enthusiasm for the thing she's describing. Sometimes she just stops, then moves off in a different direction. But underneath the apparent lack of structure, there's a recognisable argument made up of specific, logical points. What you need to do is listen for those points and note them down. Don't let your mind wander with her digressions. As you concentrate on the main features, the shape and direction of the lecture will become clearer and the conclusions will relate back to the earlier points. You can then reorganise and expand your notes to make it all easier to remember.

Dr Bellingham is rather shy and tends to mumble her lectures rather than deliver them. She's obviously an expert in her field, and in tutorials she's great value. But faced with a huge lecture class she goes back into her shell and fails to project her voice. This isn't such an easy one to give advice about because if you can't hear her, there's not much you can do. You could sit near the front or, if it's really bad, try to get an appointment with her to explain the problem. It's possible that she doesn't realise that she can't be heard. A more subtle approach is to make eye contact with her, smile and look interested. The idea of that is to make her feel more confident that she's having an impact and she may relax and speak more clearly.

Professor Oswald can't keep still. He starts at the lectern, with his notes in front of him, but pretty soon he's wandering about, waving his arms, fiddling with his sleeves and generally doing all sorts of distracting things. All you can do really is try to blot out these irritations and focus on the flow of information. You could, of course, keep your eyes on your notes and not watch him, but then you might miss some signals. It might be that he moves away whenever he starts a new phase of the lecture, or maybe the hand-waving happens only when he's making a particularly important point. Body language is part of communication; watching as well as listening to the lecturer as you take notes may help you to get more out of the lecture.

Professor Caldecott is an unashamed techie. She loves gadgets and all her lectures are always illustrated with slides, video, PowerPoint presentations, audio examples. Her choices are good and she manipulates the different media skilfully. Potentially, her presentations, especially the PowerPoint ones, are more useful than a traditional lecture. She always either distributes handouts or puts them on the VLE. Unfortunately, not all techies do the same. With visual illustrations you need time to examine them in more detail. If there aren't any handouts, ask if they can be made available. That way, you can study slides, print them out if you want, maybe discuss them with classmates. If it's a PowerPoint slide which is packed with information, one of you could make a note of what the lecturer says about it while the other copies down the information on the slide. You can share the notes later.

Dr Moorcroft has a very high opinion of himself. He specialises in medieval poetry and believes that there's only one way to interpret it – his own. He's so self-assured that he rarely gives his classes the broader picture. There's little doubt that he's an expert in his field, but the field's quite narrow and it needs to be balanced by alternative interpretations. So listen to what he's saying, but listen also for any references he makes to other people's work on a topic. Then, after the lecture, go to the library, look in the catalogue for recent publications on the same topic and check out other 'big names' in the field. If he doesn't mention any names in the lecture, search out any articles he's written in journals and get the names from the references there.

 **tip**

For some, a slow, systematic delivery is death warmed up, for others it's perfect. A dynamic, flash-bang-wallop performance may inspire some and embarrass others. You'll experience many types. The important thing is to adapt to them and not let them get in the way of the content.

The structure and language of lectures

The range of lecturing styles may be bewildering, but most of them share common features which you can anticipate. They're usually signalled by obvious terms and expressions, the sort of things we've been calling sign-post words. So what you should do is not only listen to what's being said but also consider it, think about it, evaluate it. It'll help you to decide what type of notes to take.

Typical 'lecture language'

Let's try to pinpoint the sort of shape a lecture might take and how its changes of emphasis and direction might be signalled. There are, of course, a near infinite number of expressions that could be used and the ones we've chosen are simply examples. Equally, different lectures have different aims and their structures differ accordingly. These guidelines, though, will help you to listen for and recognise these types of phrase and make better notes. You'll be more aware, for example, when you're about to be given a list, when a definition is particularly important or when a point is given extra emphasis.

At the beginning of the lecture

Lecture element	Possible phrases or expressions
Outlining the topic to be covered	'In today's lecture I'll be considering ...'
Defining the aim of the lecture	'I'm going to look at a number of aspects of ...'
Lecture format	'I'll begin by ... and then I'll go on to ... and I'll end by ...'

In the body of the lecture

Providing a definition	'I'm going to start by defining ...'
Giving examples	'Let's look at some examples of ...'
Describing processes	'The first stage is ...'
Describing events	'To begin with ... then ...'
Describing position	'At the centre is ...'

Presenting a theory or an argument

Identifying key support points	'This viewpoint is supported by ...'
Explaining the perspective of each point	'This means that ...'
Justifying the evidence	'It can be seen from this evidence that ...'
Presenting a counter-argument	'The opposing viewpoint is that ...'
Drawing logical connections	'It's therefore clear that ...'
Identifying main issues	'The critical factors are ...'
Stressing importance	'It's essential that ...'
Repeating a point for clarification or emphasis	'Let me put that another way ...'
Moving on to a new theme	'Passing on to the next theme in my discussion ...'

At the end of the lecture

Concluding – reiterating the key messages	'To summarise the main aspects I've covered, let's remind ourselves of ...'

How to listen better

Think about where you sit in the lecture theatre. If you're near the front you'll hear better, but you may not have such a good view of any visual aids. Many students head straight for the back rows – that may be good for a laugh or even a little nap, but it won't do your learning much good. If you find some individuals distracting, don't sit near them.

Become familiar with the jargon. There are almost always technical terms and other sorts of jargon associated with particular disciplines. It's best if you know them beforehand. Just read the relevant chapter in the textbook.

Get organised beforehand. You don't want to be looking for pens and paper when the lecture's started.

Don't try to take down all the lecturer's words as if they were dictation. That may be necessary sometimes, but the lecturer will probably indicate that and speak more slowly. For the rest of the lecture, listen to the main points of what's being said and jot them down in your own words.

What next?

Analyse the styles ...

... of your various lecturers and decide which strategy will help you get the most from each one. Use the general suggestions in the examples we've given to adjust your approach if necessary. It might be interesting to ask a friend to use the same strategy and compare notes afterwards to see how effective it is.

 **recap**

Lecturing styles.

The structure and language of lectures.

11 Listening and taking notes

We know that, whatever the discipline, lectures aim to present a topic for study by introducing and stressing key points and developing understanding through explanation, argument, examples or suggestions for further reading. Your job is to distil all that into notes which capture the essence of what's said in terms you understand.

Condensing what you hear

Lectures don't give you the 'answer' to a topic or a comprehensive explanation of it; they're more like guidelines and hints to make it more accessible to you. They give you essential pieces of information in a particular order for each course. Quite often, they're only an introduction to the topic. For some subjects, they're compulsory because professional bodies insist that, to qualify as a member of their association, you must prove you've attended the necessary classes.

Your role in lectures

You won't get everything you need for a complete understanding of the subject or enough to help you revise for your exams just from sitting in on lectures. So you need to get involved. If you take notes that are comprehensive and comprehensible, you'll be deepening your understanding and using your critical faculties. You'll also have a set of notes that may be useful when you start making notes from set texts. It's part of the whole learning process.

brilliant tip

For every lecture, note the date, the lecturer's name, and the topic and aims of the lecture. Remember also to number your pages.

You'll go to lots of lectures, sometimes several in a day, so you need to have a good idea of why specifically you're taking notes on them. This may seem obvious, but if you form a clear idea of your aim, it'll help you to take the sort of notes that suit you best. You may want to have a record of what was said for future reference and exam revision. Perhaps the idea is to grab the main points so that you can follow them up in your reading later. They could be a good example of how to build an argument, a sequence of ideas or a process. We could multiply the examples, but in the end the choice depends on you.

Approaches to note-taking

There are several questions to ask about what might affect your note-taking. Are you able to listen for specific information and identify and follow the thread of an argument or discussion? How neat is your handwriting? What's your learning personality or style? What's the lecturer's style? What's the subject and does it have any particular conventions? They'll all affect what you write and how you write it.

Later, we'll look at the different formats you might consider for when you're making notes from your reading, but you won't have that luxury with lecture notes. There, you'll have to be more spontaneous because you're following someone else's train of thought and you don't get much chance to dwell on particular points. In a way, that means you have less control over how you structure your notes. But the more lectures you go to, the more you'll develop note-taking methods that suit your learning style.

> ## ⊛ brilliant tip
>
> - Listen for and note the key ideas. Don't try to write down every word because it's impossible and you'll miss out on understanding ideas, explanations and examples.
>
> - Make sure you use a style that will produce notes that you'll still understand in six days, weeks or months.
>
> - Refine your system with such tricks as underlining or highlighting points the lecturer emphasises, using asterisks (*) for special points or to mark words you need to look up, and writing sub-headings or keywords in capital letters.
>
> - Create and/or copy special abbreviations for your subject.
>
> - When you jot down a thought of your own prompted by something the lecturer said, mark it with a special symbol.

Some lecture formats and how to cope with them

Let's look at some typical lecture formats and consider how we can get the most out of them with our note-taking.

A 'straight' lecture

In this case, it's a monologue with no handouts or special visual aids. So the key is obviously to listen carefully and note:

- the aims, outline and structure of the lecture
- any references to authors and other sources which you can then consult
- important personalities, dates or events mentioned
- signpost words that indicate changes of direction and shifts of emphasis
- how an argument is structured and the supporting evidence
- the stages of a process or sequence of events
- points that are repeated or emphasised
- the summarising points during and at the end of the lecture.

A lecture with overhead transparencies

Use the same techniques as for the straight lecture but also copy down the points shown on overheads to use as the framework on which to expand your own notes. As we suggested earlier, you could also consider working with a friend. One of you can copy the slide while the other takes notes on what the lecturer's saying about it. When you merge the notes afterwards, you'll get a more comprehensive record of what was said. It also means working together, discussing the notes and clarifying points. It's a good way of reinforcing your learning.

A lecture with printed handouts

First, a warning. Handouts carrying notes about lectures aren't a substitute for attending the lecture. Lecturers will expand certain points, add examples to clarify things and may also add information not covered in the handout. But handouts are a valuable note-taking aid.

If you're given one before or at the lecture:

- use it in addition to your own note-taking
- mark key points with highlighters
- write your own notes or add examples or ideas in contrasting colours.

If you get it after the lecture, use your own notes to expand its contents.

A lecture using PowerPoint software

These are usually slick, professional presentations with clearly listed points and good detailed images of graphs or diagrams. The problem is that it's difficult to make a note of so much detail. If this is your experience, use the techniques we mentioned for the straight lecture and ask if it's possible to download the slides before or after the lecture. This needn't be too expensive because you can choose to print out slides with two, three, four, six or nine to a page using black and white rather than colour.

Some note-taking formats

Linear

The usual note-taking format is the obvious, linear one, where the notes follow the structure of the lecture. You can make them clearer by sub-dividing and numbering them like this:

1.   Heading

1.1   first point

1.2   second point

2.   Heading

2.1   first point

2.2   second point

This technique is fine for most lectures, especially those where processes, procedures or sequences are being followed, and they're very easy to read back.

Keyword

The keyword format is also straightforward. This time you write a keyword for each phase of the lecture in the left-hand column and the notes relating to it beside it on the right. You end up with a quick overview of the lecture's argument in the left-hand column and details in the right. This is good for lectures with clear structural divisions.

Matrix notes

For these, you create a matrix with the various topics of the lecture listed in the left-hand column and different viewpoints across the top. You can then enter the notes in the appropriate box (row+column). This is useful if the declared aim of the lecture is to compare and/or contrast different viewpoints of several different topics.

Concept maps/mind maps

For these it's better to turn your notepad so that it's in the landscape position. Write the topic in the middle of the page, then add notes around it, linking them by a line to the centre. As more and more notes are added, some will expand on things you've already written, so rather than linking them to the centre, you'll link them to the point they're developing. The central topic gradually gets surrounded by the various points the lecturer makes (and points of your own which you may add).

It's useful if the lecturer tends to back-track, repeat points and re-emphasise them. The problem is that it can become cramped and it works only if your writing's smallish and neat.

 dos and don'ts

DO ...

... try to read some background information on the topic before the lecture. You could use a textbook or a good encyclopaedia.

... consult the disability support service about any special needs you may have. If you're dyslexic or you have a hearing or sight impairment, or any other disability, you may be able to ask to be given lecture notes or handouts before lectures.

... choose a seat from which you can see the whiteboard, projection screen or television monitor easily.

... choose A4 notepads. That's the standard size for handouts and printers so it'll make filing easier. Narrow-lined paper with a margin lets you get more on each page. Depending on your subject, you may need blank paper for diagrams and mathematical calculations, but apart from that, the choice is yours. If your handwriting's neat, you won't need lined paper and you'll get more on the page; if it's untidy, lines will keep it neater.

... store your notes carefully and use a labelling system that makes them easy to find. Get into the habit of filing notes immediately after the lecture so that you don't find them at the bottom of your rucksack or sports bag after the exams are over.

DON'T...

... rely on internet sources for background; they can be unreliable, inaccurate and misleading.

... sit near the door, at the back of the room (where the talkers and latecomers usually congregate) or underneath noisy air-conditioning vents.

... choose small, reporter-style notebooks. You'll be taking so many notes that they'll fill up in no time.

Writing up notes. Yes or no?

Whether you decide to write up your notes after a lecture is up to you. The important thing is to know why you're doing it. It takes time, so is that time wasted? Some people say that it's an essential part of the learning process; it helps them to understand the subject better and to remember things. Others find that there are more important or more urgent things to do with that chunk of time. If all you're doing is making them look neat, colourful or simply pretty, then you're definitely wasting your time.

What next?

Find out when and where ...

... all your lectures are held and jot them down in your diary or on your wall planner. Confirm the details regularly on notice boards and the VLE because schedules and/or locations sometimes change. If it's in an unfamiliar place, go and find it beforehand so you know where to go on the day.

Check the availability of ...

... handouts, overhead or PowerPoint slides.

Work on your ...

... note-taking skills. At first it may be difficult, but you'll get better with practice. You could even try taking notes from a news broadcast on radio or television, experimenting with different techniques and layouts. You could listen to the six o'clock news, for example, then check your notes against a similar broadcast at nine or ten.

 **recap**

How to take notes.

The different lecture formats.

What to do and not to do.

12 The complexities and benefits of teamwork

Working in a team is not only an effective and rewarding way to learn; it also can help to prepare you for your career. So we'll look now at the role you and others might play in a team and some essential teamwork skills.

Teamwork and you

You may play team sports at university, but there are times when the team will be formed for academic purposes. Usually that will mean working together to solve a problem and/or produce some outcome such as a poster or a report. You and your team mates may be assessed by your tutors or sometimes by each other.

Teamwork's a broad concept, stretching from sport to fundraising groups, social events to the workplace. And, of course, it's at the base of all social organisation. So it obviously pays to know something about how it works and how you can contribute.

▶ brilliant example

Teamwork at university

- Preparing a group poster
- Writing a joint report
- Problem-based learning
- Practical and project work
- Running a society or sports club.

Team roles

There are several distinct team personalities and we tend to fill the role which suits us best. Group work at university can help you find your preferred role and become a good team member. It could influence your eventual choice of career. You'll learn something even if you're given a role that isn't your 'natural' one. You may also be asked to play multiple roles or switch from one to another as the project progresses.

It's important not to feel that any one role is superior. The obvious assumption is that the 'team leader' is the star. But some leaders can be poor at coming up with ideas and weak at putting them into practice, so if having ideas and making them work is the object, the team will have to rely on others. In fact, the whole object of a team is to combine different skills to achieve a common goal. So let's look at the sort of people and skills we might need.

The leader

She may be calm and authoritative, have a fair, balanced view of things and use good judgement. She's good at spotting other people's talents and at delegating. She may also be less creative or intelligent than other team members and have no special expertise. However, if she's the manipulative type, she can be a dynamic go-getter but too impatient for results. She's good at getting others going, troubleshooting and imposing a pattern. She's realistic, gives a sense of purpose and drives the team effort. But she can be headstrong, emotional and impatient with others.

The creative type

This is the intelligent, ideas person, who sees solutions to problems, often through unusual approaches. He's extrovert and enthusiastic in his investigations of new information and ideas. He uses resources well. He may prefer to work in isolation, though, and some of his ideas may not work. He could also be over-optimistic and have a short attention span.

The organiser

She works hard and energetically, using discipline and common sense to solve problems. She's the one who turns ideas into actions and makes sure things get done. She's conscientious and well organised and has high standards. She has a clear notion of objectives and how to meet them. Her weaknesses may be that she lacks flexibility and is resistant to new ideas. Her obsessiveness about details may make her so anxious about controlling the quality and outcome of the work that she does too much of it herself.

The worker

This could be a social type who gets pleasure from supporting and helping others. She's sensitive to their feelings and provides cohesion to the team. Her diplomatic skills make her very good for team spirit, but she's not a good leader or decision maker. Alternatively, she could be the kind of person who brings professional expertise which is essential for solving the specific problem facing the group. But her outlook may be narrow and she can get bogged down in technical detail and fail to see the big picture. If she's that single-minded, she probably won't suffer fools gladly.

The critic

There's always someone who can step back in a detached and unemotional way and analyse what the team's doing. This isn't always negative input. He's good at evaluating the ideas and making sure they're appropriate and workable. However, he may lack drive and have a low work rate and his critical comments could demotivate others.

So, in general terms …

- If you prefer action, you should concentrate on putting ideas into practice, implementing decisions and getting the job done.
- If you prefer people, you should be a co-ordinator, a resource investigator or a teamworker.
- If you're a thinker, you should generate new ideas, check and evaluate decisions and actions, or offer specialist support.

brilliant tip

If you like to be in control of how things are progressing, it can be stressful for you to hand over tasks to others. But in a team, you have to accept that different approaches may be valid. If they (or you) make mistakes, you'll all learn from them.

Essential teamwork skills

Communication

The success of any team depends on its ability to communicate. The larger the group, the more important this becomes. Everybody needs to know what's expected of them by both the team and the teaching staff who've set the task. You all need to decide on time frames, team roles, arrangements for meetings and the sharing of information or files. Early on, it's important to hold face-to-face meetings, but after that you can keep in touch with email, mobile phones and discussion boards. One of the first things you should all do is agree on and set up good communication channels and exchange email addresses and contact details.

Compromise

Give and take is central to good communications. For the team to function properly at all its levels, you may have to make concessions. You may object to the role you've been given, you may not have chosen the other team members and may not even like some of them. The value of teamwork is in overcoming such feelings for the sake of the group and the desired outcomes. You'll need to be self-aware and flexible, diplomatic and tactful. Be ready to give and take criticism constructively and not turn it into some personal affront. If you're a perfectionist, get used to the idea that some of the things the group does will fall well below your normal standards, but that may be necessary for it to achieve its aims.

Time management

There are always deadlines to meet, so the co-ordinator, in consultation with everyone else, will need to plan things. If you've all got different timetables and responsibilities, it may be hard to arrange mutually suitable meeting times. If that's the case, break down the objective and set intermediate targets – milestones if you like. Time management is part of being successful, so set diary dates as early as possible.

Focus and commitment

Teamwork calls for time and effort. Each member must show commitment and a high work rate to get the best results. If individuals don't all keep their eyes on the group's goals and targets and make sure it meets them, the overall mark may suffer. One of the duties of the leader is to make it easier and desirable for all members to keep that focus.

 **example**

The more people there are in a group, the more complicated the set of contacts becomes. See for yourself by drawing circles on a scrap of paper. Each represents a member of the group. Start with three in a triangle and draw lines linking each member with the other two. Now use four to make a square and draw the lines again. Add a fifth to make a circle and do the same thing. By now the tangle of lines should make our point clear.

Good teamwork in action

- If difficulties arise, discuss them right away, either within the team or with the staff supervising the task. If you don't they can grow into insurmountable problems.

- Team members should have enough time to complete the task. If that's not possible, you may have to modify the task or the method you've agreed to use. The outcome may be less ambitious, but still good.

- Members must feel motivated all the time or the group will lose momentum. It's up to the leader to see to this by reminding everyone of the importance of and the rewards for doing a good job.

- If people are given roles which don't fit best with their personality, they may feel uncomfortable and perform less well.

- Clashes of personalities are normal. One member thinks another's not pulling his weight, another is acting like he doesn't belong, or is maybe made to feel that way. If this happens, talk about it earlier rather than later.

How to behave

- Be considerate. Respect the abilities and contributions of others.

- Be positive, praise other members' work whenever you can and don't be dismissive of their ideas.

- If you need to be critical, make it constructive criticism and don't antagonise people.

- Don't form cliques.

- If someone seems weak in some areas, they may be strong in others.

- Check your own conduct, your contribution and how effectively you're playing your role.

Communicate

- Talk to others and encourage them to talk to you.

- Share phone numbers, email addresses and reply promptly to messages.

- Talk through all problems earlier rather than later.

- Remember that some team members may be shy or nervous.

- If your team has to 'defend' its work, make sure you contribute.

- Don't monopolise discussions or impose your views. Learn to listen to others and recognise that their opinions are legitimate and valuable.

Make a real effort

- Don't be a lazy team member.

- Produce work of the highest quality you can.

- If you feel you're doing too much or more than others, call the group together, explain the problem and try to work something out between all of you.

- Think of the reward on offer and work accordingly. Remember that good marks in assessed coursework can affect your overall grades.

- Always keep the final objective of the exercise in mind.

Assessment and evaluation

- Find out exactly how you'll be assessed and use the information to the team's advantage.

- If part of the process involves assessing other team members, be fair.

- If someone doesn't deserve good marks, don't just give them out of loyalty or misguided friendship.

- When it's over, think about what you learned from it – not just the subject but your own behaviour and teamwork in general.

What next?

Reflect on your ...

... last teamwork activity. What were your major contributions? What role or roles did you adopt? How did the team perform as a whole? How could you use the experience to change your approach to the next team exercise?

Focus on ...

... the various ways of communicating, especially if the group is relatively large.

Decide what ...

... your ideal role is. Are you action-orientated, people-orientated or a thinker. Try asking a friend or someone you've worked with in a team what they think. But don't be surprised if their answer's different from yours.

 **recap**

Team roles.

Essential teamwork skills.

Making sure that your team works well together.

13 The tutorial way of getting involved

Tutorials are classes with small groups of students who, together with a tutor, discuss a topic or tackle problems related to a particular aspect of their course. They're an excellent way of getting you more closely involved and delving more deeply into your subject.

Small is beautiful

Most tutorials involve 5–12 students, although in some universities they're one-to-one sessions. The tutor's role is to encourage discussion or, for problem-solving tutorials, to help students who are having difficulties of some sort with their studies. The tutor may also have to make an assessment of your participation and performance.

Your tutors won't necessarily be the people who deliver your lectures. They could be academics who are brought in for the sole purpose of taking tutorials, or perhaps postgraduate students who are studying in your department. The value of tutorials is that they're more than just extra classes about your chosen subject. It's a meeting between intelligent people with their own opinions and concerns. No doubt most of the discussions will feature some aspect of your course, but in the process of interacting with your peers and the tutor, you'll be increasing your knowledge, developing interpersonal skills and communication strategies and helping to increase your self-confidence.

Types of tutorial

There are essentially two types of university tutorial. In subjects related to arts, social sciences, law and social work, for example, there's usually a preset topic which is discussed freely. In scientific and engineering disciplines and numerical subjects such as accountancy, tutorials may be more closely related to lectures and practicals. Students discuss answers to a series of problems or calculations under the guidance of a tutor. Whatever your discipline, you'll need to prepare for these classes and make sure you participate.

You'll get regular tutorials during the term or semester. Details of dates, times and venues will be listed in your course handbook, given on the departmental notice board or posted on the VLE.

brilliant tip

It may be useful to prepare for the tutorial with others, especially if it involves working through examples or problems. If the problem's tricky, you might find a solution together. If you don't, then asking for help from the tutor as a group will make sure that the problems are dealt with thoroughly.

Preparation

Before each tutorial, you'll need to prepare to contribute. If it's for a practical or numerical subject, you'll need to do at least some of the following:

- tackle the full set of problems or do the prescribed reading
- submit answers on time
- think about any difficulties you've had with the tutorial problems or about possible issues that might come up in the discussion
- reflect on how this topic or these problems fit into the wider course structure.

For discussion-style tutorials in non-scientific subjects, you'll need to have:

- done the required reading
- identified and analysed the topic or theme
- thought about the main issues
- looked at the topic from different angles and considered arguments for and against.

Tutorials and lectures

If you have an informal meeting with a lecturer to go over a particular piece of work or ask for an explanation of a point in a lecture which you haven't understood, that's not really a tutorial. In fact, the link between tutorials and lectures depends on the subject you're studying and your department's policy. Your tutor may not know what your lectures are aimed at and so won't be able to discuss your queries with any confidence.

Getting involved

It's possible that you meet the other students in your group only during that class and not in any others. And if there's a time lapse between tutorials, you may feel reluctant to get involved in discussions and problem-solving with comparative strangers. That sort of feeling's normal. It's too easy to assume that everyone knows more than you do, but they're probably feeling the same way. No two students are the same and it's swapping ideas with others, hearing their opinions, supporting or challenging them that makes tutorials so rich and stimulating. Some of the most satisfying learning experiences come from exchanges in tutorials.

Speaking up

Most communication is a two-way process – speaker and listener. The only difference in tutorials is that there are several listeners, all with views of their own and something to say. You'll get more out of the situation if you're both speaker and listener, so you'll need to develop some skills in interpersonal communication. We've invented some familiar tutorial types and suggested the sort of contacts they have with others.

 **example**

The quiet one

Lizzy's a quiet student – shy, retiring. She sits in the tutorial, head down, taking notes. She's bright and has her own ideas about topics, but you rarely hear a word out of her. Usually, she speaks only if she's asked a direct question. Then, as often as not, she just shakes her head or says 'I don't know'. The tutor and the others try to help her by asking her opinion directly or by asking her to comment on what someone else has just said.

The know-it-all

Tom is obnoxious. He knows everything (or thinks he does). He's got opinions on almost any subject that comes up and he's not afraid to voice them. He's usually done the reading, but he rarely thinks very deeply about it, or else he's done the problems but left out key steps. He's chipping in all the time with 'In my opinion ...', 'I think ...', 'If you ask me ...'. The way the others react to him is to say 'I think you're taking rather a narrow view on this. What about ... ?'

The star

Jez likes to be the centre of attention. He's determined to be the star and his pushiness prevents others from asking questions or contributing. It's no surprise to hear him saying something like 'This can be broken down into ten areas. The first one is ... , the second one is ... , the tenth one is ...' and so on. The only way to make him pause is to interrupt him with 'Could I come in here?' or 'Actually, I have a similar point to make.'

The talker

The only person who manages to shut Jez up is Val, but she's just as bad. She tends to hog the conversation. She does the reading, and thinks about it, so she's got plenty to say. But she goes on and on. She's so keen to tell you what she thinks that she seems to forget that other people might have points to make, too. She just pours out the words 'My understanding of this theory is ... furthermore ... on the other hand ... I'd also like to say that ...' On and on. But the tutor and the others make her pause at least by saying 'Could we hear other views?' or 'Let's summarise what you've said so that we're sure we've understood you.'

The interrupter

Mind you, Val doesn't always get her own way, not when Alistair's in the class. Alistair's not a good listener. Even if someone else is talking, he interrupts them or talks over them, with stuff like 'If I could come in here ...' or 'I can't let that go without challenging it ...'. The others get fed up with him and are constantly saying 'Let me finish' or 'You're not sticking to the point.'

The uncertain one

Chris always seems unsure of herself. In fact, she's very bright, but she's got no confidence in her understanding or abilities. And she doesn't ask many questions either. The only time she offers an opinion is when she's asked directly. Even then, she usually comes out with 'I'm not sure' or 'I don't think I know'. The only way to get her going is with a direct question like 'How would you tackle this?' or by trying to boost her confidence with things like 'That's a really good point. I agree with you.'

The dropout

It's difficult to know why Derek's there. He's got no interest in anything. He says he only took the subject to make up his module numbers when he matriculated. He's always looking out of the window, clicking away at his mobile. All you get out of him is 'No idea. I'm only here until the union opens' or 'This is really boring, innit?.' No point trying to draw him out, so everybody ignores him.

The balanced one

Finally there's Sarah. She seems to have got the balance right. She contributes a lot, but she also listens to what others are saying. She's done the reading, sorted out some of the ideas, but she's not always sure of some of the points. So she asks about them. You always hear 'Could you explain ... ?' and 'What do other people think about it?' It actually makes the others open up a bit more. They say she's made an interesting point and ask her to expand on it, and the rest start chipping in.

Problem-solving tutorials

To prepare for problem-solving tutorials, think about the underlying principles involved in the exercises. Ask yourself how the examples fit in with the rest of the studying you're doing, especially your lectures. Make sure you've done all the examples beforehand. Make a note of the ones that caused difficulties or raised questions in your mind so that you can discuss them fully with the tutor.

Don't clam up because you feel your question's stupid. There'll be others in the group who are thinking exactly the same thing. Get your question in early on in the session. Ask it before others who haven't prepared properly take the conversation on to unimportant topics with trivial or irrelevant questions.

↗ brilliant dos and don'ts

DO ...

... make sure that you contribute. It's better to say something that you know something about rather than be asked a direct question by the tutor about something on which your knowledge is a bit shaky.

... make your points clearly and objectively. You may hold strong views on a subject, but you'll have to support them with evidence and argument, not emotion.

... be aware that your ideas are as valid as anyone else's. Everyone's contribution to the discussion is equally valuable.

DON'T ...

... take criticism personally. The tutorial is an objective academic exercise; it would be very dull and even pointless if everyone agreed.

... just speak, listen too. In a tutorial everyone has the right to speak and be heard. You may not agree with some of what you hear, but listen to what others have to say and notice the merits as well as the flaws in their argument.

... assume that your tutor is expressing a personal view when she makes a point. She may be taking up an opposing position (known as 'playing devil's advocate') just to get the discussion going.

What next?

Check when and where ...

... you have tutorials and put all the details in your diary or on your wall planner. If you're not sure of the location, find it beforehand so that you know where to go on the day.

Draw up a work plan ...

... that includes doing the preparatory reading or examples for your tutorials. It'll have a big effect on your performance.

Identify tutorial characters ...

... like those we described earlier. Could you use any of the conversational gambits we noted there to stop people monopolising the debate, encourage the quiet ones to contribute and generally create a more balanced discussion?

And ask yourself ...

... what kind of character you are. Do you need to change how you contribute? Think about body language, conversational strategies and any other aspects of the experience that could help you to participate fully and get real benefits from your tutorials.

 **recap**

Types of tutorial.

Preparation.

Participation.

Student types.

Strategies for dialogue.

14 The essence and importance of critical thinking

The ability to think critically is probably the most valuable skill you'll develop at university. It's an ability with uses and applications in all walks of work and life. So we need to do some thinking about thinking.

A logical approach to analysis and problem-solving

Is it actually possible to think better? Are there theories or techniques that can help? Well, most university teaching is based on the assumption that you can and there are. Basically, you need to recognise what it is and practise it.

You won't get good marks simply by having a good memory, recalling facts and churning them out. At university you're expected to analyse those facts, reach an opinion about them and support it with evidence and argument. If you're systematic and methodical about doing this, it'll help with all sorts of tasks, from the easy to the more challenging.

brilliant definition

The first reaction to the words 'critical' and 'criticism' is usually to assume they're negative. But critical thinking is positive. It means considering all aspects of a topic and then making a careful judgement about it. Critical thinking is good, creative thinking.

Thinking about thinking

A famous educational psychologist, Benjamin Bloom, and some of his colleagues listed six steps in learning and thinking in education:

- knowledge
- comprehension
- application
- analysis
- synthesis
- evaluation.

Their analysis was very detailed, but for our purposes it's enough to understand what these different phases mean in more general terms. They can be seen as a natural progression. It's probably obvious, for example, that the things you did at school involved mainly knowledge, comprehension and application. At university, you'll need to do more analysis, synthesis and evaluation. That's easier to understand if you think of the types of exercises you'll be expected to do:

- essay writing in the arts and social sciences
- problem-based learning in medicine and nursing
- engineering problems based on real-life machines and buildings
- scenarios in law
- project-based practical work in the sciences.

All of these call for basic knowledge, understanding and an ability to apply that knowledge and understanding. But they also expect you to look more deeply into ideas and theories, bring together different thoughts and make judgements about the results. In other words, you must be able to analyse, synthesise and evaluate. In subjects such as art and design, architecture, drama or English composition, synthesis might be replaced by creative thinking. But creative thinking is also critical thinking.

In fact, some of the instructions you get for writing assignments and other forms of assessment hint at the sort of thinking the examiner's expecting from you. You're often asked to 'discuss', 'compare', describe', 'analyse' and so on. There's no rule to link any of them with a specific type of thinking, but they can guide you.

 examples

Knowledge

If you know a fact, you can recall or recognise it, but you don't necessarily understand it at a higher level. So the words 'Define', 'Describe', 'Identify' and similar expressions are asking you to use knowledge.

Comprehension

Comprehending a fact means that you do understand what it means, which puts you in a position to 'Contrast', 'Discuss' or 'Interpret'.

Application

Knowing and understanding a fact means you know how to use or 'apply' it to 'Demonstrate', 'Calculate' or 'Illustrate'.

Analysis

The next step is being able to break down knowledge into parts and show how they fit together, so you can 'Analyse', 'Explain' and 'Compare'.

Synthesis

Synthesising is the ability to select relevant facts from your knowledge and use them in different ways or different contexts, to create something new. That's what you need to do when asked to 'Compose', 'Create' or 'Integrate'.

Evaluation

After all of that, you're in a position to evaluate facts and information and arrive at a judgement. You can then 'Recommend', 'Support' and 'Draw a conclusion'.

Be careful, though. This isn't a set of fixed 'rules'. For example, if you're asked to 'describe' something in the sciences, you may simply have to note what you observe – element A was added to element B and resulted in reaction X. The same word in architecture, however, might call for much more complex skills and theoretical perspectives.

The 'six steps' in practice

In order to illustrate more clearly the nature of the different phases, let's apply them to three general types of discipline – law, arts subjects and numerical subjects.

Law

Knowledge – you know the name and date of a case, statute or treaty, but don't understand its relevance.

Comprehension – you understand both the principle of law in the legislation or case and its wider context.

Application – you're able to identify situations to which the principle would apply.

Analysis – you can see how the facts of a particular scenario relate to the principle and use that knowledge to uncover the extent of its application.

Synthesis – using reasoning and analogy, you can predict how the law might be applied in other circumstances.

Evaluation – you're able to consider the various options and use your judgement as a basis for advising a client.

Arts, e.g. history or politics

Knowledge – you know that a river is an important geographical and political boundary in international relations, but you don't know why.

Comprehension – you understand that the river forms a natural barrier, which can be easily identified and defended.

Application – you can use this knowledge to explain the terms of a peace treaty.

Analysis – you can see that the fact that the river is a boundary is important for signatories to the peace treaty in terms of their possible gains or losses of territory.

Synthesis – you can relate this awareness to the recurrence of the same issue in later treaties and its possible implications.

Evaluation – you can discuss whether this boundary was an obstacle to resolving the terms of the treaty to the satisfaction of all parties.

Numerical subjects

Knowledge – you can write down a particular mathematical equation, without understanding what the symbols mean or where it might be applied.

Comprehension – you understand what the symbols mean and how and when to apply the equation.

Application – if you have the background information, you can use the equation to obtain a result.

Analysis – you can explain the theoretical process involved in deriving the equation.

Synthesis – you can take one equation, link it with another and arrive at a new mathematical relationship or conclusion.

Evaluation – you can discuss the limitations of an equation based on its derivation and the underlying assumptions behind this.

A system for critical thinking

OK, so you have a particular problem and you feel that critical thinking will help you solve it. It could be an essay question, something arising from problem-based learning, or even something as ordinary as deciding what type of car to buy or where to rent a flat. The points discussed below will help you to organise your thinking in a methodical way. They're not in themselves a solution; they're simply stages you might go through to reach a conclusion. Reject them, adapt them, change their order, but think about them and get what suits you best from them.

What's the problem?

First of all, you need to be sure that there really is a problem or that it really is what you think it is rather than something else. Write down a description of it and be very precise with your wording. If it's a specific question you've been given, analyse its phrasing carefully, look for alternative meanings. If you're working in a group, everyone should agree on a single interpretation.

How do you approach it?

Try some 'brainstorming', either on your own or with others or the group. That may throw up some possible solutions or viewpoints. Look at it from all possible angles and write down everything you come up with, even if you're not sure it's relevant or important. If you use a spider diagram or mind map, that might help you to make associations and multiply the ideas you're having.

When you're satisfied that you've had a thorough go at exploring lots of ideas, try to arrange them into categories or sub-headings. Alternatively, you could group them as arguments for and against a particular viewpoint. Once you've got them relatively organised, you can start eliminating the ones that are trivial or irrelevant and sort the rest into some sort of order of priority.

Back up the information with evidence

Now that you've narrowed (or maybe broadened) your focus, make sure you understand the facts. You'll probably need to collect more information and ideas to extend your response, so find some examples or suggest a range of interpretations or approaches which support your viewpoint. You might only need to use dictionaries and technical works to find out the precise meaning of key words; or you might discuss your ideas with your peers or a tutor; or you could read a few texts to see what other people have said about the topic.

Assemble your case

You've gathered lots of information, so it's time to make sure it's all relevant and does apply to your question. Look at the question again, check that you really do understand it, and start organising what you've collected. Some of it will support your argument, some of it will oppose it. Maybe a table or grid would help you to get it organised and see the balance you have between for and against. If any of the material is dubious, get rid of it. You want the strongest possible case, with no trivial or irrelevant distractions.

Build to a conclusion

By this stage, you've done so much thinking about it and gathered so much material that you'll probably have formed a strong personal viewpoint. What you have to do now is build your discussion with a view to making that your conclusion. You know what you want to say, so just say it. But be careful. It's too easy to slip into making value judgements or using other terms or expressions of opinion that aren't supported by the evidence you have.

Value judgements are statements that reflect the views and values of an individual rather than any objective reality. Someone who supports a cause calls it a pressure group, but to a person who disagrees with it, its followers are 'activists'. Depending on which side you are, conservationists may be called tree-huggers and vice versa, freedom fighters are terrorists. The words don't just have a meaning, they imply an attitude and quite often it's negative. In a discussion, how valuable or 'true' is the claim that 'teenagers are unreliable, unpredictable and unable to accept responsibility for their actions'? Value judgements are subjective, often biased opinions. It's important for your conclusions to be objective and supported by facts.

 brilliant definitions

Fallacy – a fault in logic or thinking that means that an argument is incorrect.

Bias – information that emphasises just one viewpoint or position.

Propaganda – false or incomplete information that supports a (usually) extreme political or moral view.

Fallacies and biased presentations

Critical thinking demands a sensitivity to language. Arguments and discussions are mostly reasoned, dispassionate affairs, but even in such contexts, the choice of words reveals more than the speaker or writer sometimes suspects. If you can spot them, you'll be able to think not just about the argument itself but also about the way it's being conducted. If troops are massing on a border, it's legitimate to talk of them being a 'threat'. But if you add the word 'sinister', you're making assumptions about the reasons why they're moving into position and speculating on their intentions. In other words, you're not just an observer but someone who's becoming involved in the processes taking place.

The obvious areas in which faulty logic and debating tricks are used are those of advertising and politics. Analysing the methods of persuasion and misdirection they use is a useful way of practising your critical skills.

As well as being aware of how others use words, try to balance your own style and choose your words with care. It's very easy to slip into bad habits. 'Absolutes' such as 'always', 'never', 'all' and 'every' are such familiar expressions that we can use them without really thinking of how they affect our meaning. Each of them means that there are no exceptions. You should use them only if you're absolutely sure of facts that imply 100 per cent certainty.

A review of critical thinking

- It should be obvious by now that critical thinking is a practical, hands-on process, not just abstract theorising. So make sure you appreciate and apply those practical aspects. Focus on the task in hand. Once you start reading around a subject or discussing it with others, it's easy to get distracted and stray from the point.

- Write down your thoughts. As you do so, you'll be forced to clarify them and maybe refine them. Apart from that, even though we think we'll remember a good idea, it often drifts away and we can't recall it. So make it permanent; write it down. As you review it later, you'll see it more critically and it can lead you to fresh ideas.

- Lots of students lose marks because they simply quote facts or statements, without trying to explain their importance and context or even saying why they've included them. That suggests that they maybe don't understand what a quotation means or implies. Your work will be more interesting and persuasive if it's analytical, not descriptive.

- When you do quote evidence from other sources, it's very important to use appropriate citations. This shows you've read relevant source material and helps you to avoid plagiarism. Make sure you find out which style conventions your university uses and be consistent in how you use them.

- Refresh and expand your own ideas by discussing things with others – staff and students. They might have interpretations and opinions which haven't occurred to you. Bounce ideas off one another.

- Keep an open mind. You may start with preconceived ideas or sound convictions about a topic, but try still to be receptive to the ideas of others. You may find that your conviction isn't as secure as you first thought.

- And if there's not enough evidence to support any conclusion, say so. There may well be times when both sides of an argument are equally valid. Recognising that is as valid as deciding that one side or the other is 'correct'.

Critical thinking isn't just an academic exercise; it's about who you are. Shallow thinkers rush to conclusions, generalise, oversimplify. They make the arguments personal, resort to stereotypes, make value judgements and hide behind fallacies. Their results are usually inconclusive and unsatisfactory.

To think more deeply you need to keep asking yourself questions, even if the topic's been sorted out or you feel you understand it. Look beneath the surface. Decide whether the sources you're using are dealing with facts or opinions; look out for assumptions, including your own; think about why writers write the way they do. And when you quote from a source, don't just repeat what it's saying, focus on what it means.

What next?

Practise seeing ...

... both sides of an argument. Choose a topic, maybe something you feel strongly about. Write down the supporting arguments for both sides, paying particular attention to the arguments opposite to your own.

Look at the instruction words ...

... in past exam papers. Which ones are used most frequently? What exactly are they asking you to do and what level of thinking will you need to show in your exam answers? If you're unsure about any aspect of it all, ask a subject tutor to explain.

Look into the often entertaining ...

... world of fallacies and biased arguments. There are websites that list different types of them with examples. Just type 'fallacy' or 'logical fallacies' in a search engine; you'll learn from what you read, and it'll help to improve your analytical and debating skills. And it'll probably make you laugh.

 **recap**

Thinking about thinking.

The six steps.

A system for critical thinking.

A review of critical thinking.

15 Libraries are more than collections of books

When you choose your various courses, you'll be given reading lists of recommended texts. But they're just part of the written word resources you'll need. Remember we stressed that, in this new learning environment, you're independent and have to take responsibility for your own choices. So you'll be expected to locate additional material for yourself, which means developing the skills to recognise where the gaps in your reading are and how to plug them.

How to use the library

You might be thinking this is an unnecessary chapter. After all, we all know what libraries are and what you do in them. You go there, borrow a book, and that's it. Maybe, but university libraries are much more than collections of books and journals. For students, they're a major resource with information in many forms. As well as the items they carry on their shelves, they represent electronic gateways to a massive amount of online information. With so much material at your fingertips and such specific topics to research, you need to know how to focus on what's available, what's relevant and how to access it in its most useful forms.

Join the library

The first, obvious step is to make sure you're a member with borrowing rights. So, once you've matriculated, find the university library and activate your membership. Register for one of the tours which the librarians organise. They'll take you round, identify the places and facilities that are available, and you can ask them questions. While you're there, check out any leaflets or maps which you can use later when you're finding your own way round.

The moment you join, you're on the library system and there's a record established in your name. It's usually done electronically and you'll be able to check which books you've borrowed, which are due for return and other relevant information.

More than books

As well as books, most university libraries have copies of some newspapers, periodicals and academic journals. There'll be many kinds of reference materials, perhaps slides, photographs, videos and DVDs. There'll also be areas set aside for particular types of study. The most obvious are the quiet study areas, but there may also be places for group work where you're allowed to discuss things. Photocopiers and printers will probably be available, along with computing terminals and possibly a wireless network. You'll have access to online catalogues and, of course, the library staff are there to support you, either in person or through the library website. So there's definitely more than books.

The materials (including books) that are carried will depend on what degrees are being taught, any teaching specialisms, the research interests of staff and what collections may have been left to the university. Each library is unique and you may find archive materials that aren't available anywhere else.

brilliant tip

Some reading lists are long and the books on them are expensive. If you need to refer to a particular book frequently and/or it relates closely to your lectures and coursework, it's obviously worth buying your own copy. But if not, check to see if it's in the library and how many copies they carry. (You may have problems if all the other students in your class need to consult the same thing at the same time.)

Digital and web-based resources

Today, vast amounts of material are accessible online in just about every area of interest. Libraries have subscriptions to e-book repositories, e-journals, e-newspapers and online dictionaries and encyclopaedias. Your institution will have its dedicated system of letting you access these digitised and web-based resources and you'll probably need a password. It'll pay you to get to know the details of your system as early as possible. These are resources that are available 24/7 from any computer connected to the internet. They may also allow more than one person to access an e-book at the same time. Some e-book facilities, such as ebrary, have extra tools which let you search, make notes and consult linked online dictionaries to check the meanings of words.

There are now many electronic databases which make it easier to get access to information from public bodies, and most of them are available online. For example, you can look at statistical population details on the National Statistics website (www.statistics.gov.uk), and any papers and publications produced by the Houses of Parliament at www.parliament. uk. Access to academic journals and other material will depend on whether your library subscribes to them or not, so find out which search engines and databases are available to you.

Paper-based resources

The most obvious of these are the books:

- Your prescribed texts link with the content of your courses.
- General textbooks provide a broader overview of the subject.
- Supplementary texts discuss topics in greater depth.

Then come the many different kinds of reference books:

- Standard dictionaries help with spelling, pronunciation and meaning.
- Bilingual dictionaries translate words and expressions in two languages.
- Subject-specific dictionaries define important terms relating to a particular discipline.

- Thesauri (which is the plural form of thesaurus) give you synonyms, i.e. words similar in meaning to the one you're looking up. A–Z versions are easier to use than the original *Roget's Thesaurus*.

- General encyclopaedias provide a quick overview of or introduction to a new topic.

- Discipline-specific encyclopaedias have in-depth coverage of specific topics.

- Biographical dictionaries and other material are excellent sources of information on both contemporary and historical figures.

- Yearbooks and directories carry up-to-date information on organisations.

- Atlases provide geographical and historical information.

Finally, there are newspapers and journals:

- Newspapers, both daily and weekly, cover contemporary issues.

- Periodicals and academic journals are publications which are specific to a particular discipline or subject. They usually appear three or four times a year and provide new ideas, reports and comment on current research issues.

- Popular periodicals such as *Nature, New Scientist* and *The Economist* deal with broader issues and emerging trends in the fields of study indicated by their titles.

Shared library resources

Many university libraries share resources with those of neighbouring institutions. They're all linked to the British Library too, which is the national library of the UK. This receives a copy of every publication produced in the UK and Ireland, and its massive collection of over 150 million items increases by 3 million every year. Some university libraries are known as European Documentation Centres (http://ec.europa.eu/europedirect). They hold important documents of the European Union.

Getting to know the system

You'll have plenty to be thinking about without having to worry whether books are on the shelves, overdue, on short- or long-term loans and all the rest of it, so find out the rules you need to know as a borrower.

(?) brilliant questions and answers

(Q) How many books can I borrow at any one time?

(A) That depends on your status. Staff and postgraduate students can usually borrow more books than undergraduates.

(Q) How long can I keep the item I've borrowed?

(A) It depends on what it is. Normal loans are usually for several weeks. But there may be a big demand for some books because they're prescribed texts, so they may be put on a short-loan system. That means you can take them out but have to hand them back earlier than with 'normal' books – maybe in a matter of a few hours, but usually it's a few days.

(Q) What's the fine if I keep it longer than I'm supposed to?

(A) It depends on the sort of book. If it's a short-term loan, the fine will be higher than 'normal' loans. It may just be a few pence, but think about it. If you've got ten books you should have handed back two weeks ago, that'll cost you £10 or more.

(Q) How can I renew the loan?

(A) By phone with most libraries and, more and more, online. Check your university's home page.

Electronic book tagging

Most universities operate a system of electronic 'book tagging' to make sure that resources can't be taken out without being logged out to a particular user. This means that all books need to be 'de-activated' before you can take them outside the library.

Regulations and codes of conduct

You'll see notices on leaflets and websites telling or reminding you of the library rules. They're important because they're there to protect the resources and also regulate the studying environment for you and all the other users, asking you to be aware of the needs of others studying around you. In particular, they spell out your legal responsibilities under copyright law and tell you how much you can photocopy from a specific book or document.

brilliant tip

If your library uses a card system for photocopying, write your name and a contact number on the card they issue to you. It's all too easy to leave it on a machine.

Information literacy skills

What's information literacy? Well, it's all about realising you need information and knowing where to find it and how to use it. It may sound pretty basic, but there are more steps in the process than you might think at first. You need to be able to:

- recognise that you need a piece of information
- think of ways to plug that gap
- decide how you're going to find and access the information
- compare and evaluate information you get from different sources
- organise, apply and communicate information to others according to what's required of you
- synthesise and build upon existing information to help expand it and create new knowledge.

It's worth taking a moment to think about these different stages, recognise the differences between them and ask yourself how competent you are at each of them. To help you answer that question, consider some of the basic skills you'll need to master.

- You'll need to be familiar with how electronic catalogues work in order not to waste time in fruitless searches. Most let you search by author, title or subject, but there may be other alternatives on your system.

- When you identify the book that you want from the catalogue, you'll want to know which shelf it's on. So you need to take a note of two things: the location (because the book might even be in another site library) and the number, which may be a sequence of letters and/or numbers depending on the system your library uses. It's on the spine of the book and books are all arranged in sequence in stacks. At the end of each stack you'll find the numbers of the first and last books in the sequence they contain. If you can't find what you're looking for, library staff will help you.

- Sometimes a book may not be available in your own library and you may want to borrow it from another UK library. There's usually a librarian who's responsible for inter-library loans so that's the person you need to consult. Be careful, though, as there's usually a fee to pay for this and you're the one who has to pay it.

- We spoke earlier of the various e-resources you might use. Normally, you'll access them through the library's website. Some are open-access, but for others you'll need a password so that publishers can check that your library has subscribed to a particular resource and that you have access rights. Systems vary, but usually there'll be special training sessions in lectures or arranged independently in the library. There's a wealth of material; don't be fazed by it. Ask a librarian to help you find your way around it all.

brilliant tip

Imagine your lecturer has mentioned an article by someone called Nichol which you should read. You look up the name, but there's no sign of the article. That may be because she may be called Nicol, Nicoll, Nickol or many other variations of the surname. So, if you haven't seen a name written down (in your course handbook, for example), try different options to get the one you want.

Look further afield

Find and join the local public library. It may have some texts relevant to your course and they won't be in such heavy demand as those in the university library. Some university libraries have agreements with other, similar ones in the area, including national libraries. This obviously extends the resources available to you and you should take advantage of such arrangements. You can use the facilities and sometimes even borrow books from partner libraries.

Explore all the library locations available to you. You may find some with different study areas that are more convenient or that suit your moods, learning preference or personality. You may prefer peace and quiet or work better if there's some activity around you as you study.

And make sure you know about all the alternative library facilities on your campus. There may be satellite libraries on different parts of the site or in different buildings. Some of these may be departmental libraries with specialist resources. They may also hold duplicates of books in the main library.

Of course, finding information on the shelves and online is only the first step. It's important to know how best to use it for your studies. Next you need to evaluate it and use it appropriately in your academic writing, note-making and revision. The reason we mention this here is that it helps enormously if, when you find the information you need, you note the details of where you found it. We'll deal with how to do that later, but it's never too early to point out that plagiarism is theft. So, if you use material from a specific book, article or other publication, always acknowledge where it came from and who wrote it.

brilliant example

There are two main cataloguing systems; the one your library uses will be explained in leaflets or during the library tour.

The two systems are:

- the Dewey decimal system, in which each book is given a number. For example, editions of Shakespeare's *Hamlet* are filed under 822.33
- the Library of Congress system, which uses an alphanumeric code, so the same editions of *Hamlet* would be filed under PR2807.

There may be small variations in how these are interpreted, so the important thing is to find out exactly how your own library's system works.

What next?

Try to go on a library tour …

… and if you see or hear things you don't understand, ask about them. In many ways university libraries are different from public libraries and they've got much more to offer. If your university doesn't organise tours, see if you can take a virtual tour through your university library's website.

Get to know the electronic library resources …

… particularly any which are specific to your own subjects, and explore the shelves covering your subject area. Find this area by looking in the library catalogue and the information on the book stacks. When you do, browse through what's there. You may find interesting books and catalogues which you might not have come across otherwise.

When you find something in a book …

… which isn't on your list of recommended reading, make sure it's a reliable source. Check that it's by someone qualified to write about the subject, with good academic credentials, and that it's not out of date.

---

brilliant recap

The range of facilities and resources.

Getting to know the system.

Regulations and codes of conduct.

Information literacy skills.

Looking further afield.

---

16 Taking an active approach to information

Nowadays, we have access to more information than we can handle. It's important, especially for those involved as teachers or learners, to evaluate evidence, data and opinions with great care. That's why we're now going to look at where information and ideas come from, how to check whether sources are reliable, and the differences between fact, opinion and truth.

How to filter and select reliable material for discussion

Whatever subject you're studying at university, you've got to be able to evaluate information and ideas. It's a skill which has many forms and applications and which will differ according to the task in hand. You may be analysing information to test its truth or accuracy, or the reliability or potential bias of the person or organisation which produced it. Or you may be evaluating it in relation to some argument or case. You may also come across evidence which contradicts it or even find conflicting arguments which are based on the same information. It's a complex process and it'll be up to you to sort out the conclusions to which the bulk of the evidence leads. So let's look first at where ideas and information come from and what they actually are.

The origin of information and ideas

Facts and ideas come from someone's research or scholarship. They might be descriptions, concepts, interpretations or numerical data. And you know of their existence only because they're out there in the public domain, which means that they've been communicated or published. The place in which they first appear is called the primary literature. If they're modified and reappear, they do so in what's known as the secondary literature. You need to understand and know this when you're doing your analysis and evaluation of information and deciding how to cite evidence or references in your written work.

Assessing sources of 'facts'

Not all 'facts' are true; they could be misquoted, misrepresented, frankly untrue or based on a false assumption. That's why you need to be so careful with lots of web-based information because you can't know whether it's been properly tested or edited. So, if misquotation and misinterpretations are so frequent, it's logical to say that the closer you can get to the primary source, the more likely you are to be nearer the truth of what was actually said or written. Mind you, you then have to ask who wrote it and who paid them to do so. That's why an important element in assessing sources is to investigate the ownership and provenance of the work. In other words, find out who wrote it and where and why they did so.

The author

So who wrote it? If it is signed or there's a 'byline' identifying the author, you can check his credentials to decide whether his ideas can be trusted. If he turns out to be an authority in the area, the decision's easy. If you're not sure about him, a bit of research, such as typing his name into a search engine, might help. Mind you, just because he's Professor Such-and-such, it doesn't mean what he writes is definitely true. But if you know he's someone whose opinions on the subject are based on years of research and experience, you'd probably stick with him rather than quote some anonymous author on a website. And if the source you're reading doesn't identify the author, it could mean either that he's not willing to take responsibility for the content or that there's a reason for him to hide.

Provenance

Provenance means 'where it came from'. If the author's place of work is mentioned it could tell you whether there is likely to have been any academic study behind what he's written. If he works for some public organisation, he may have to follow particular rules of publication and perhaps have his work checked over by a committee before it's published or distributed. Authors in that sort of setup are more likely to get into trouble if their material turns out to be scurrilous or incorrect. And if he's writing for a company, a political party or some other vested interest, how much pressure might have been put on him to bend the facts to suit their message?

brilliant tip

In most published academic sources, author and provenance are easy to find. The information may even be printed just below the title. With the web, though, it's a different story. But check the information in the header, body and footer of the document for clues.

The nature of evaluation

In 'scientific' subjects you'll need to interpret and check the reliability of data before you can set up and test meaningful hypotheses, so evidence-based evaluation is an essential skill which underpins the whole scientific approach.

In 'non-scientific' subjects, ideas and concepts are important, but they need to be supported. So you may need to carry out an objective analysis of information and arguments in order to build your own position and back it up with evidence.

Facts, opinions, truth

With a large reading list and lots of viewpoints, it's easy to get confused and mix up fact, opinion and truth. In many fields, such as arts and social sciences, there's often no 'right' or 'wrong' answer. Instead what you get is a range of stances or viewpoints. So it's quite possible that your answer may be quite different from those of your fellow students and possibly even from that of your tutor. But as long as you construct your own argument and support it with evidence, you'll get credit for it. The easy option is to follow the party line and regurgitate what you've heard in lectures.

That may be fine, but equally the lectures may have been deliberately constructed to provoke discussion and hint at alternative interpretations. Follow your own path. Even if your tutor doesn't share your conclusions, she'll mark your work according to the way you've presented it.

In some subjects, such as history, politics and economics, it's easy to stray into opinionated and biased conclusions; they may even be what we identified earlier as 'value judgements'. If you submit viewpoints such as these without reliable evidence to support their accuracy and relevance, you may be marked down.

Discussing the nature of truth could lead us into deep waters and philosophical confusion. We don't need to go into the murky world of politics (the word 'murky' makes that a value judgement, by the way) to know that truth has many faces and that 'factual' statistics can prove opposing things. In discussion and debate, you can agree that something is true only when all sides of the argument accept it. If you can show that a particular line of argument lacks credibility or is unacceptable in some other way, it'll strengthen the arguments against it.

Of course, the central features of this question are the notions of objectivity and subjectivity. Objective judgements are those based on a balanced consideration of the facts, whereas subjective judgements are based on the opinion of the individual making them. In the academic world, the preference is for detached, objective writing. But that doesn't mean you can't have opinions. On the contrary, you'll be encouraged to form your own views on all sorts of topics. The key is to produce valid reasons for them.

Primary and secondary sources

Primary sources, as we said earlier, are those in which ideas and data are first communicated. They may be published in the form of papers (articles) in journals and they're usually refereed by experts in the authors' academic peer groups. These people check for accuracy and originality and report their findings back to the journal editors.

Books (and, more rarely, articles in magazines and newspapers) can also be primary sources, but it depends on the type of information they contain.

They're not formally refereed, but they are read by editors and lawyers to check for errors and any allegations which are unsubstantiated or might be considered libellous.

Secondary sources are those that quote, adapt, interpret, translate, develop or otherwise use information drawn from primary sources. It's this recycling process that makes them secondary, rather than the medium in which you find them. In the academic world, they include reviews, textbooks and magazine articles. As people adopt, modify, translate and develop information and ideas, they may, intentionally or otherwise, alter the original. Most authors don't deliberately set out to change the meaning of the primary source, but it can happen. Others may, again consciously or unconsciously, alter the impact of their reporting by quoting evidence on one side of a debate and ignoring the other.

But not all modifications which occur in secondary sources are necessarily 'bad'. They could involve correcting errors in the original or adding valuable new ideas and content to it.

▶ brilliant example

On 30 September 1999, the world record for the men's 100 metres was 9.79 seconds. That's a fact. It's been lowered several times since then, but the statement itself is still true. Some world records may have been created by athletes who took performance-enhancing drugs. That's an opinion. There may be evidence to back it up, but it's a controversial area and proofs are elusive. The different opinions on drug misuse are open to conjecture, claim and counter-claim, and they can't all be true. If you were handling this topic for an exercise, you'd need to identify the difference between fact and opinion and base what you write on that knowledge. Accept that there's controversy, but keep a clear distinction between the facts, the truth and your opinion of the evidence.

How reliable is your information?

Here are a couple of checklists to help you decide how reliable your information is. The more satisfactory and positive answers you can give, the more reliable you can assume the source to be.

Authorship and the nature of the source

- What's the author's name?
- What qualifications does she hold?
- Who employs her?
- Who paid her to do the work?
- Is this a primary or a secondary source?
- Has it been refereed or edited?
- Is the content original or derived?
- Does the source cite relevant literature?
- Have you checked a range of sources?

The information and its analysis

- Is the source cited by others?
- Is when the source was written important with regard to the accuracy of the information? For example, was it written at the time the events occurred or later and therefore with hindsight?
- Have you focused on the substance of the information presented rather than its packaging?
- Is the information fact or opinion?
- Are there any logical fallacies in the arguments?
- Does the language used indicate anything about the status of the information?
- Could there be any numerical errors?
- Are the statistics used to analyse the data appropriate?
- If there are graphs, are they constructed fairly?

The provisional nature of information

Some things which were once considered incontrovertible facts now seem ridiculous. Centuries ago, people thought the Sun orbited the Earth (and their observations even seemed to confirm it). Yet, there are things which seemed absurd, such as the idea that continents could float and drift, which are now accepted as facts. There are also massive changes in social 'truths' which, over a long period, can alter the whole framework and terminology of discussion. Any debate on slavery, for example, or the emancipation of women would now be very different from its counterpart a couple of hundred years ago. This is why the academic world encourages challenges to accepted fact and opinion. An open and enquiring mind is an asset as long as it supports its views with sound, up-to-date reference points.

Researching and presenting your argument

- Your grade will probably depend on how convincing your argument is and how well you use supporting evidence. So what is this 'evidence' we keep mentioning? Well, it comes in many forms, from statistical/ numerical sources through quotations to direct observation. Wherever you got it, ask yourself if it's relevant and valuable. And always note where you got it in your writing. If you don't, the marker may recognise it as someone else's idea and you'll get no credit for it. You may also be accused of plagiarism.

- Don't just highlight your side of the argument; try to produce a balanced conclusion. Be open about counter-evidence that doesn't seem to support your case. Explain what others of a different persuasion think or might think, and then say why you've arrived at your conclusion.

- Choose your sources carefully. Try to read and cite the primary source if you can. Don't rely on a secondary source to do this for you because the author may be using information selectively to support his case, or interpreting it differently from how you might.

- If you're not certain about something, 'triangulate' it by making cross-referencing checks. That means looking at several sources and comparing what they say. Make them as independent as possible. There's little point in comparing an original source with one based directly on it. If you find the different sources agree, it may make you feel more confident of your position; if they don't, you may need to decide which viewpoint is the more persuasive.

- How old is the source? 'Old' doesn't necessarily mean 'wrong', but ideas and facts may have altered between when it was written and now. Can you trace changes through time by comparing the sources you have? Are there any important events, works or changes in methods which may influence conclusions?

- Look at the range and quality of citations provided by the author. They may show how much research she carried out beforehand and prove that her ideas or results are based on genuine scholarship. If you're not sure how good the work is, have a look at some of these references. Are they up to date? Do they refer to independent work, or is she mainly quoting herself or one particular researcher?

- Look beneath the surface – at substance rather than presentation. Just because information is in a glossy magazine or on some well-constructed website, it doesn't necessarily mean it's good. This doesn't necessarily tell you much about the quality of its content.

- Analyse the language she uses. Is it subjective or objective? Personal opinion or objective conclusion? Are there any signs of propaganda or bias in expressions such as 'everyone knows …', 'I can guarantee that …'? Does she distort the evidence to suit her case, or use exaggeration, ambiguity, journalese or slang? Your analysis will help you to evaluate the quality and probable reliability of her work.

- However reliable it seems to be, it's probably a good idea to be a little sceptical about the facts or ideas involved and question the logic of arguments. Even information from primary sources may not be perfect; at the time it was written a particular approach may have seemed legitimate but may no longer apply or may lead to different conclusions. Even if you're finding the viewpoint very attractive, try not to identify too strongly with it. You need to stay detached when you're assessing its merits and flaws.

- Look for fallacious arguments and logical flaws. Analyse the method being used to convey the facts rather than the facts themselves.

What next?

Analyse the nature of your sources …

… each time you're given a reading list for a tutorial, assessment exercise or background reading. Decide whether the sources on it are primary or secondary, and why. If they're secondary, do they quote any of the primary sources? Try to get a copy of one of the primary sources and see if it tells you anything about the nature of knowledge in your discipline, where it comes from and how it can be modified during translation.

brilliant recap

The origin of information and ideas.

Assessing sources of 'facts'.

Facts, opinions and truth.

Primary and secondary sources.

The reliability of information.

Researching and presenting your argument.

17 Learning how to read

Whatever you're studying, it's sure to involve lots of reading. There may be bits you can skim through and there'll definitely be bits you need to linger over to deepen your knowledge and understanding of topics. In this chapter we'll look at some skills which will help you to read more efficiently.

Reading and understanding

Most of the books and chapters you'll be reading as part of your studies will be written in a fairly formal, traditional academic style. Sometimes that can mean they look and feel like heavy going. Big, unfamiliar words, long sentences, an apparent lack of passion – all these things can make reading feel like hard work. But all these materials have been written by people who want to communicate information and/or a point of view, so they're carefully organised to make their points. If you learn how text is structured, you can use that knowledge to help you read it in a way that'll make it understandable and yet save you time. That's what we mean by reading more efficiently.

brilliant tip

Most of the time when you're reading for study, you'll be taking notes. It's possible to do both at the same time, but that may not work well because your notes could end up just being a rewrite of the text. If you scan the relevant section of text first, it'll give you a clearer idea of its content and how it fits into the argument and you'll be able to write more meaningful (and probably much shorter) notes.

The overall organisation of the text

You'll be dealing with different sorts of texts. They may be recommended by tutors or books and articles you find for yourself when you're expanding your lecture notes or revising. Whatever the source material, the best strategy is to do a quick survey (not a read) to get an overall idea of what's in it. There are various ways of doing this:

- Does the title sound as though it'll be about the things you're looking for?

- Is the author a well-known authority on the subject?

- Does the 'blurb' on the cover confirm that it's relevant to your needs?

- When was the book published? Will you get up-to-date information from it?

- Look at the list of contents. Does it cover the topic areas you need? Are the chapter titles very general or quite detailed?

- Is there a comprehensive index and is it easy to use? Take a quick look for specific references to the material you want.

- And finally, what does the text look like? Is it easy to read and easy to navigate using sub-headings?

These are your starting points. Once you've worked through this list you'll have a better idea of whether that particular piece is valuable for you. It may be that you decide you need to read the whole book, or there may just be certain chapters or pages that cover what you're looking for. Equally, you may decide that there's nothing there which you need at present.

Why are you reading?

This may seem a strange question, but it's part of what you need to do to help focus your reading. Before you start the actual reading, make up your mind exactly what it is you're looking for and adapt your approach accordingly.

? brilliant questions and answers

Q Are you looking for a specific point of information?

A If so, use chapter titles, sub-headings or the index as a guide and read only the relevant pages. It'll speed up the whole process.

Q Is the idea to expand your lecture notes by using a textbook?

A If so, you'll read in a different way, perhaps using points from the lecture to direct your attention. You might also be taking notes, which, again, will alter your reading technique.

Q Are you reading in order to appreciate the author's style or the aesthetics of perhaps a poem or a work of fiction?

A If so, you'll read more slowly, taking time to reflect on the choice of words and expressions, and you may re-read certain parts.

The structures of academic writing

Academic texts usually follow the same basic pattern. Each part of the argument, as well as the overall piece, consists of an introduction, the main body of the text and a conclusion. Both the introduction and the conclusion may consist of one paragraph or several. Each paragraph, including those in the main body of the text, has its own particular point to make or develop and each starts with what's called a topic sentence, which indicates what the paragraph contains.

brilliant example

The typical layout for a piece of work consisting of five paragraphs looks like this:

Introduction (Topic paragraph)

Main body (Paragraphs 2, 3 and 4, each beginning with a topic sentence)

Conclusion (Terminator paragraph)

The way these paragraphs and the sentences within them fit into the overall argument is usually signalled by 'signpost words'. They guide the reader through the logical structure of the text. For example, the word 'however' warns you to expect that whatever follows it will contrast or conflict with whatever went before it, and if you see 'thus', you'll know that you're about to read a consequence of what went before because it means 'as a result of this'. So look out for signpost words; they'll help you to identify general meanings, changes of direction and the underlying argument.

A quick way of getting a general overview of the text is to read topic and terminator paragraphs, or even just the topic sentences. Unfortunately, that won't be sufficient to supply your needs, but it'll get you focused on what you're likely to gain from your reading of the whole piece.

Another technique is to scan quickly through the text for keywords related to your interest. You may notice that several occur in particular paragraphs, which suggests that those paragraphs are worth reading in detail. If there are headings and sub-headings, they'll be very helpful in the same way.

brilliant tip

We're looking at the structures of texts in order to help you to decode them as a reader. It's as well to remember that, if you want to make your work easier to decode (by a marker, for example), you should use the same layouts and techniques. For both reader and writer, the better the material is structured, the more effective it is at conveying information.

brilliant example

Here's a more detailed example of a piece of writing with the structural features we've been talking about highlighted for you. We've put the topic sentences in italics and the signpost words in bold.

(INTRODUCTION, OR TOPIC PARAGRAPH)

Technological advances and skilful marketing have meant that the mobile phone has moved from being simply an accessory to a status as an essential piece of equipment. From teenagers to grandmothers, the nation has taken to the mobile phone as a constant link for business and social purposes. As a phenomenon, the ascendency of the mobile phone, in a multitude of ways, has had a critical impact on the way people organise their lives.

(BODY TEXT)

Clearly, *the convenience of the mobile is attractive.* It is constantly available to receive or send calls. While these are not cheap, the less expensive text-message alternative provides a similar 'constant contact' facility. At a personal and social level, this brings peace of mind to parents because teenagers can locate them and be located by them at the press of a button. **However**, in business terms, while it means that employees are constantly accessible and, with more sophisticated models, can access internet communications also, there is no escape from the workplace.

The emergence of abbreviated text-message language has wrought a change in everyday print. **For example**, pupils and students have been known to submit written work using text message symbols and language. Some have declared this to mark the demise of standard English. **Furthermore**, the accessibility of the mobile phone has become a problem in colleges and universities where it has been known for students in examinations to use the texting facility to obtain information required.

The ubiquity of the mobile phone has generated changes in the way that services are offered. **For instance**, this means that trains, buses and restaurants have declared 'silent zones' where the mobile is not permitted in order to give others a rest from the 'I'm on the train' style mobile phone conversation.

While the marked increase in mobile phone sales indicates that many in the population have embraced this technology, **by contrast**, *'mobile' culture has not been without its critics.* Real concerns have been expressed about the potential dangers that can be encountered through mobile phone use.

One such danger is that associated with driving while speaking on a mobile. A body of case law has been accumulated to support the introduction of new legislation outlawing the use of hand-held mobile phones by drivers whilst driving. The enforcement of this legislation is virtually impossible to police and, **thus**, much is down to the common sense and responsibility of drivers. **Again**, technology has risen to meet the contingency with the development of 'hands-free' phones which can be used while driving and without infringing the law.

A further danger is an unseen one, namely, the impact of the radiation from mobile phones on the human brain. Research is not well advanced in this area and data related to specific absorption rates (SARs) from the use of mobile phones and its effect on brain tissue is not yet available for evaluation. **Nevertheless**, although this lack of evidence is acknowledged by mobile phone companies, they advise that hands-free devices reduce the SARs levels by 98%.

Mobile phone controversy is not confined only to the potential dangers related to the units alone; some people have serious concerns about the impact mobile phone masts have on the area surrounding them. The fear is that radiation from masts could induce serious illness amongst those living near such masts. **While** evidence refuting or supporting this view remains inconclusive, there appears to be much more justification for concern about emissions from television transmitters and national grid pylons which emit far higher levels of electro-magnetic radiation. **Yet**, little correlation appears to have been made between this fundamental of electrical engineering and the technology of telecommunications.

(CONCLUSION, OR TERMINATOR PARAGRAPH)

In summary, *although it appears that there are enormous benefits to mobile phone users, it is clear that there are many unanswered questions about the impact of their use on individuals.* At one level, these represent an intrusion on personal privacy, whether as a user or as a bystander obliged to listen to multiple one-sided conversations in public places. **More significantly**, there is the potential for unseen damage to the health of individual users as they clamp their mobiles to their ears. **Whereas** the individual has a choice to use or not to use a mobile phone, people have fewer choices in relation to exposure to dangerous emissions from masts. **While** the output from phone masts is worthy of further investigation, it is in the more general context of emissions from electro-magnetic masts of all types that serious research needs to be developed.

Speed-reading

The basic techniques of speed-reading were developed in the 1950s by Evelyn Wood, an American educator. She set up institutes to teach students skills which enabled them to read hundreds of words a minute.

Her methods have been used in many fields where busy people need to read and understand lengthy papers as quickly as possible. US presidents Jimmy Carter and John F. Kennedy were famous for their speed-reading.

The techniques

People who read quickly don't read each word as a separate unit. They use their peripheral vision which, if you stare straight ahead, is what you see at the edges of your vision to the right and the left. By doing this, they take in groups of words at a time. So, instead of reading:

Students need to read many books in the course of studying

they read:

(Students need)   (to read many books)   (in the course of)   (studying)

In other words, rather than moving their eyes 11 times, once for each word, they move them 4 times. It's obviously a more efficient and less tiring way of reading. Studies have also shown that people who read slowly are less likely to gather information quickly enough for the brain to understand it, so reading slowly may actually make comprehension more difficult.

Before we go any further, maybe you'd like to check your own reading speed. (Although not if you're just using it as a displacement activity.) There are two possible methods – one measures how much you can read in a given time, the other how long it takes you to read a specified amount of text.

In Method A you'll read for a particular length of time.

- Choose a chapter from a textbook. Don't use a newspaper or journal because the text there is often printed in columns.
- Calculate the average number of words to a line, e.g. if there are 50 words in five lines, that's 10 words per line.
- Now count the number of lines per page. Let's say it's 41.
- Multiply the number of words per line by the number of pages – that's $10 \times 41 = 410$ words on each page.
- Start at the beginning of your chosen text and read for a set period of time – let's say 4 minutes – without stopping. Note the point on the page at which the time runs out.

- Let's assume that you managed 2½ pages in 4 minutes. To find out how many words that is, multiply 410 (the number of words per page) by 2.5 (the number of pages you read). That gives you 1025 total words read.

- Now divide that by 4 (the number of minutes you read) and it shows that you've averaged 256 words per minute (wpm).

Method B uses a text of a known length.

- Choose a text and count the number of words in it. Let's say it's 744.

- Time how long you take to read it. We'll say 170 seconds.

- To find how many minutes that is in decimal form, divide it by 60, which gives you 2.8.

- Now divide the total words by 2.8 and you get a reading speed of 266 wpm.

Since you're a student and you do quite a bit of reading, you probably already use a version of fast reading to some extent, but there are ways of improving your technique.

Eye gymnastics

Here's an exercise which helps to train your eyes to use your peripheral vision when you're reading. As you do it, your eyes will be forced to jump from one group of words to the next, focusing on the centre each time. Try to read the text quite quickly from left to right in the normal way. If you feel some discomfort behind your eyes, it means they're adjusting to this new way of moving. Just keep practising. You can use this text as a piece of training equipment just as you'd use a treadmill or a barbell.

Learning to read quickly	is a skill	that needs to be developed.
If you have to read	a new piece of text	you will find it useful
first of all	to read	the first paragraph
and the last paragraph	of the text.	From this
you should be able	to gauge	the context
and general outline	of the relevant topic.	While it is true

that all academic texts   should be fully edited   before publication,

it does not follow   that every text   follows these conventions

However,   a well-written piece   of academic writing

should follow this pattern   and, as a reader,   you should exploit

this convention   in order to help you   to understand

the overall context   before you embark   on intensive reading

of the text.

When you are about to   take notes from texts   you should not begin

by sitting   with notepad ready   and the pen poised.

Certainly   make a note of   publication details needed

for your bibliography,   but don't try   to start taking notes

at the same time as   beginning   your first reading.

It is better   to read first,   reflect, recall

and then write notes   based on   what you remember.

This gives you   a framework   around which

you ought to be able   to organise your notes   after you have read

the text intensively.   People who start   by writing notes

as soon as   they open the book   will end up

copying   more and more   as they get more tired.

In this case   very little   reflection or learning

is achieved.

Finger tracing

Another technique is finger tracing. As its name suggests, it's when you run your finger along under the line of text you're reading. It follows the path of your eyes across the page, starting and stopping a word or two from either side. This keeps your mind focused on what you're actually reading and stops you skipping back to previous sentences or jumping forward to the text that follows, and it helps to increase your eye speed. Some people use a bookmark or ruler held just under the line they're reading; it's a useful guide and works in the same way.

Try this exercise:

- Choose a reading passage about two pages long. Note your starting and finishing time and calculate your reading speed using Method B.

- Take a break of 40–60 minutes, and then go back to the text and run your finger along the lines much faster than you could possibly read it.

- Now do the same thing again but slowly enough for you to be just able to read it. Note how long it takes you this time and work out your wpm again. You'll probably find that you're faster this time round.

- Now do the same exercise at the same time of day over a week, using texts of the same sort of length and complexity.

Speeding up and slowing down

The average reading speed is around 265 wpm, but various factors may make that slightly slower for university students. Texts may be more difficult, their terminology unfamiliar, and they may be discussing quite complex concepts which need to be absorbed. All these things can slow down a reading. But the more familiar you become with your subjects and the issues being covered in your course, the faster you'll be able to read.

As well as trying to get faster, you should think about things which might slow you down. They could include:

- distractions such as background noise, TV, music, talking

- sounding each word as you read it aloud

- reading word by word

- being over-tired

- poor eyesight – your eyes are too important to neglect, so get them tested; reading glasses can make a big difference to your studying comfort as well as to your speed-reading

- poor lighting – if you can, read using a lamp that can shine directly on to the text; reading in poor light causes eye strain, which makes it harder to concentrate and cuts down your reading time.

Other strategies

- *Skimming.* Let your eye run quickly down a list or over a page looking for a key word or phrase, just as you do when looking for a name in a phone book. That's the way to find a specific piece of information you're looking for.

- *Scanning.* Let your eye run quickly over a chapter this time. It'll give you an idea of what the chapter's about before you start.

- *Picking out the topic sentences.* Read the topic sentences to add more detail to the overview you got from scanning. It'll help you to understand what's being conveyed before you study-read the whole text.

- *Identifying the signpost words.* They'll guide you through the logical process mapped out by the author.

- *Recognising clusters of words which go together grammatically.* As you read, group words in clusters according to their natural sense. It's what you did in the eye gymnastics exercise and it'll help you to make fewer eye movements.

- *Taking cues from punctuation.* Full stops, commas and the other punctuation marks are valuable clues when it comes to understanding a text. They separate chunks of meaning, indicate points to emphasise, mark transition points and help comprehension in many other ways. As reader and writer, you should never underestimate the importance of punctuation.

Speed with comprehension

Measuring speed on its own gives a false result. It's all very well having a wpm of 300 or whatever, but if you don't understand what you're reading, you're wasting your time. So speed-reading needs to be matched by a good level of comprehension. There are ways of testing your understanding to make sure you've understood the main points of what you've been reading. The one we'll look at is called the SQ3R method, which stands for Survey, Question, Read, Recall and Review. It's also useful when you're revising for exams because it helps to develop memory and learning skills simultaneously.

With the SQ3R method, you can't just read on autopilot and not retain much; you have to process the material as you go along. Let's go through the five stages: S, Q, R, R, R.

Survey

- Read the first paragraph (topic paragraph) and last paragraph (terminator paragraph) of a chapter or page of notes.
- Read the topic sentences of all the paragraphs between them.
- If there are headings and sub-headings, focus on them.
- Study graphs and diagrams for important features.

Question

- What do you already know about this topic?
- What's the author likely to tell you?
- What specifically do you need to find out?

Read

- Read the entire section quickly to get the gist of it, using finger tracing if it helps.
- Go back to the question stage. Check and revise if necessary the answers you gave then.
- Look for keywords, key statements, signpost words.
- Don't stop to look up unknown words – get it read.

Recall

- Turn over the book or your notes and try to remember as much as possible.
- Make important pattern headings/notes/diagrams/flow charts. We'll discuss how in the next chapter.
- Look at the text again and see how accurate your recall was. Do this after every 20 minutes of reading.

Review

- Take a break, then try to recall the main points.

Reading online

You can always print out material you get from the web and use the techniques we've been describing to read it, but printouts cost money and anyway using up paper unnecessarily is environmentally unsound. Then again, you may need to assess the material before committing yourself to printing it out. So, for a lot of the time, you'll actually be reading directly from the screen. When you do that, there are several points to consider:

- Web page designers often divide text into screen-sized chunks, with links between pages. This can make it hard to get an overall picture of the topic, so before you form a judgement about the material, make sure you've read all of it.

- Writers of web-based material often go for a punchy style, with bulleted lists and snappy messages. They use graphics and effects to highlight what they want you to retain. This may make reading easier, but it may also sacrifice the sort of details you need in academic work.

- It's so easy to check things online that there's a danger that you might over-use its resources. That would perhaps give your work a more modern bias and it could also lead you away from genuine academic sources.

- On the positive side, you can use the skimming method we described and make it even quicker with the 'Search' function to skip to key words.

- If you're likely to be sitting at a terminal for long periods, make sure you're positioned well, with your eyes more or less level with the mid point of the screen.

- Take lots of breaks. Get up, walk around, stretch and relax a bit before going back.

- If you wear glasses, it may help to have an extra pair especially for reading on-screen material. Check with your institution's health and safety office or an optician.

- If you do decide to print out a resource, look for an icon that gives you a 'print-friendly' version.

Reading effectively and with understanding

After everything we've said, it must be obvious that reading isn't the simple process that most people assume it to be. You need strategies and practice to make it work for you. So start by thinking about why you're reading. Look at the material you've already collected on the subject, such as lecture notes, which can remind you of how a topic was presented, what arguments were used or how a procedure was followed. Decide whether you're trying to get a general overview or identify additional specific information. And when you've decided that, use a technique and material that suits your needs and a reading speed that fits the type of text you've chosen. For example, an interesting article in a newspaper won't demand much in the way of intensive reading whereas an important chapter in an academic book will.

Get the general message before focusing on the difficult bits. Not all texts are reader-friendly. If you come across a section of text that's difficult to understand, skip over it. Forcing yourself to read and re-read it won't make it any clearer. Read on and then, when you come to a natural break in the text – the end of a chapter or section – go back to the hard bit and try again. It'll probably make more sense now because you've got a better feel for the context. The same advice applies to new or difficult words. Don't stop every time you come across one; read on and try to get an idea of what it might mean from the rest of the text. You can look it up when you've finished and add it to your personal glossary.

Follow up references in your text. Be aware of any citations to other authors you find there. They won't all be relevant to the aim of your reading, but it's worth making a quick note of any that look interesting as you come across them. You'll usually find the full publication details at the end of the chapter, article or book and you can use them to find and read them when you've finished the current text.

brilliant tip

Take regular breaks. If you try to read continuously over a long period of time you'll retain less. You can concentrate well for 20 minutes and more, but after 40 minutes, the mind begins to wander. Take plenty of rests (but make sure they don't start getting longer than the actual studying periods).

What next?

Check your reading speed ...

... using the two methods we've described. If you think it's slow, try out some of the techniques and exercises we've outlined. Decide which ones suit you, use them for a while, then check to see if your speed's improved.

Practise surveying a text ...

... using a book from your reading list. Rather than simply opening it at a particular page, spend 5 or 10 minutes surveying the whole book. Think about how the author has organised the content and why. Remember this as you read the text, and reflect on whether it's helped you to understand and absorb the content more easily.

Remember that ...

... grammar, punctuation and spelling provide useful clues to meaning. Look for these visual cues and use them to help both your speed and comprehension.

---

brilliant recap

Surveying a text's overall organisation.

How to examine the structure of the writing itself.

Speed-reading techniques.

Reading online resources.

Combining speed with understanding.

18

Turning reading into notes

Most courses provide recommended reading lists. They'll probably include textbooks, journal articles and web-based materials. Sometimes you'll get specific references to topics covered in these texts, but at other times it'll be up to you to find the relevant material for yourself. When you do, you'll want to make a note of it in a form that's easy to create and just as easy to understand when you return to study the point or revise for exams later. In this chapter, we'll look at both general and specific aspects of making notes.

The need for notes

With lectures, tutorials and your own reading bombarding you with information, there's just too much of it for you to retain. So you need ways to compress it or maps which take you to the particular topic you're looking for. Notes fulfil both these functions. As you move through your studies you'll develop skills and techniques which suit you. They'll depend on your subject, your learning style and the time that's available both for making and then organising them.

brilliant tip

Develop good habits and you'll save lots of time both with note-making and consulting them later. So right from the start, remember two techniques:

● Before you do anything else, make a note of the full details of the source. That means the author's name and initials, the title, the publisher and the date and place it was published. Don't forget to add the chapter and pages these particular notes refer to. This is crucial if you're going to be quoting any of it in your written work.

● Make your notes personal by using underlining, highlighting, colour coding, numbered lists, bullet points, mnemonics or anything else which helps you to find your way around them. Choose a distinctive layout, maybe with boxes for important points. If you're consistent with this, it'll make the different aspects of your notes instantly recognisable.

What should be in them?

The main reason you make notes is for writing an assignment or revising for exams. If it's for an assignment you may just look for a few specific topics, but for an exam the notes will need to be much more comprehensive. So the first thing for you to decide is why you're actually making the notes. There are many possible reasons. You may want to:

● create an overview of the subject

● record a sequence or process

● analyse a problem

● isolate the logical steps of an argument

● compare different viewpoints

● borrow quotes to support a point you're making

● add your own ideas to the text or comment on the points it's making

● link something in the text with points that have cropped up in a lecture or tutorial.

As you can see, they're very varied and their style, detail and depth will alter according to their purpose.

The majority of people probably start with a sheet of paper in front of them and a pen clutched in their hand. They open the book, start reading and begin jotting down 'important' points as they go along. The trouble with that is you end up writing out whole chunks of the text and it doesn't encourage you to think much about what you're reading; it goes from the page to your notebook without dwelling long in your head. So, once you've decided why you're making notes, get used to following a routine:

- Decide what style and layout are best for the particular task you're doing.

- Scan the section you'll be reading.

- Establish what the writer's trying to do. Is it a narrative of events or a process, a statement of facts, an explanation, a presentation of a logical argument, an analysis of a problem, a critique of an argument?

- Work out his approach and viewpoint and decide how it relates to what you're looking for.

Then, as you're making your notes, jot down ideas of your own which may be triggered by the text and highlight any links you see with other texts and lectures.

Finally, don't just copy the author's words, use your own. It's his meaning you want, not his words. But if you do want to copy something directly from the text, put it in quote marks and note carefully the page on which you found it.

Note-making formats

When you think about making notes, it's perhaps automatic to assume that you start on line one and add notes as you work down the page. This is fine, but there are different formats for different purposes. If you wanted, for example, to stress the two sides of a particular argument, it might be more helpful to have two columns side by side, one carrying points for, the other points against. Or if you were brainstorming and just jotting down disparate ideas for an assignment, they wouldn't necessarily follow a connected, linear sequence. In that case, it might make sense to use a mind map or spider diagram, where you write them down as they occur, placing them near ones which are similar or in a separate area and using lines to connect notes that may belong together.

In fact, we can identify seven basic note-making formats, although there are variations on all of them.

Keyword notes

This is a fairly obvious and common format. Topics are identified by a keyword which is jotted down on the left, maybe in the margin. Then all points relating to that topic are written opposite it. It means that you can quickly find a specific part of the argument and all its aspects are gathered conveniently together. But it does depend on the source text having a systematic structure. If it doesn't, you may find you've moved on to other topics and then there's a reference back to a previous one, so you have to jump back in your notes, you might lose the thread of your reading, there may not be enough space left on the page, and so on.

Linear notes

Another obvious format. Once again, it helps if the text is presented logically. This time, instead of keywords, you use numbers. But not just 1, 2, 3 and so on. Think of 1 as a keyword and 1.1, 1.2, 1.3, 1.4 as the various points relating to it. Again, it's a good way to gather and organise material, but as before, if you come across something that you want to add under an earlier number, it may be hard to find room for it in the sequence.

Time lines

This has limited use as a format. It consists of setting a time line on the left and noting events or the stages in a process opposite the appropriate times and/or dates. Once again, it's difficult to go back and insert material at an earlier time. However, it does give a strong visual aid if the object of the note-making is to remember sequences.

Flow charts

This is another way of making a relatively simple visual representation of what may be a complex process. You might, for example, be reading about the development of a piece of equipment from its original conception (and the conditions in which it was conceived) to its production. A flow chart would allow you to break down the whole process into, for example, preliminary discussions, research phase, various forms of testing, final trials, production and operational application. Arrows leading from one phase to the next would trace a clear path through the process. It's a format that's useful in specific circumstances, but it does need a lot of space and it may also have circuitous little flows weaving around the main one.

Concept maps/mind maps

In a way, these are a sort of 'flash-bang-wallop' style of note-making. The paper is usually set in landscape rather than the usual portrait format, and ideas, concepts and statements are spread all over it, with lines connecting those which might be linked together in terms of meaning or impact. The advantage is that they hold all the information on a single page, but they can get very messy as the information multiplies and there are sometimes so many points and lines that they're hard to follow. Before you use them in earnest, make sure that they're right for your particular learning style.

Matrix notes/grid notes

Creating a table or matrix is obviously useful if your notes are recording different viewpoints, approaches and applications. It would, for example, be perfect if you were dealing with a problem that consisted of different elements and involved several contrasting viewpoints on those elements. An article on traffic problems might have separate columns for the views of the government, the police, local businesses and the local community. The various rows in the grid could then be labelled to test their attitudes to pedestrianisation, parking fees and fines, congestion charges, commercial access and car-sharing schemes. It gives a quick, easy-to-use overview of the issues and how they combine or contrast, but there's not much space to develop notes or add extra information.

Herringbone maps

This may sound a strange label, but it's the perfect image for a format that lets you lay out opposing sides of an argument. Imagine the usual cartoon version of a fishbone, with a spine down the middle and bones sticking out on either side. On one side, the 'bones' carry statements for an argument; on the other are the statements against. It's simple and effective. But it's also limited. There's no obvious place for statements that are ambiguous or refer to things other than the for and against stances. And you might find you need a very long herring as you read more and more of the text and make more and more notes.

Getting personal

We keep referring to books, articles and online sites as resources, but the same word applies to your notes. Never throw them away; you've spent lots of time collecting them and they're excellent when it comes to revising. In fact, you may well find that by the time you get to the exams, they'll refresh your memory of the subject and even make it clearer than it was when you were writing them. They've distilled its essence and stripped away any confusions there might have been on the first read of the text.

brilliant tip

Don't try to cram too much information on to a sheet. Leave white space around lists or other important items of information. It'll not only help you to remember the information more easily but also leave space for any extra details you might want to add later.

In fact, the visual aspects of your notes are important. They should be memorable, recognisable. Be careful, though – don't turn the business of making them look good into a displacement activity. The idea isn't to make them look pretty or create some sort of art form out of them; it's to create patterns, colours and shapes that trigger your recall.

Find ways of abbreviating what you write. Use familiar abbreviations such as NATO or DNA and the common ones like e.g., i.e., etc., but develop your own shorthand too. You could use maths symbols, text messaging techniques or words from other languages. When we started writing this book, the word 'university' was occurring quite frequently (naturally enough) so we used the auto-correct function to represent it with a single key – the hash sign. You can do the same thing with a pen – writing one little symbol instead of ten letters saves ages.

You can also save time by photocopying the relevant pages. This is useful if you don't need many notes on a particular topic or maybe when there's a lot of demand for a particular book and it's on short loan in the library.

It's easier to get a photocopy and highlight the key bits or add your notes in the margins. In this case, though, it's important to remember that copyright law means that there are restrictions on photocopying. Check what they are by looking at notices in your library.

Another point about photocopying is that it's basically passive and therefore less useful as a way of learning. Learning calls for involvement, so note-making should be an active process. We've stressed before that it's important to think as you write. Don't just use your notes to summarise what authors have said; think about their meanings, evaluate the facts and their ideas, make connections between different sources, between your reading as a whole and the task you've been set.

What next?

Look for a general dictionary ...

... that gives a comprehensive list of abbreviations and see which ones might be useful for you. Also, check a subject-specific dictionary for lists of specialist abbreviations. You'll not only be able to use them yourself but you'll know where to look if you come across one that's unfamiliar as you're reading.

Everyone has a different method ...

... of note-making and we've actually suggested that you should personalise yours to suit your style. So compare your notes with those of a classmate, on the same piece of text if possible. Talk about what you've chosen to note and why; it'll help both of you to appreciate any differences in reasoning, understanding, logic.

Don't hesitate to try ...

... different styles. A strategy that works well for some things may be less good for others. Also, as you progress, the sorts of books you read may change and call for different approaches. So find a style that suits you, but always be open to new things. Stay flexible.

 **recap**

Why are you taking notes?

What are notes for?

Some different formats.

Personalise your note-making.

PART 4

Developing the necessary writing skills

19 Getting started with academic writing

It may seem an obvious thing to say, but writing and thinking are very closely allied. You'll find that assignments at university challenge you to write in different forms, forms which are dictated by the type of thinking the question asks you to do. So here we'll look at the first stages of getting and organising material to plan the structure of your submission.

First steps

All writing exercises are designed to ask you three questions:

1 How well do you know and understand a topic?

2 How skilled are you at researching a specific aspect of it?

3 Can you organise information and evidence in a structured way to articulate and support your arguments?

Time management again

You'll find the submission date in the course handbook, so it's easy to work out how long you've got before you have to hand in your essay. Do that and then, according to the way you prefer to work, try to break down that time into segments, each of which you allocate to a particular activity. The sequence might be:

- working out what's being asked
- thinking about it and jotting down some ideas
- consulting lecture and tutorial notes or online resources

- doing some preliminary reading
- organising the material you've collected
- doing any additional reading that's necessary
- writing the first draft
- doing other things to get some distance between you and the work
- reviewing and rewriting
- editing, proofreading and printing out or writing the final copy.

Leave yourself extra time for the unexpected and don't forget that during the same period you'll be going to other lectures, doing more reading for different topics, relaxing and having to meet other commitments.

Breaking down the task

It's worth taking time to make sure you understand exactly what you're being asked to do. So, once again, ask yourself some questions.

What's the instruction?

We tend always to speak of 'essay questions', but many assignments are not questions but instructions. They're introduced by a word which is telling, not asking, you to do something – describe, analyse, assess, consider, etc. So the first thing to do is make sure you interpret the word properly.

What's the topic?

This is maybe obvious, but it's worth making sure you identify exactly the specific topic and its context. It's all too easy to see a particular word or expression and jump to conclusions about what's being asked. Your job is to stick to the topic, not wander off on some personal interpretation of just one element of it.

What's the aspect of the topic?

Most topics have many facets and trigger lots of different opinions and responses. Make sure you understand and can define the specific focus that the person who set the question is asking you to apply.

What restriction is imposed on the topic?

Even though you've identified the precise aspect, there may be elements of the question that limit it or ask you to consider it in the light of other things. These are the things which restrict the area in which you can operate.

As you do this preliminary breakdown of the task, it's worth jotting down your decisions. That'll help you identify the parameters within which you need to stay and it'll stop you wandering wherever your thinking takes you. You'll stick to the point. It's also the first step towards deciding how you'll approach structuring your response. All of which adds up to time well spent and, in the end, time saved.

▶brilliant example

The assignment is: Assess the importance of post-operative care in the rehabilitation of orthopaedic patients.

The instruction tells you to 'assess' the topic, which is 'post-operative care'. The particular aspect of it is not its cost, effectiveness, desirability or anything else; it's its 'importance'. But that doesn't mean its overall importance in society or to every post-operative patient. There are in this case two restrictions which help to narrow the field of research: its value in the 'rehabilitation' of 'orthopaedic patients'.

Instruction words

Instruction words vary from subject to subject. As a general guide, we can suggest that they're asking you to do one (or more) of four things:

1 Do: create something, draw up a plan, calculate.

2 Describe: explain or show how something appears, happens or works.

3 Analyse: look at all sides of an issue.

4 Argue: look at all sides of an issue and provide supporting evidence for your position.

We obviously can't give an exhaustive list, but some of the more common instruction words are as follows:

Account for	Give reasons for
Analyse	Give an organised answer looking at all aspects
Assess	Decide on value/importance
Comment on	Give your opinion
Compare [with]	Discuss similarities; draw conclusions on common areas
Compile	Make up (a list/plan/outline)
Consider	Describe/give your views on the subject
Contrast	Discuss differences/state your view
Demonstrate	Show by example/evidence
Discuss	Give your thoughts and support your opinion or conclusion
Evaluate	Decide on merit of situation/argument
Exemplify	Show by giving examples
Explain	Give reason for – say why
Give an account of	Describe
Illustrate	Give examples
Outline	Describe basic factors
Show	Demonstrate with supporting evidence

The topic

Once you're sure that you've pinpointed exactly what's being asked of you, it's time to start generating ideas about it. Making a map of some brainstorming is a good way to begin. Jot down thoughts as they occur, link them to other associated thoughts, try to think of points of view contrary to them. All you're doing is jotting down some headings which you can expand later through more thinking or extra reading. The headings may also be the beginnings of a structure, but at the moment just write whatever occurs to you. But be careful, don't be tempted to wander into areas which are outside the topic and the restrictions. The important thing about this is that what's on the page are your ideas and not those taken from books or lectures. Your reading may have influenced them, of course, but they're your own initial responses to the task. They arise from you doing some critical thinking.

Research

Now that you have some initial material on paper, it's time to start developing it further and adding more detail. You're ready to move to the research phase. Thanks to the initial brainstorming, you already have a few areas you need to investigate so you can narrow your focus to concentrate on them.

Reading lists

An obvious first source is your reading list. There you'll find both basic and more detailed texts. You don't really have to read all of them, but they're valuable, targeted resources and you're bound to find material which is relevant to your topic there.

brilliant tip

If there's time, reading whole books will obviously be useful, but in the case of reading for a particular assignment, it makes more sense to read selectively. Look at the contents page and the index to find the relevant sections.

General or subject encyclopaedias

These can give you a quick insight into background information and also help to point you towards more detailed texts. Electronic versions may be available through your university library.

Library resources

You can use the electronic catalogue to find books and/or articles on your topic. It's also useful to look at the shelves devoted to the specific thing you're researching. You may also come across titles which weren't suggested as fitting your search words but which may be relevant for you.

Handouts/PowerPoint slides

Since the topic of your assignment is probably related to something that's been dealt with in lectures, it's likely that you'll find key issues and ideas, problems and solutions in the information provided by the lecturer.

Lecture notes

This is where the habit of writing the lecturer, topic and date on each of your lecture notes will help you to find the relevant information very quickly.

Ebrary

Once you're familiar with how to access and use it, it's an efficient way of locating information and usually a very reliable resource.

E-journals

This is a source of information which is reliable and probably the most up-to-date writing on your topic.

Whichever of these resources you're using, it's another example of applying critical thinking. As you read and make your notes, you're making choices, deciding what's relevant and what's not, spotting arguments for and against a point of view. And the more you do that, the better you'll understand the topic and the clearer your ideas will become. You'll be looking for facts, examples, information to support a particular viewpoint, and counter-arguments to balance your analysis, and your initial brainstorm will be growing accordingly, but always within the scope of the task which you identified at the start.

brilliant tip

If you're stuck, try asking the basic questions which trainee journalists are advised to use: Who's involved? What are the problems/issues? When, where, why and how did it all (or will it all) happen?

Time to analyse

OK, by wide, general reading, you've now collected lots of information on the topic. It's time to sort through your notes and ideas and analyse them to decide what's relevant and what isn't. Once again, you'll need to apply your critical thinking. At university, you need to do more than just reproduce facts. You need to build an argument and support it with evidence. So, once you've discarded what's irrelevant, you'll have to organise the rest into different approaches, viewpoints, arguments and counter-arguments. The underlying aim is to present a tight, well-argued, well-supported case for your viewpoint.

By the way, when we say 'discard', we don't mean throw it away. The material may not be relevant in this particular instance, but the topic may come up again in a different form and the 'discarded' material may then be relevant. So never throw away notes – apart from anything else, they're all valuable when you're revising for an exam.

Wider considerations

Use a wide range of sources. Don't rely on handouts and notes from a single textbook. You'll get credit for showing that you've looked further afield and found material outside the recommended reading.

Keep a record of what you read. There'll probably be times when you know you read something somewhere that's relevant to the topic you're researching, but you can't remember what or where it was. When you make notes, part of your routine should be to include in them the page number, chapter, title, author, publisher and place of publication. You'll be able to find them more quickly and citation and referencing will be much easier.

When you did your time management plan for the assignment, one of the suggested areas was time allocated for reading. It's all too easy to use 'Oh, I need to do more reading' as an excuse not to start the actual writing. So, when you allocate reading time, make it realistic. Give yourself plenty of time, but then stick to it and make yourself move on to the next phase.

What next?

Look through our list of instruction words ...

... and decide which ones are asking you to do, describe, analyse or argue. Now do the same thing with some or all of the assignment titles you've been set or ones from past exam papers. In each case, decide which of the four types of approach is needed. Sometimes you may have to do more than one in the same question. For example, you may have to describe something before you can analyse it.

 **recap**

Understanding what's needed.

Time management.

Breaking down the task.

Instruction words.

Research resources.

20 The bare bones of academic writing structures

Whichever type of writing assignment you've been set, you'll structure it according to a basic format by starting with the general (the introduction), moving on to the specific (the main body) and then moving back again to the general (the conclusion). We're going to look at this structure and examine its elements in more detail.

The basic format

Let's look first at the standard framework of introduction, main body and conclusion, and suggest how you might organise your writing within it. We'll survey some other academic formats in the next chapter.

Introduction

This is the first contact your reader makes with you, so you want to create a good impression. It needs to be clear and organised and tell him what to expect in the pages that follow. It gives him an idea of how you handle language and helps him to focus on what you're going to write and the direction in which you'll be taking him. So, in overall terms, it needs to do three things:

1 Give a brief general explanation of the topic and its context.

2 Outline what you understand it to mean.

3 Describe how you're going to approach it.

Part of the third point may be that you warn the reader that you'll be concentrating on certain aspects of the subject rather than giving an exhaustive account of all of it. This may be because it's a complex issue and, if you're having to work to a word limit, you can't do justice to all its aspects. Whatever the reason, it's important to indicate this to the reader/marker so that he understands exactly what to expect and why. You can acknowledge that there are many strands to the topic but explain that you're going to focus on what you consider to be the important ones in the context of the question.

When you've finished writing the assignment, revisit your introduction to make sure it's still an accurate description of what you've actually done. As you write the main body of the text, new ideas often occur and it's easy to get drawn into exploring them. This is fine, but you need to alter the introduction to accommodate them.

brilliant tip

You may have a good idea of what your argument will be, but until you've written the whole text, you can't be absolutely sure of the points you'll make or the balance you'll achieve between them. For this reason, it might help you to leave the introduction until you've written the main body of your assignment. Once you know what you've said, you'll find it much easier to introduce it. So, if you're struggling with the introduction, consider a different writing sequence: main body, conclusion, introduction.

Main body

This section consists of all the points you'll be making in your argument and presentation of the materials. Its structure indicates how you're organising the content. As you move from point to point, you may need to generalise, describe, define or give examples as part of your analysis. Try to be as clear and brief as you can, and always keep the reader with you by giving plenty of indications (using signpost words) of any changes of direction and the introduction of new themes or opposing arguments.

As you're writing your first draft, you may find sub-headings useful. They help to keep you focused on exactly where you are in the development of your argument and stop you wandering off the point or getting out of sequence. In most disciplines, they're not acceptable in the final draft which you hand in, but that's not a problem because you can replace them with a topic sentence, which will act as a link with the previous paragraph or an indication of a change of emphasis or direction.

Conclusion

This summarises everything that's gone before. It ties up any loose ends and reminds the reader of where he's been and what the main conclusions are. Once again, it can consist of three elements:

1 A reminder of the question and the important features on which you've concentrated.

2 A summary of the specific evidence you've presented to support your views.

3 A statement of your overall viewpoint.

Its function is obviously different from that of the introduction, but so is its language. In the introduction, you should try to be clear and avoid jargon or technical words as far as possible. But since you've probably used technical or more sophisticated terms in the main body as you looked at the subject in more detail, it's appropriate to use that more complex terminology in the conclusion. Don't introduce any new ideas at this stage; your conclusion should be a distillation of the points you've covered in the main body.

Sometimes students rush their conclusion. It might be because there are other things they have to do, or they're fed up with the subject, or they're tired or perhaps just relieved to be near the end of it. Resist this temptation. The conclusion is the thing that creates the final impression in the mind of your reader/marker. Give it your full attention and leave some time after you've written it to look back over it and check that it's correct and has the impact you want.

As you're writing, you'll get absorbed in each stage of the argument and its presentation. The points you're making will be very clear to you, but when you move to the next point, that takes over, and when you get to the end, you won't have such a clear idea of each step you've taken. So, at the end of each phase of your argument, try jotting down its main ideas and your 'mini-conclusions' about them. If you write them on a separate piece of paper, you'll have a ready-made outline of the main body which will be the perfect plan of your overall conclusion.

Keep the right balance

It would obviously be absurd to have an introduction which covered the same number of pages as the main body, or a conclusion consisting of three lines. The most substantial (and longest) element of your writing should, of course, be the main body. There are no hard and fast rules about the length of the introduction or conclusion, but they should be as short as you can reasonably make them without leaving out essential information. It's all too easy to sweat over the introduction and spend time outlining the context and anticipating points, then leaving yourself too little time and space to deal with the rest of the essay and the conclusion. Keep the proportions right.

Word limits

Tutors set word limits on essays not to save them having to mark acres of text but to train you to be precise and concise in your writing. The limit forces you to analyse the topic more carefully to decide what to keep in and what to leave out.

It's important to note that falling short of the word limit is just as bad as going over it. Some students keep a running total of words they've used and as soon as they reach the minimum word limit, they stop abruptly. This is not a good approach. It unbalances the overall piece and simply gives the impression that you've run out of ideas. The ending's poor and many points may be left unresolved.

Word count shouldn't really feature when you're writing your first draft. Make it part of the reviewing and editing process. That's when you cut and reshape your writing to make it tighter and clearer.

It's always better to write too much and then have to cut than to write too little and try to pad it out. If your text is seriously past the limit, it might be possible to make an appendix. You could choose some elements to cut, then shorten them and reformat them as bullet points. They're still included in the word count, but bullet pointing them makes them shorter. You can then add them to the end of the essay as an appendix (or, if there's more than one, several appendices). All it needs is a note in the main body telling the reader that there's further information on a particular point in Appendix A (or whichever the relevant appendix is). Before trying this, though, make sure it's acceptable in your department. Check your course handbook or ask a member of staff.

Another way in which you can reduce the count is by thinking about citations. In many disciplines you're expected to include references to publications or experts in your field of study. In law, this could be cases; in the arts and humanities, it could be work by a distinguished academic. But you don't have to quote long pieces of text. Summarise their ideas in your own words (but make sure you acknowledge your source). It's all part of developing the necessary writing skills and techniques.

brilliant tip

Most word processors count the words for you. Microsoft Word also has a 'floating' toolbar which shows the total as you write or edit. To access it, go to the Tools menu and choose Tools > Word Count > Show Toolbar. But be careful – looking at it after every few sentences wastes time.

What next?

To help you get the right balance ...

... in your writing, look at chapters in textbooks and see how much space they give to introducing the chapter and drawing conclusions.

Take a piece of your own writing ...

... or a textbook which has sub-headings and practise converting them into topic sentences. Decide which is more effective – the topic sentence or the original sub-heading – and think about why you chose one rather than the other.

Look at some of your own old ...

... or even recent exercises and try to identify whether you've included the basic elements and sub-elements of the standard writing format we've identified. Is there a clear division between the introduction, main body and conclusion? What's the balance like between them? Does the introduction cover context, specific focus and statement of intent? Does the conclusion state your position clearly with the reasons why you've arrived at it? If any of the answers is 'no', work out how you could improve things. It's all part of improving your writing (and thinking) style.

 **recap**

The basic format of academic writing.

Introduction, main body, conclusion.

Getting the right balance.

Word counts.

21 How to create a plan

We've dealt with gathering the material and looked at the basic framework of a typical piece of academic writing. We can now look at how to bring the two together and choose how to organise your notes and ideas into an outline plan that will present them clearly and effectively.

Creating a plan

If there were a one-size-fits-all plan, we'd describe it, but unfortunately there's not. People think and write differently and any particular approach may suit some but not others. Some plan meticulously, others simply sketch a bare outline. Too much detail can prevent ideas expanding, too little may leave gaps. The ideal is a plan which is devised specifically for the project in hand and has just enough detail to lead you through the argument with confidence and still enough flexibility for you to adapt it as you write.

Establish the main themes

You did your brainstorming and then added notes and ideas to it as you read more. Look at the material you have and decide whether there are any themes or issues that stand out. One way of doing this is to highlight all the items that are related, using a different colour for each category or theme. When you've done this initial sorting of the material, think about the instruction word again and see whether you should start organising it on the basis of description, analysis or argument.

The basic structural approaches

You want your piece of work to flow smoothly through its various points and present a logical, structured argument. To achieve this, you can choose one of the most commonly used structural models: chronological, classification, common denominator, phased, analytical, thematic, comparative/contrastive.

Chronological

This is a description of a process or sequence, such as outlining the historical development of the European Union. It's a kind of writing that's most likely going to be entirely descriptive.

Classification

Classification means putting objects or ideas in order. Let's say you're asked to discuss transport by examining ways of travelling by land, sea and air. That already gives you three classifications and each can be sub-divided into commercial, military and personal modes of transport. You could then sub-divide even further by considering, for example, how they're powered. To some extent, how you divide and sub-divide is subjective, but the approach does give you the chance to describe each category at each level in a way that allows some contrast. It's particularly useful in scientific disciplines and any context which lends itself to starting with the general and moving on to the more specific. ('Travel' is general, 'a two-masted sailing boat with back-up engines powered by solar panels' is specific.)

Common denominator

This lends itself to topics where there's a common characteristic or theme. If, for example, you were given an assignment which asked you to 'Account for the levels of high infant mortality in developing countries', the implication is that there's something missing in these different countries which results in children dying. So the common denominator is deficiency or lack. Your plan might, therefore, group its material under the headings:

● Lack of primary health care

● Lack of health education

● Lack of literacy.

Phased

The phased model is for when you're identifying short-, medium- and long-term aspects of an issue. It's a sequential approach. The example this time is a task that tells you to 'Discuss the impact of water shortage on flora and fauna along river banks'. You could divide the various factors which contribute to the shortages into:

● short-term – the river bed dries out in the summer and so annual plants die

● medium-term – oxygenating plant life is damaged and wildlife numbers fall

● long-term – the water table gets lower and lower and certain amphibious species decline.

Analytical

Analysis means examining an issue in depth and it's used to consider complex issues. Suppose you were asked to 'Evaluate potential solutions to the problem of identity theft'. Your approach might follow an outline plan like this.

● Define identity theft and give an example.

● Explain why it's difficult to control.

● Outline legal and practical solutions to the problem.

● Weigh up the advantages and disadvantages of each.

● Say which ones you would favour and why.

brilliant tip

Analysis is useful for many kinds of essays, reports, projects and case studies and also when you can't identify themes or trends. There's a method called the SPSER model, which stands for Situation, Problem, Solution, Evaluation, Recommendation. It works as follows:

● Situation: describe the context and give a brief history.

● Problem: describe or define the problem.

● Solution: describe and explain the possible solution(s).

● Evaluation: identify the positive and negative features for each solution and give evidence and/or reasons to support your viewpoint.

▶

● Recommendation: identify the best option in your opinion and say how you came to your conclusion. (This element may be omitted, depending on whether you're asked to provide a recommendation or not.)

Thematic

This is similar to the phased approach, but in this case the identifying characteristics are not sequences but themes. Each question will produce its own themes, but possible examples could be:

● social, economic or political factors

● age, income and health considerations

● gas, electricity, oil, water and wind power.

Comparative/contrastive

Comparing and contrasting derives from the themed approach. For example, consider a task that asks you to 'Discuss the arguments for and against the introduction of car-free city centres'. It's the perfect opportunity for using a grid-style way of organising your notes into positive and negative aspects for the main interested parties in the debate.

	Positive aspects (P)	Negative aspects (N)
1 Pedestrians	Greater safety; clean.	Lengthy walk; poor parking.
2 Drivers	Less stress; park and ride facilities.	High parking fees; expensive public transport.
3 Commercial enterprises	Quicker access for deliveries.	Loss of trade to more accessible out-of-town shopping centres.
4 Local authority	Reduces emissions.	Cost of park and ride.
5 Police	Easier to police.	Reliance on foot patrols.

Interestingly, you can write your assignment in two different ways using this plan. The introduction and conclusion will be similar in each case, but the way of constructing the main body will be different.

1   After the introduction, move vertically down the 'positive' column. Now do the same with the 'negative' column, and then write a short conclusion to establish the balance between them. (So the main body sequence is: P1, P2, P3, P4, P5, N1, N2, N3, N4, N5.)

2   After the introduction, look at pedestrians and examine the positive and then the negative aspects for them. Now do the same with each of the other categories of people, then write your conclusion. (The main body sequence this time is P1, N1, P2, N2, P3, N3, P4, N4, P5, N5.)

brilliant tip

The choice is yours. However, be careful if you're using this approach in an exam. If you use the first method (P1, P2, P3, etc.) you may run out of time and either not get to the negative aspects or maybe have to rush them, which will make your answer unbalanced. But, using the second method in the same circumstances might mean that you don't get round to considering the attitudes of the local authority or the police.

Expanding your outline

The outline plan is the basis for what you write. Follow it through, making sure you don't miss out any points. Check, too, that the links between sections that you noted in the plan are clear in the text so that the reader is led logically through your argument.

Try for balance

It may be that you have consciously to discard some of the techniques you used at school. The tendency there is for written work to be descriptive rather than analytical. You can still be descriptive, but be careful to restrict it to just what's needed for the task, and if the instruction requires you to analyse or argue, make sure this is the main focus of what you write.

Explain your approach

The models we've described are fairly standard and easily recognisable approaches to academic writing assignments, but it's still important to tell your reader early on, usually in your introduction, which one you intend to use.

Write 'your' answer

In subjects with a mathematical content, there are clearly correct and incorrect answers, but in many other disciplines this isn't the case and so you're not looking for the 'right' answer but 'your' answer. The way you handle the subject, structure your argument and provide evidence to support it is what counts, and that's what determines the sort of mark you'll get.

What next?

Look at a chapter in a basic textbook …

… and analyse the structural approach the author has taken. Note how much space she gives to 'scene-setting' using description and to the other components of the text, such as analysis, argument and evaluation.

Read over some of the essay titles …

… or report assignments you've been set and try to decide which of the approaches we've been describing might be best for each one.

Take some of your coursework tasks …

… or past exam papers and find the ones that have been framed as questions. Now try converting them into 'instruction' tasks and decide which of the do–describe–analyse–argue categories they fit into.

 recap

Establishing the main themes of your plan.

Seven basic structural approaches to written assignments.

Expanding the outline.

22 Quotations, citations, references and bibliographies

Academic writing at all levels is much more formal than most other types of writing and you need to learn the basic rules and follow them. Many of them relate to how you use and acknowledge material you've found in the work of others. There are several referencing styles and the one you use will depend on your university's preferred option. We'll take an overview of them here and outline the four main ones and how to use them.

Acknowledging the work of others

Every kind of academic paper, from essay to thesis, refers to work done on the topic by others in the past. It's normal – in fact, it's essential – to read widely on topics and benefit from what others have discovered or proposed. And whether you quote directly from their texts or simply paraphrase their ideas, you must tell your reader exactly where you found the material. The reader must be able to locate your source for herself.

So you do two things:

- Indicate the source in the body of your text at the point where you refer to or quote it.
- Give full details of it in a footnote, endnote or separate reference list at the end of your paper.

 **definitions**

Citation – the use of the idea presented by an author and expressed in your own words to support a point in your own work.

Quotation – the use of words taken directly from the source.

Bibliography – a listing at the end of your work of all the source materials you've consulted. You don't need to have used them all directly in your text. In some styles the word 'bibliography' is used instead of 'reference list'.

Reference list – all the books, journals, web and online materials you've referred to in your paper. It's usually placed at the end.

Referencing styles

You'll find your department's preferred style in your course handbook, or it may be recommended by your lecturer or supervisor. If there's no stated preference, the choice is yours, so you need to have an idea of the sort of variations there are. That's why we'll now look at the four most popular styles and highlight how they work. To make it all simpler, we'll invent a book, its author, publication date and publishers. Let's be pretentious and call it *The Existential Lay-by* by K. J. Shiels, published by Pekinese Press, Cambridge in 2007. None of the 'quotations' from it is intended to be accurate or even to make much sense; they're there simply to provide examples of how citations and quotations work.

When it comes to how you format the source for inclusion in your reference list or bibliography, however, there are so many possible variations (multiple authors, articles in newspapers, journals or collections edited by someone else, online resources, broadcasts and so on) that it would be confusing to list them all here. Instead, we suggest that once you know which style your university prefers, you use a search engine to consult one of the many excellent sites which lay out examples of each very clearly. The search terms Harvard style, Vancouver style, etc. are all you need.

Harvard

This is maybe the simplest, quickest and possibly the easiest to adjust to of the four.

- When you refer to the source in your text, you put the author's name and the date in brackets at the end of the sentence, e.g. Not all philosophies are sensible (Shiels, 2007). Note that this isn't a direct quote from Shiels but a paraphrase of his viewpoint.

- You can also make the author's name part of your sentence, putting the date in brackets immediately after it, e.g. Shiels (2007) argues that existentialism and absurdism occupy different points on the spectrum of despair.

- If you quote directly from the book, you must also add the relevant page number, e.g According to Shiels (2007, p. 23) 'dialectical materialism predicated a linear narrative which has today been undermined by the phenomenon of hypertext'.

- The way to identify the book in your reference list or bibliography is: Shiels, K. J., 2007. *The existential lay-by*. Cambridge: Pekinese Press. (Note: Everything, including the punctuation marks, must follow this exact pattern. The same applies with every other referencing style.)

Modern Languages Association (MLA)

- When you refer to the source in your text, you put the author's name and the page number in brackets, e.g. Not all philosophies are sensible (Shiels, 126).

- You can also make the author's name part of your sentence, putting the page number in brackets at the end of the sentence or clause, e.g. Shiels argues that existentialism and absurdism occupy different points on the spectrum of despair (79).

- If you quote directly from the book, you must put the name and page number at the end of the sentence, e.g. 'dialectical materialism predicated a linear narrative which has today been undermined by the phenomenon of hypertext' (Shiels 23).

- The way to identify the book in your reference list or bibliography is: Shiels, K. J. *The existential lay-by*. Cambridge: Pekinese Press, 2007.

Vancouver

This is a numerical system with full-size numerals in brackets after the citation or quotation. Each number refers to a work listed in the bibliography or reference list, where the sources themselves are numbered 1, 2, 3, etc. It makes the text easier to read because there are no names or other bits of information interrupting the flow. However, if the reader wants to know the source of the reference, he has to stop reading and turn to the bibliography to find it. If you cite or quote more than once from a particular source, each time you put the same number in brackets, so if you're quoting from Shiels and two other imaginary writers, Ebeneezer Black and Billabong White, and the quotations/citations come in the order Black, Shiels, Shiels, White, Black, White, Shiels, the sequence of numbers in brackets will be (1), (2), (2), (3), (1), (3), (2).

The way to identify the book in your reference list or bibliography is:

Shiels K. J. The existential lay-by. Cambridge: Pekinese Press; 2007.

Chicago

This style uses footnotes. The first time a particular source is cited or quoted, the full bibliographical information is given in a footnote. Each time it's used after that, abbreviations are used. The sequence might be as follows:

- It has been claimed that not all philosophies are sensible[1] (Shiels, 126). The footnote will read:
  [1] K. J. Shiels, *The existential lay-by*. (Cambridge: Pekinese Press, 2007), 25. (This means the reference is to page 25.)

- We'll assume that you're quoting or citing from other references and that they take up footnotes 2, 3 and 4, so the next time Shiels is sourced, the footnote will read:
  [5] Shiels, *op. cit.*, 27. (*Op. cit.* means 'work already quoted' and 27 is the page number.)

- If there are no other references between this and the next Shiels one, the footnote will read:
  [6] Shiels, *ibid.*, 159. (*Ibid* is short for *ibidem*, meaning 'the same'. It's indicating that it's the same Shiels text you've already quoted but this time the reference is to page 159.)

- The way to identify the book in your reference list or bibliography is: Shiels, K. J. 2007. *The existential lay-by*. Cambridge: Pekinese Press. (Notice that the layout of the full bibliographical information is formatted differently here than it was in the footnote.)

What's it all for?

This may seem fussy, but there are good reasons for giving full information about the quotations and citations you use. Ideas in books and articles belong to the people who express them. They themselves may have got them from others, but if you're using their version, you must acknowledge that you're borrowing from them. Even if your aim is to disagree with them, you must still give them credit for what is their intellectual property.

Noting what sources you used will help your reader to understand how you put your argument together and where it fits into general studies of and opinions about the topic. By knowing the sort of influences you responded to, he'll be better able to place your work and form opinions about it. It will also show him how much reading you've done and the scope of your knowledge of the subject. This will be useful if he's assessing your work or advising you on further reading or sources that are more relevant. Finally, it will give him the information he needs if he wants to read the source material for himself.

Reference lists are part of an academic discipline. Quite often, if you fail to provide one, you'll lose marks.

brilliant tip

If you have a quotation contained inside another one, in British English you put the whole quotation in single inverted commas and the contained quotation in double inverted commas. To demonstrate this, here's another quote from our fictional author Shiels: 'Philosophy consists of more than Shakespeare's notion that "There's nothing either good or bad but thinking makes it so" but the words are a valuable starting point.' In American English, that becomes: "Philosophy consists of more than Shakespeare's notion that 'There's nothing either good or bad but thinking makes it so' but the words are a valuable starting point."

Using information within your text

There are two ways of introducing the work of others into your text: by quoting exact words from a source or by citation, which involves summarising or paraphrasing the idea in your own words. Remember that in both cases you must acknowledge the source of the material.

Quotations

In this case, it depends whether the quotation's short or long. If it's short, put the exact words in single inverted commas within your own sentence. If we make xxxx your words and zzz the words of the quotation, this gives us: xxxx xx xxxx 'zzzz zz zzzz zz zzzz' xxx xxxx x xxx. If it's a long quotation, say 30 words or more, you don't use inverted commas. Instead, you separate it from your own text by indenting it and using single spacing for it, like this:

Xxx xxxx x xxx xxxxxxxxx xxxxxxx xxxxx xxxx:

> Zzzz zz zzzzzz z zzzz zz zzzzzz zz zzzz zzzz zzzzz zz zzz zzzzzzzzzzzzzz zz zzzzz zzzzz zzzzzzz zzzzzzz zzzzz zz zz z zzzzzz z zz zzzzzzzz zzzz zz zzzzzzzz zzzzzzzzzzzz zzz zzzzzzzzzz
>
> (source reference)

Xxx xxxx x xxx xxxxxxxxx xxxxxxx xxxxx xxxx

If you deliberately miss out some words from the original, you show you've done so by filling the 'gap' with three dots. This is called an ellipsis. For example, if the quotation in the last example started somewhere other than at the beginning of a sentence, you'd write:

Xxx xxxx x xxx xxxxxxxxx xxxxxxx xxxxx xxxx:

> ... zzz zz zzzzzz z zzzz zz zzzzzz zz zzzz zzzz zzzzz zz zzz zzzzzzzzzzzzzz zz zzzzz zzzzz zzzzzzz zzzzzzz zzzzz zz zz z zzzzzz z zz zzzzzzzz zzzz zz zzzzzzzz zzzzzzzzzzzz zzz zzzzzzzzzz
>
> (source reference)

Xxx xxxx x xxx xxxxxxxxx xxxxxxx xxxxx xxxx

If the words are left out of the body of the quotation, an ellipsis is still used but it's enclosed by square brackets to show that there wasn't an ellipsis in the original, e.g. 'zzz zz zzzzzz z zzzz zz zzzzzz [...] zzzz zzzz zzzzz zz zzz'.

brilliant tip

Cutting words out of a quote which aren't relevant to the point it's supporting helps to keep it brief and focused. But you must never omit words that change the sense of the quotation. If the quotation was 'The prospect of entry into a federal European Union is not universally acceptable', leaving out the word 'not' would change its meaning completely and misrepresent the views of the author.

Citations

There are two basic ways of citing text, one which stresses the information, the other which stresses the author. If we use the Harvard method for identifying the sources, examples of the two methods would be:

- Philosophical advances are almost entirely dependent on linguistic evolution (Shiels, 2007).

- Shiels (2007) claimed that philosophical advances were almost entirely dependent on linguistic evolution.

In the first, the statement reads as if it's a generally accepted 'truth' which he's articulating; in the second, it may still be a 'truth' but by putting the author at the beginning, it makes it seem more like his opinion.

Footnotes and endnotes

We've already seen how footnotes are used in the Chicago referencing style. Their more general use is to provide additional information or add a comment or discussion point which would interrupt the flow of the argument if it was included in the text. They're at the bottom of the page on which the link appears. Endnotes are collected together at the end of the whole text. Before using them, you should check what your department's policy is.

Software referencing packages

These are flexible programs and can create your reference list in several different formats. But unless you're very familiar with them, does it really make sense to spend time learning how to use such complex tools and key in the data to 'feed' them? It would probably be quicker and produce the same results if you typed a list straight into a word-processed table and sorted it alphabetically.

Making citing and listing references easier for yourself

It must be obvious by now that citations and quotations are crucial to the production of good-quality academic writing. So get into good habits from the start. Whichever way you prefer to make and copy notes – electronically, photocopying, writing – make sure you always include all the necessary bibliographical information. If you don't, it'll take ages to find it later.

Choose or find out which reference style to use as early as possible. Don't switch between systems. Whichever you choose, follow its conventions to the letter, including all punctuation details. Once you've done so, add works to your reference list as you read them. Just set up a table or list and type in the relevant details as soon as you cite the source in the text. Using a table makes the formatting easier and lets you insert new records very easily.

Even if you're not sure whether you'll use a quotation you're noting down, you should still record full reference details with it. You may have an excellent memory, but it'll still take time to locate the source and note down its details later. And if your memory's not so good, it'll be a very frustrating process.

What next?

Find out which referencing style ...

... is recommended for your subjects. These may be different from one discipline or tutor to another. Some subjects such as law, history and English literature often use specialised methods of citation and referencing. Usually, you'll get some training on what's needed. If you don't, look at the way the referencing has been done in the books on your reading lists. If you compare it with the examples we've given, that should help you to identify the style by name.

Look at textbooks or journal articles ...

... in your subject area to see if they deviate from the four styles we've listed. Sometimes you may find they've modified them in some way. If so, or if you're still unsure about what style to use, ask your tutor about it.

 **recap**

The importance of referencing.

The four main styles.

Why do you need to do it?

How to use quotations and citations.

23 Never ever plagiarise

Plagiarism and copyright are two related topics that are extremely important academically and legally. They may seem complex at times and they're often misunderstood by students. But if you don't find out what they mean and how they could affect your university career, you could be risking serious disciplinary action.

Plagiarism is stealing

If you take someone else's ideas and pretend they belong to you, that's theft, plain and simple. The problem is that over recent years technological advances such as digital scanners, photocopiers and file-sharing have all made it much easier to cut and paste and copy things. You may even do so without knowing you're doing it. So it really is in your interests to get to know exactly what's involved so that you know when you need to acknowledge intellectual property. Apart from anything else, wouldn't you rather develop your own ideas than steal other people's? Isn't that why you're at university?

 brilliant definitions

Plagiarism – using the work of someone else as if it were your own without acknowledging the source. (Note: 'work' here includes ideas, writing and inventions – not just words.)

Intentional plagiarism is a very serious offence. Universities impose a range of penalties depending on how severe the case is. It may just be a reduction in marks or it could be exclusion from the university or a refusal to give you a degree. You'll find the sanctions imposed by your institution in your departmental or school handbook.

With such severe possibilities, it's hard to believe anyone would still deliberately set out to cheat in this way. But part of the problem is that you may be plagiarising without knowing you're doing it. It's the sort of thing that happens when you've read something a while ago and forgotten you've read it. Then along comes an essay topic which is about that subject and some ideas come into your head which you assume to be yours whereas in fact they're memories of your original reading. The best way to avoid this is to be scrupulous about noting down full details about each source as you consult it.

You can, of course, use other people's ideas and words; in fact, it's good academic practice to do so. But you must always acknowledge the source. If you think an author has said something particularly well, quote her directly and provide a reference to the relevant article or book beside the quote. The academic convention for direct quotes is to use inverted commas (and sometimes italics) to identify it as original material taken directly from a source.

brilliant tip

We're not just talking about stealing from books and articles. Copying a friend's or a classmate's essay or some other piece of work is cheating, too. And both people involved may be punished for it. If you let someone copy your work, you're as guilty as he is. So if you're tempted to be Mr Nice Guy and 'help out' someone else in this way, resist. It's not worth the risk.

Cutting and pasting

It's plagiarism if you cut or copy something from a source such as a website, for example, and paste it into an essay without citing it. There are very sophisticated programs now which can scan a text and identify sections which have been copied from elsewhere. More and more, universities and departments are using them to eliminate such practices.

How to avoid plagiarism

OK, so you've identified the source material that you want to use. What you need to do now is decide how you're going to use it. Does the bit you want to cite support an idea, or contradict one, or is it neutral? You'll probably also need to decide whether you'll quote the material directly as it's written, summarise it or paraphrase it. So let's see what these three options mean and how they work best.

Quotations

You can select a short quote, which you include in your own text, or a long one (maybe 30 or 40 words), which will be separated from your own text by being indented and sometimes italicised too. We gave examples of these in the previous chapter. In British English, short quotes are contained within single quotation marks; American English uses double quotation marks.

Be careful. Too much quotation is basically plagiarism, even if you acknowledge the sources. Think about it: if your work is just big chunks of someone else's joined by short links of your own, it's not really yours, is it? Try to keep quotes well under 10 per cent of the total.

Summarising

This offers a broad overview and gives a brief version of the main points. It's less detailed than a paraphrase and the ideas should be expressed in your own words. You can keep any technical terms, but other ideas should be expressed using a different sentence structure and vocabulary from that of the original.

Paraphrasing

This condenses the material of the original but in more detail than a summary. Once again the words you use must be your own and the rule about technical terms is the same as for summarising.

Whichever approach you take, you must on each occasion use your chosen citation and referencing style to note the author, date, title, place of publication, publisher and relevant page number(s).

How to paraphrase

As we said, you want to convey the main ideas of the original, but using your own words, not the author's, so …

1 Read the text to get its general meaning. Speed-reading topic sentences first of all may help to get you started.

2 Turn over the text and note down its main ideas.

3 Now read the text more carefully.

4 Turn it over again and make more detailed notes about the main ideas.

5 Take down full bibliographical details for your reference list.

Sometimes it helps to start with the conclusion of the text and look back over the main ideas with that in mind. This makes you focus on ideas rather than on exact words.

In both paraphrasing and summarising, you need to show that you've not only read the material but evaluated it. In other words, you've been using critical thinking. The important thing is to present the ideas from the original in a fresh way, to penetrate the meaning rather than just read the words.

Let's now take a short piece of text and illustrate what to do and not to do when you paraphrase and/or summarise. We'll take an exercise that involves a comparison between e-books and traditional books. Let's say we're reading Watt, W. (2006) *The demise of the book*. Dundee: Riverside Press. (p13) and we come across the following useful paragraph:

> E-books are a function of the internet era and make access to otherwise unattainable material possible to wide audiences. The globalisation of literature means that individual authors can present their work to a wider audience without incurring abortive publication costs. This facility constitutes a considerable threat to publishers of traditional books.

Here's how *not* to paraphrase it:

> E-books are part of the internet *age* and allow people from all over the *globe* to use them. This *means that writers show* their *writing* on the internet and so they *do not have such high publishing costs*. This *feature* means that *publishers of old-fashioned books* are *under threat* (Watt, 2006).

The words in italics are simply synonyms for words in the original. It's a lazy type of paraphrasing and it remains so close to the original that it constitutes a form of plagiarism. We've cited the source, but all we've done is stolen the meaning without thinking much about it or attempting to analyse its ideas. A better paraphrase would be:

> Watt (2006) notes that there is concern amongst publishers of hard-copy printed books that the advent of e-books marks the end of their monopoly of the literature market, since authors can publish directly on the internet, thus avoiding publishing costs.

This shows that we've not only read the ideas of the original but actually understood them.

Now let's use the same text for summarising. First, how *not* to do it:

> It has been suggested that '*e-books are a function of the internet era*' and that '*globalisation of literature*' allows authors to '*present their work to a wider audience*' without having to incur '*abortive publication costs*'.

This time, the italics represent direct quotes from the original and so about 60% of 'our' summary belongs to the author of the original. Again, it's too much and is a form of plagiarism. We've used quotation marks, but we've given no indication of where we've taken the quotes from. A much better summary might read:

> With the advent of e-books, individual authors are faced with new approaches to publication of their work (Watt, 2006).

The importance of copyright

When you see the copyright symbol © it tells you that someone is making it clear that the words you're reading belong to them. But just because you don't see any such symbol, it doesn't mean that anyone can quote it without acknowledging the source. The material may still be copyright. We're dealing here with a highly complex legal situation and what we say can give only general indications of what's involved.

Nonetheless, it's important for you to be aware of the nature of copyright and avoid infringing it. Once again, that is stealing. Under the law, your work is protected and others can't use it without your permission. In the UK, that protection applies during the author's lifetime and for 70 years afterwards. That's why you usually see © accompanied by a date and the owner's name at the start of a book.

So you need to be sure that you're not breaking the law when you're photocopying something, digitally scanning it or printing it out without the owner's permission. This isn't as harsh as it sounds because educational copying, for non-commercial private study or research, is usually allowed by publishers. But it's better to stay safe and make sure you copy only a small amount of material under what's called the 'fair dealing' provision. There's no precise legal definition for this, but it means just using very short extracts and acknowledging the source.

brilliant tip

The laws as we're describing them apply to what's classified as 'private study or research' and that means exactly what it says. If you're using the material for commercial or other uses, such as photocopying a funny article for your friends, that's illegal. So is copying software and music CDs (including 'sharing' MP3 files).

How much can you copy?

It's safer to ask at your library or in your department to find out exactly how much you can copy and what the general copying rules are. In general, you shouldn't copy more than 5 per cent of the work involved, or:

● one chapter of a book

● one article per volume of an academic journal

- 20 per cent (to a maximum of 20 pages) of a short book

- one poem or short story (maximum of 10 pages) from an anthology

- one separate illustration or map up to A4 size

- short excerpts of musical works – not whole works or movements.

In each of these cases we're talking about single copies. You're not allowed to make multiple copies of any of these or hand over a single copy for multiple copying to someone else.

Even if you're copying from something you bought and which you therefore own, such as a book or CD, if you copy it or a significant part of it without permission, you're infringing copyright. The same rules apply to text, music and/or images on the internet. Some sites do offer copyright-free images, but you should check the home page to see if there's a statement about copyright or a link to one.

How to avoid the copying traps

- If you're copying material by electronic means, always make sure you quote the source. It's only too easy to highlight some text, then copy and paste it into a file and move on. If you then use it in your work without saying where you got it, you could be in trouble.

- We've stressed and re-stressed the need to write full details of sources when you're making notes. Do this on the same piece of paper that you used to summarise or copy them out. When you take down phrases and extracts, using the exact words of the original, always put quote marks around them. When you look at them later, you may not remember that they're direct quotes and it's important to acknowledge that they are in any material you submit. You may not use them in your final draft, but even if you just paraphrase them, you still have to cite the source.

- Look again at the examples of good and poor paraphrasing we noted earlier. Don't paraphrase a source too closely; if all you're doing is taking key phrases and rearranging them, or just replacing some words with synonyms, that's still plagiarism.

- Don't use too many quotations. A text which simply strings together chunks of other people's ideas will probably make for dull, uneven reading and will certainly be guilty of plagiarising.

- Double-check all your 'original' ideas. Your individual take on a subject may represent a fresh, unique insight into a topic, but equally it might be something you read months before which has just resurfaced. Think carefully about possible sources and, if you're not sure, check with people such as your tutor or supervisor to see whether the idea's familiar to them, or look at relevant texts, encyclopaedias or the internet.

What next?

Double-check your department's ...

... (or university's) plagiarism policy. This should tell you what the rules are and how you might break them. It'll also give you information on how to cite sources.

Read the notices in the library ...

... about photocopying or, if there aren't any, ask about it.

When you're making notes ...

... highlight and put quotations marks around all direct transcriptions. And (yes, we're saying it again) add full details of the source whenever you take notes from a textbook or other paper source.

 **recap**

The various forms of plagiarism.

How to avoid it.

Paraphrasing, summarising and quotations.

The complexities of copyright.

How to avoid the copying traps.

24 The conventions of academic writing

As we warned in the introduction, the book you're reading is definitely *not* written in an academic style. Its aim is to be more or less conversational, addressing you personally and using contractions (you're, we've, this'll) to create a fairly relaxed reading experience. Academic writing has its own aims and the appropriate conventions to help to achieve them. Success at university will depend upon you recognising those conventions and learning how to use them. So now we'll attempt to define the basic aspects of academic style and language and suggest what you should and shouldn't do.

Academic language and conventions

Most of the ways you'll be assessed at university will involve the submission of a piece of written work. It could be an essay, a report, a project portfolio, a case study, a dissertation or several other forms of linguistic presentation. Whatever they are, you'll have to write them all in an appropriate academic style. There'll be some differences between 'scientific' and 'humanities' styles, but they share some common features and that's what we'll focus on.

Academic style

As soon as they hear the words 'academic style' many people immediately assume that it means convoluted sentences, long words and boredom. That may be true of the worst types of academic writing, but it's a false assumption. Basically, academic style aims to use language precisely and objectively to express ideas. It must be grammatically correct, and it's more formal than the styles you find in novels, newspapers, emails and everyday conversation. But it still aims to be clear and simple. Most of all, it avoids illogical or emotionally charged expressions and presents its findings objectively. Its tone is impersonal, its vocabulary succinct and 'correct'.

brilliant tip

The academic world thrives on sharing research and learning and there's an old gag that says that the USA and Britain are 'two countries divided by a single language'. Academic writing in the UK is nearly always in British English (BE), but you'll probably read lots of material written in American English (AE). The obvious differences are in spelling – 'colour' (BE) and 'color' (AE) – but there are also differences in vocabulary. In the USA, your 'lecturer' (BE) is your 'professor' (AE) and an author may write 'we have gotten results' (AE) rather than 'we have obtained results' (BE). Some disciplines are trying to standardise their terminology. In chemistry, for example, 'sulphur' (BE) is now spelt 'sulfur' (AE) on both sides of the Atlantic. The differences don't pose a problem, but you should be aware of them.

The need to be objective

However enthusiastic you are about a subject, you mustn't let your personal feelings show through. Apart from anything else, they might cloud your reasoning and create an impression of bias when what you're supposed to be doing is presenting a reasoned, balanced analysis or report. The important thing is the substance of your argument; therefore you need to use impersonal language. So don't use personal pronouns, i.e. words such as I, me, you, we, us, and use the passive rather than the active voice, in other words, write about the action, not who's doing whatever it is.

To make this clearer, let's give some examples:

● 'Pressure was applied to the wound to stem the bleeding' is passive.

● 'We applied pressure to the wound to stem the bleeding' is active.

● 'The results were compared with those of the previous experiment' is passive.

● 'I compared the results with those of the previous experiment' is active.

In each case, the second example may seem clearer, more 'natural', but you could also argue that starting with 'we' or 'I' puts the emphasis on who's doing it rather than on the action. By getting rid of 'we' or 'I', the passive construction keeps the emphasis clinical, dispassionate, factual.

You can also achieve that sort of objectivity by changing the verb in the sentence to a noun, so that:

'I **applied** pressure to the wound to stem the bleeding'

becomes:

'The **application** of pressure to the wound stemmed the bleeding'

and

'We **compared** the results with those of the previous experiment'

becomes:

'A **comparison** was made with the results of the previous experiment.

(In each case, the noun and verb are in bold.)

There are other ways of maintaining an impersonal style. For general statements, you can use a structure such as 'it is ...', 'there is ...' or 'there are ...' to introduce sentences. But be careful. Look, for instance at this sequence:

'Statistics show that survival rates amongst casualties are higher when the preferred treatment is amputation.

It is important for the patient to ...'

The 'it' at the beginning of the new paragraph seems to refer to the word 'amputation', which is very misleading. A new paragraph should introduce a new point. To avoid this, you need to change the sentence round and perhaps begin the new paragraph with 'The important point for the patient is to ...'.

The same potential for misunderstanding occurs when you use 'this is ...' or 'these are ...'; 'that is ...' or 'those are ...'. Words like 'it', 'this', 'these', 'that' or 'those' often refer to words, objects or ideas in preceding sentences. When you use them, make sure there's no ambiguity about their meaning.

The more assignments you write, the easier you'll find it to juggle text in this way and the more sensitive you'll become to the flexibility of language.

Using the right tense

You should always use the past tense to describe or comment on things that have already happened. In everyday speech we often use the 'wrong' tense, for effect or to add drama or immediacy to a description of something that's happened. Imagine there'd been an incident the previous evening. It would be quite normal to hear someone describing it in this way: 'He's standing there and I'm wondering what he's going to do. Then suddenly, he gets in his car and drives off.'

However dramatic the events you may be describing in an academic exercise, you must avoid allowing these habits to creep in. If you were writing a TV documentary, it would be fine for the voice-over to say 'Napoleon orders his troops to advance on Moscow. The severe winter closes in on them and only a few of them manage to survive and return home.' But if it's an academic essay, it must read as 'Napoleon *ordered* his troops to advance on Moscow. The severe winter *closed* in on them and only a few of them *managed* to survive and return home.'

There are times when the present tense obviously is appropriate. When you're describing your results in a report, for example, you'd write 'Figure 5 shows …' rather than 'Figure 5 showed …'.

Using the right words

Good academic writers think carefully about their choice of words. They're looking for precision; they want their meaning to be clear, unambiguous. In colloquial language, we're usually happy to be approximate with our meanings. Take the way we use two-word verbs, for example. What does the verb 'turn down' mean? You can turn down your collar, turn down a side street, turn down the volume, turn down an offer, turn down the radio, turn down the bedcover. And the same applies to almost all such verbs – run over, look up, make up, and so on. They're called phrasal verbs and they have several meanings, some of them surprisingly remote from one another. (You can make up a story and make up someone's face.) It's the sort of looseness that's dangerous in academic writing and you should always try to find a word which leaves no space for misinterpretation.

> ## ☀ brilliant tip
>
> Quite rightly, there have been questions about how to use gender-specific language. In the past, it was almost always he, him and his. We explained in the introduction how we intended to avoid the problems this causes by using he, she, him, her, his and so on in an arbitrary way. If you don't, and you try to be politically correct all the time, you end up with sentences such as: 'A lecturer must give himself or herself time to prepare his or her lectures so that he or she can be confident that his or her meaning is clear to his or her students.'
>
> That's awful. But just as bad is the 'S/he will provide specimens for her/his exam' format. One way round it is to make the sentence plural, as in: 'Lecturers must give themselves time to prepare their lectures so that they can be confident that their meaning is clear to their students.'
>
> Whichever technique you use, it's important to be aware of the need to remain correct but without creating constructions which are so clumsy that they actually get in the way of meaning.

From non-academic to academic

Let's see how to change a non-academic text into one that's academically acceptable. At first it reads:

> In this country, we've changed the law so that the king or queen is less powerful since the Great War. But he or she can still advise, encourage or warn the prime minister if they want.

The points that need correcting are as follows:

- 'this country' isn't specific
- 'we've' is a personal pronoun and the verb has been contracted
- 'but' is a connecting word and shouldn't be used to start a sentence, so the grammar's weak
- the word 'law' is imprecise because it has several meanings
- 'king or queen' duplicates nouns

- 'he or she' and 'they' are pronouns which don't relate properly to one another and are misleading
- 'can still' is an example of informal style.

If we correct these flaws, we get a much tighter, more focused text:

> In the United Kingdom, legislation has been a factor in the decline of the role of the monarchy in the period since the Great War. Nevertheless, the monarchy has survived and, thus, the monarch continues to exercise the right to advise, encourage and warn the prime minister.

The changes are:

- 'the United Kingdom' is more specific
- 'legislation has' is impersonal
- 'nevertheless' is a powerful signpost word
- 'legislation' is tighter than 'law'
- 'monarchy' is a singular abstract term
- 'monarch' replaces the duplication of 'king or queen'
- 'continues to exercise' illustrates the more formal style.

Language and clear thinking

The way in which you put your ideas on the page or screen actually helps you to form and clarify them. Until you put them into words, you're not sure yourself of their exact nature. So developing your writing skills and your sensitivity to language is fundamental to the whole learning process. You should be prepared to play with language, experiment with words and phrases, change the order of words within sentences and sentences within paragraphs. Look at the difference between:

> Shakespeare was great because he wrote many excellent plays.

and:

> The power and poetry of his plays made Shakespeare one of the greatest of all writers.

It's a trivial example, but the difference is obvious and it lies in the choice of words and the order of the ideas. The more you learn to manipulate words in this way, the more you'll be able to:

- exploit the flexibility of the language to make your meaning clear and precise

- show that you can group ideas in a logical way

- hold the attention and interest of your reader.

The fundamentals of academic writing

We're going to look at some elements of academic (and non-academic) writing that can cause or maybe help you to overcome difficulties. In a way, they constitute a series of Brilliant Dos and Don'ts, but it might be confusing to mix them together, so instead we're organising them as an alphabetical list.

Abbreviations and acronyms

Some abbreviations can be used in academic writing, for example, those that express units, such as, °C, m^2 or km/h; but avoid abbreviations such as e.g., i.e. and viz. in formal work. They're fine, however, for note-taking.

Acronyms are a different form of abbreviation. They take the initial letters of an organisation, a procedure or an apparatus and use them as words in their own right. So instead of writing out the World Health Organization in full every time, you write WHO. The academic convention is that the first time that you use the name of one of these organisations or procedures in your text, you write it in full with the abbreviation in brackets immediately after it. After that, in the same document, it's sufficient to use the abbreviated form. For example: The European Free Trade Association (EFTA) has close links with the European Community (EC). Both EFTA and the EC require new members to have membership of the Council of Europe as a prerequisite for admission to their organisations.

Sometimes, for example in formal reports, as well as using them in this way you may need to include a list of abbreviations.

'Absolute' terms

Be careful when using absolute terms such as always, never, most, all, least and none. You can use them, but only when you really are absolutely certain of what you're claiming.

Clichés

Languages are constantly developing and expressions come and go. Clichés are examples of language which may be useful but which sometimes have become so familiar that they're used without really thinking what they mean. So be aware of when you use them and, where possible, replace them with something less general or less long-winded. For example: first and foremost (first); last but not least (finally); at this point in time (now). This procedure is the gold standard of hip replacement methods. (This procedure is the best hip replacement method.) In that last example, 'gold standard' is an absurd, counter-productive term. It would perhaps be acceptable in a financial context but has no place in a surgical procedure.

Colloquial language

We've already mentioned this, and we might stress again at this point that the book you're reading is breaking most of the rules we're describing. But again (See? We began a sentence with 'But'), that's because we're deliberately using a colloquial style. It has no place in an academic paper. Nor has a sentence such as: Not to beat about the bush, increasing income tax did the chancellor no good at the end of the day and he was ditched at the next Cabinet reshuffle. A far more acceptable version would be: Increasing income tax did not help the chancellor and he was replaced at the next Cabinet reshuffle. Colloquial language is vibrant, expressive, but it has no place in sober academic discourse.

'Hedging' language

We keep stressing the need for academic language to be precise. There are times, though, when it's impossible to say definitely that something is or is not the case. That's when you can use verbs that allow you to hedge your bets. In other words, you can state something without subscribing to either side of the argument in question or present several different viewpoints without committing yourself to any particular one of them. That's what we're calling 'hedging' language.

It's very simple: you present the reader with a construction which makes them feel that you're suggesting a hypothetical, or imaginary, case. And you do this by using expressions such as 'it seems that …', 'it looks as if …', 'the evidence suggests that …' and so on. You're not committing yourself, but you're suggesting that something is possible, maybe even probable.

You can actually take it a stage further, too, by using verbs known as modal verbs – can/cannot, could/could not, may/may not, might/might not. If you use them with other verbs they actually increase the sense of uncertainty. For example: 'These results suggest that there has been a decline in herring stocks in the North Sea' can be made even more tentative by saying 'These results could suggest that there has been a decline in herring stocks in the North Sea.'

Jargon and specialist terms

Jargon can be impenetrable. Some of that used in the commercial world seems fine to begin with but rapidly loses its impact through over-use. In academic disciplines, however, jargon doesn't always have the same pejorative associations. Subjects use language in a way that is exclusive to their particular discipline and students quickly adopt the terminology because it describes objects, systems, ideas and events very precisely. However, it's wise to be aware when you're using terms which might be described as jargon and which might not be understood by non-specialists. In such cases, you should explain the terms. Apart from anything else, it helps you to be sure that you understand them yourself and know how to use them in context.

Rhetorical questions

As the word 'rhetorical' suggests, these are powerful linguistic weapons when it comes to delivering speeches. They can be useful in academic writing, but they should be used with care and not too frequently. If you're in any doubt, don't use them but instead turn them into a statement. For example: 'How do plants survive in dry weather?' becomes 'It is important to understand how plants survive in dry weather.' (And, of course, since it's not a question any more, there's no question mark.)

Split infinitives

The mission of the Star Ship Enterprise is 'to boldly go where no man has gone before'. That's the most famous of all split infinitives. The infinitive of any verb is the 'to ...' bit and consists of two words – to eat, to dance, to go – and splitting them means putting another word (usually an adverb) between them. The 'correct' version would be 'to go boldly'. However, although there are still many who deplore such a 'mistake', it's rapidly becoming accepted. Having said that, academic writing tends always towards the 'correct', so it's probably better to avoid splitting the infinitive in your work.

Value judgements

We've already mentioned these, but it may be easier now for you to understand why they're inappropriate for your university assignments. We've been stressing the need for an objective, impersonal approach. Value judgements express views rather than facts. If you say that 'Louis XIV was a rabid nationalist' without supporting your claim, you're just voicing your opinion. However, if you say 'Louis XIV was regarded as a rabid nationalist. This is evident in the nature of his foreign policy where he ...' you're distancing yourself from the claim and also providing some evidence to support it.

Playing with language

People are often surprised at how writing can be changed significantly and improved simply by rearranging the order of words or phrases.

Heads and tails

If you experiment by shifting elements around within a sentence, you can sometimes make it much clearer and much more powerful. Moving a phrase or clause from the tail end of the sentence to the beginning or vice versa often alters the emphasis and gives prominence to the aspect that needs to be stressed. Consider this statement:

> The medical profession spent time and energy on activities in which they had little expertise because they were faced with the need to deliver a complete range of services with a greater attention to cost control as a result of the administration's directive.

It's too long, it just adds one bit of information after another and it leaves a muddled impression. The reader has little idea of which of the various elements is more important than the others. In the end, it all just tails weakly away. Let's move things about:

> Faced with the need to deliver a complete range of services with a greater attention to cost control as a result of the directive, the medical profession spent time and energy on activities in which they had little expertise.

It's still too long, but it's slightly better. At least now we've separated it into two distinct elements – the things that are causing the problems and the way the profession responds to them. But it's still unwieldy; the first half, for example, gives the reader no chance to pause and just keeps piling element upon element. Let's give it one more try:

> The result of the directive was that the medical profession, faced with the need to deliver a complete range of services with a greater attention to cost control, spent time and energy on activities in which they had little expertise.

It's the best so far. The various elements have been brought into better relationships by starting with the directive, then wrapping its requirements inside the main point, which is the fact that the medics were doing things they knew little about. We could go on tweaking it, but we've done enough to make the point, which is to show how taking identical elements and rearranging them changes meaning and emphasis.

Long and short sentences

We'll talk more about the length of sentences in the next chapter but, for the moment, let's see how lengthening or shortening them affects their impact on the reader. We'll take what we called 'the best so far' from the examples above:

> The result of the directive was that the medical profession, faced with the need to deliver a complete range of services with a greater attention to cost control, spent time and energy on activities in which they had little expertise.

It's still one long sentence. Let's split it:

> The directive required a complete range of services to be delivered with a greater attention to cost control. The result was that the medical profession spent time and energy on activities in which they had little expertise.

Perhaps this does make it clearer by allowing the reader to pause between the two separate pieces of information and absorb them separately. Yet, the separation destroys the power of the link (and implied conflict) between the two. And if you think a lot of shorter sentences would be easier to understand, try this:

> The directive required a complete range of services to be delivered. It also insisted on greater attention being paid to cost control. The medical profession had little expertise in this. As a result, they wasted time and energy on it.

It's as bad as, maybe even worse than, the original long, rambling effort, so there's no obvious rule about long is bad, short is good. Again, though, the point is when you've written something, come back to it later and see whether you can improve your message by moving its component parts around.

Honing your academic style

If you were desperate for a loan and writing to your bank manager, you wouldn't be all matey or use slang or txt-msging. If you were writing a love letter, you wouldn't use impersonal, formal language and the passive voice. Of course not, because the bank manager and the object of your affections would be expecting a particular sort of vocabulary and tone. Well, academic writing is aimed at a particular type of reader and he'll also have his expectations. So think about your audience. Your readers will probably be marking your work; they'll want to see knowledge and content and they'll be looking for evidence of critical thinking and the correct use of specialist terms and structures.

Don't say don't. In fact, don't use any contractions. It's all too easy to slip in the occasional 'it's' or 'it isn't'. They belong to spoken English (and a conversational style such as the one we're using in this book), but there's no place for them in academic written English.

What next?

It's very important for your English ...

... to be grammatically correct. If you're not sure whether yours is good, get a grammar book or type 'English grammar' into a search engine and choose a page which presents material in the form you need it.

Work with a friend ...

... on improving your writing styles. Swap examples of your writing, read hers and get her to read yours critically, and then discuss your findings. Talking about them will force you to identify exactly what's right and what's wrong. Feedback's a crucial part of learning and you should get it wherever you can.

As you read books and articles ...

... notice how the authors use the techniques we've been describing. Look for examples of 'hedging' language and see if there are other ways in which authors manage to avoid making absolute judgements. The more you become aware of these stylistic features, the more naturally they'll come to you in your own work.

 recap

The elements and conventions of academic style.

Language and thinking.

Dos and don'ts of academic writing.

Playing with language.

25 The basics of sentences and paragraphs

When is a sentence not a sentence? What makes a paragraph? How long should they be? Are there any rules about how to structure them? These are questions for anyone who writes in any medium, but they're perhaps especially pressing for students faced with the apparent strictness of academic language and the need to meet particular standards. It seems that most people know instinctively when they're reading 'good' writing. We're going to suggest some basic principles to help you refine your style.

The functions of sentences and paragraphs

There are many excellent grammar books available which explain the mechanics of academic writing. They deal with the many complexities and nuances of 'correctness' and construction. Here, our aim is simply to demystify the process and propose some basic guidelines on how to create effective sentences and paragraphs. It's sometimes frustrating to be told that some aspect of a piece of writing is 'wrong' and not know why. An awareness of the fundamentals and functions of sentences and paragraphs will help to overcome that frustration.

Whatever you're writing – an essay, a report, a dissertation or any other kind of assignment – the building blocks are sentences and paragraphs. But unlike most other types of building blocks, they come in different sizes, shapes and colours. As we said before, you shouldn't imagine that, for academic writing, the sort you need are complicated structures, with long, involved sentences full of impressive-sounding 'big' words. The brevity and simplicity of shorter sentences can be just as effective. Remember why you're writing: it's not to impress but to express.

 **tip**

A good way of deciding whether a sentence you've written works well and is grammatically correct is to read it aloud. Try to be simultaneously a newsreader and a listener. You may be surprised at how much easier it is to hear (non)sense than to see it.

Sentences

These are sentences:

- **Help!**
- Students **work** in the holidays.
- Universities **provide** tuition in a wide range of subjects.

A sentence has to have an active verb in it. In simple terms, verbs are 'doing' words and we've put them in bold here.

These are *not* sentences:

- Bringing the debate to an end.
- Having been at war for 100 years.

Yes, they both begin with capital letters and there's a full stop at the end of each, but the verb part in each (the '-ing' word) is in the form of a participle rather than being active. Try walking up to a group of people and saying 'Bringing the debate to an end' or 'Having been at war for 100 years.' They'd probably edge away from you looking embarrassed or scared. The sentences as they stand don't mean anything. They would if you added a bit more information. For example: 'Bringing the debate to an end is the function of the chair person' or 'Having been at war for 100 years, the states were impoverished.' (Mind you, it's still not a good idea to walk up to a group of strangers and say them.)

Simple sentences

These have at least a subject (the person or thing doing the action) and a verb, and perhaps a phrase of other information. Together they make sense as a unit. For example:

- Babies cry.

- Criminal law differs from civil law.

- Plants require sunlight and water.

Compound sentences

These are two simple sentences joined by a word such as 'and' or 'but', which means there'll be two verbs in them. For example: 'Scots law and English law are fundamentally different, but there are some areas in which they are similar.'

Compound sentences should contain only two specific elements. So consider this sentence: 'Scots law and English law are fundamentally different, but there are some areas in which they are similar, and this is taken into account in framing legislation, but the Scottish legal system still defines aspects such as house purchase and matrimonial issues.' It's obviously clumsy and far too long. It also consists of four simple sentences. It would be better to split it as follows: 'Scots law and English law are fundamentally different, but there are some areas in which they are similar. This is taken into account in framing legislation, but the Scottish legal system still defines aspects such as house purchase and matrimonial issues.'

 **definitions**

Clause – a unit of meaning built around a verb.

Principal or main clause – like a simple sentence, it would still make sense on its own.

Subordinate clause – has a similar function to a noun, adjective or adverb but would not make sense on its own.

Complex sentences

A complex sentence consists of a main clause with additional subordinate clauses. In these examples, the main clauses are in bold and the subordinate clauses in italics and the oblique strokes separate them from one another:

Gait analysis gives insights / *into the walking difficulties that are experienced* / *by people who have cerebral palsy.*

Social work legislation protects the rights of the elderly / *when they are no longer able to cope independently.*

Although Britain is regarded as a democracy, / **it has no written constitution** / *that can be cited as the basis of Constitutional Law.*

These sentences can be quite long and can contain more than one subordinate clause. Too many of them coming one after the other might give your text a heavy or monotonous feel, so try to vary the length of your sentences. That makes the rhythms of your text more interesting and helps to keep your reader's interest. As a general rule, shorter sentences expressing a single idea have a stronger impact than longer complex sentences, but if you want to balance two ideas, use compound sentences.

brilliant tip

When two sentences that should either be independent or joined by 'and' or 'but' or another conjunction are instead joined with a comma, that's known as a 'comma splice'. Avoid it. 'Fiona is a redhead, Beatrice is a blonde' is incorrect. Instead, you should write 'Fiona is a redhead. Beatrice is a blonde' or 'Fiona is a redhead, but Beatrice is a blonde.'

Paragraphs

There are such things as single-sentence paragraphs; they're sometimes used – especially in fiction and, above all, when they're short – for dramatic effect. Normally, however, and certainly in academic writing, a paragraph is made up of several sentences. It has a topic that's outlined in the first sentence and developed further within the paragraph. It ends with a sentence that either terminates that topic or acts as a link to the topic of the paragraph that follows it. So a typical structure might be:

- a topic introducer sentence, which introduces the overall topic of the text – usually this would be the opening of the very first paragraph

- a topic sentence, which introduces a paragraph by identifying what it will be about

- a developer sentence, which adds more information to expand the topic

- a modulator sentence, which acts as a linking sentence and is often introduced by a signpost word to move to another aspect of the topic within the same paragraph

- a terminator sentence, which concludes the discussion of that particular topic within the paragraph, but can also be used as a transition sentence to link to the topic of the next paragraph.

brilliant example

Anthropologists insist that there are many 'lost' tribes still living in the jungles of the Amazon. Evidence of their presence has been found in clearings and pathways and their existence has been confirmed by sightings made by local tribesmen. However, there are no signs of permanent habitable structures. Also, it is possible that some of the supposed 'observations' were simply invented by the tribesmen in an effort to impress the scientists. Thus, the present state of our knowledge with regard to these peoples relies more on speculation than on observed facts. There is a clear need for a properly funded and centrally co-ordinated expedition to make further investigations.

This consists of six sentences. Here's a list of the first word of each sentence with an indication of the sentence's function in the paragraph:

- Anthropologists – topic sentence.
- Evidence – developer sentence.
- However – modulator sentence introduced by a signpost word, which in this case indicates a conflicting theme.
- Also – developer sentence, again with a signpost word, indicating this time additional information.
- Thus – developer sentence whose signpost word indicates a consequence or effect.
- There – terminator/transition sentence.

The role of signpost words

The example shows how sentences are the building blocks of paragraphs. Each adds its own bit of information and some of them are held together by signpost words. By now, that's a familiar term for you. They're words that help the text to flow smoothly as ideas merge or contrast with one another. The list below shows some typical examples of such words and their functions. It's by no means exhaustive, but it'll give you an idea of the range available to you.

Addition	additionally; furthermore; in addition; moreover
Cause/reason	as a result of; because (mid-sentence)
Comparison	compared with; in the same way; in comparison with; likewise
Condition	if; on condition that; providing that; unless
Contrast	although; by contrast; conversely; despite; however; nevertheless
Effect/result	as a result; hence; therefore; thus
Exemplification	for example; for instance; particularly; such as; thus
Reformulation	in other words; rather; to paraphrase
Summary	finally; hence; in all; in conclusion; in short; in summary
Time sequence	after; at first; at last; before; eventually; subsequently
Transition	as far as … is concerned; as for; to turn to

Sentences are the building blocks of paragraphs and paragraphs are the building blocks of text. Just as we've seen how sentences move from introducing a topic through developing and modulating it to a conclusion, so your paragraphs build your argument, develop it, formulate contrary views and synthesise everything into a conclusion. So does that mean we can stick labels such as developer, modulator and terminator on them too?

Well, yes, but we need to be a little more subtle than that. Simply to say a text consists of a topic paragraph, three developers, two modulators, three more developers and a terminator isn't really very helpful. We need to know what sort of developments we're talking about. Are they giving examples, examining opposing viewpoints, describing a process, listing a sequence of events, defining or classifying something, illustrating causes and effects, comparing, contrasting? The possibilities are legion.

▶ brilliant example

There are two basic ways of presenting an argument, which might produce two different types of paragraph: deductive and inductive.

- In the deductive model, you state your main point first and then add supporting information or evidence.
- In the inductive model, you start with the supporting information and your main point comes as the conclusion.

Testing your writing

We've spoken about the length of sentences. There are two ways to check whether yours are structured well. First, simply read them aloud. You'll hear inconsistencies of logic or grammar. Second, if you feel you need to pause for breath in mid-sentence, you probably need to insert a comma or even a full stop followed by a new sentence.

Another benefit of this technique is to show when your sentences are all turning out to be about the same length. This is a common aspect of how some people write and the problem is that it produces a regular, monotonous effect. Your points are all presented in equally sized chunks and it becomes wearing for the reader. Rhythm is an important consideration, even within the formalities of academic style.

So vary the length of your sentences. Mixing short and long ones changes your rhythms and is more reader friendly. There's no hard and fast rule, but if a sentence runs into three or four lines of typescript, check to see whether it would read better if you broke it up into two smaller sentences.

How long should a paragraph be? Once again, think about your reader. When you're faced with solid blocks of text with no visible paragraph breaks, the impression you get is that reading might be hard work. If the information's laid out in more accessible chunks, it makes the task seem less onerous. The length of any paragraph depends on its content, of course, but you'll usually find that extra-long ones will have more than one topic in them. So, if your paragraph seems too long, read it aloud, listen for a natural break point and check to see whether that should mark the start of a new one.

And don't forget to use signpost words to help your reader navigate through the logic of your text.

What next?

Learn from the professionals ...

... and choose an extract from a textbook and analyse a couple of paragraphs, looking for introducers, developers, modulators, signpost words and transition/terminator sentences. Then do the same thing with a sample of your own writing. Is the paragraph structure balanced? Have you over-used or under-used signpost words? Have you used the same ones frequently? If so, check for alternatives in the list we gave earlier.

Look at your work as a reader ...

... rather than the writer. Ask whether it could be clearer, whether the meaning comes through, whether it's hard or easy to read. Listen to its rhythms and apply some of the tips we've suggested to make the reading experience as easy and pleasant as possible.

brilliant recap

The basic structures of sentences and paragraphs.

Types of sentence.

Types of paragraph.

Testing your writing.

26 The importance of the post-writing phases

If you want your work to be of the highest quality you can manage (which most people obviously do), you must not only take great care while you're writing it; you must also look at it critically and objectively to pick up and correct any flaws which have crept in. Even with the most meticulous professional writers, grammatical slips, misspellings and typographical errors often go unnoticed. The skills we'll consider here will help you to find and eliminate them from your writing assignments.

Make your writing make sense

Each time you finish an essay, you feel a huge sense of relief and just want to hand it in and relax. But the writing of the text is only a part of the overall creative process. The next phase, which consists of reviewing, editing and proofreading, is just as critical and can make a real difference to the finished piece of work. When you draw up your time management schedule at the beginning, try to organise it so that you leave a gap between finishing the writing and starting the editing. That will let you get some distance between you and the work and you'll be able to read it with fresh eyes when you get back to it.

When you do, you'll be looking for lots of things, such as flaws in layout, grammar, punctuation and spelling. You'll be checking to see that it's consistent in its use of terminology and in presentational features such as font and point size, layout of paragraphs, and labelling of tables and diagrams. But you'll also be looking critically at its content to make sure it's relevant and that it makes sense.

It can be a complex process, but if you don't do it thoroughly there's little doubt that you'll get fewer marks than you would have if you'd taken some time to make sure you'd got things right. Style, content, structure and presentation all contribute to the clarity and impact of what you're handing in. On top of that, the very act of learning how to edit your work properly will sharpen your powers of critical analysis.

 brilliant definitions

Reviewing – examining a task or project to make sure it meets the set requirements and objectives and makes overall sense.

Editing – revising and correcting a piece of work to arrive at a final version. Usually, this involves focusing on smaller details of punctuation, spelling, grammar and layout.

Proofreading – checking a printed copy for errors of any sort.

Choosing a strategy

How you approach this will depend on your preferences. Some people opt to go through their text just once, trying to pick up every flaw in all the different areas; others make several passes, looking each time at a different aspect – grammar, spelling, style, and so on. It's up to you to decide what works best for you. At the outset, it might help if you try focusing on each of these three broad aspects in separate sweeps through the text.

Content and relevance; clarity, style and coherence

- Read the question again and confirm that you've interpreted it correctly.

- Check what aims you set out in your introduction and make sure they've been met in your treatment of the subject.

- Be objective as you read, checking that your argument makes sense, your facts are correct and there aren't any inconsistencies.

- Cutting a text by 10–25 per cent can significantly improve its quality, so get rid of anything that's not relevant, any informal language or expressions and any gendered or discriminatory language.

- Double-check that you've acknowledged all your sources. Don't risk plagiarism.

brilliant tip

You may be surprised to hear that errors and typos which are missed on the computer screen are often obvious when they're printed out. Always use a printout for your final check. If you still find errors, it's easy enough just to reprint individual pages.

Grammatical correctness, spelling and punctuation

- If you've used titles and subtitles, make them stand out by using either bold or underlining (but not both).

- Think about how well the text flows and the different parts link together. If they don't, add some signpost words to guide the reader along.

- Check the length of your sentences and try to get a balance by mixing long and short.

- Check your spelling with both a spellchecker and, if you're unsure about something, in a standard dictionary.

- If, as you read, you feel that something's clumsy, try rewriting it in different ways, moving the parts of the sentences around, changing active to passive or vice versa or finding synonyms.

- Get rid of any 'absolute' terms which might introduce a note of subjectivity.

brilliant tip

Word processors have made reviewing and editing much easier. To make sure you get the most out of them:

- use the word-count facility
- check page breaks and the general layout with the 'View' facility before you print it out
- don't rely entirely on the spelling and grammar checker
- if staff add comments using 'Tools/Track Changes' in Microsoft Word, you can accept or reject them by right-clicking on whatever has been marked for alteration.

Presentation

- Make sure you haven't crammed the text into too tight a space, and that it's neat and legible.

- Check that your reference list is complete, and consistent with whatever style you've chosen or been told to use, and that all citations are matched by an entry in it and vice versa.

- Make sure you've included the question number and title, your name, matriculation number and course number.

- Number and clip or staple the pages together, with a cover page if needed.

- Go through all diagrams, charts and other visual materials to check that they're in sequence and labelled consistently.

- If there's any supporting material in the form of footnotes, endnotes, appendices or a glossary, make sure they too follow the right sequence.

brilliant tip

There are universally recognised symbols that are used in proof correcting. They're a sort of shorthand to indicate omissions, misspellings, grammatical mistakes and many other aspects of the text which need attention. Your tutors may use them on your essays and it's useful if you familiarise yourself with them so that you can use them yourself. You can easily find a list of the most commonly used and their meanings by simply typing 'proofreading symbols' into a search engine.

A checklist

It may help you to break down the editing into five main areas that need attention. You can then use them as a checklist and work through them systematically.

Content and relevance

- Have you done what the instruction word asked you to do?
- Have you finished the task and answered all the questions it asked?
- Is the structure you've used right for the exercise?
- Have you dealt with the topic objectively, using relevant examples?
- Are your facts accurate, and have you cited all your sources correctly?

Clarity, style and coherence

- Have you said what you meant to say?
- Does the text flow, using the right signpost words?
- Have you removed any informal language?
- Is the style academic and right for the task?
- Are content and style consistent throughout?
- Have you used the right tenses, and are they consistent?
- Have you achieved the right balance between sections?

Grammatical correctness

- Are all sentences complete, and do they make sense?
- Have you checked for any grammatical errors which you keep making?
- Have you been consistent in using British or American English?

Spelling and punctuation

- Have you corrected all 'typos'?
- Have you checked the spelling, especially of words that you often misspell?
- Have you also checked the spelling of subject-specific words and foreign words?
- Have you checked punctuation and tried reading aloud?
- Are all proper names capitalised?
- Have you divided any overlong sentences?

Presentation

- Is it close enough to the word-count target?
- Does the work look neat?
- Are the cover-sheet details correct?
- Does your presentation follow departmental requirements?
- Is the bibliography/reference list formatted correctly?
- Have you numbered the pages?
- Are figures and tables in the right format?

Reviewing in exams

In exams, you won't have the time to dwell on things, so it's all the more important to make your reviewing fast and efficient. There'll probably be time only for a skim-read, correcting as you go along. If you've missed something out, put an insert mark in the text and/or margin with a note 'see additional paragraph x', then write the paragraph, clearly marked as 'x', at the end of the answer. Similarly, if you find you've made the same error over and over again, such as always referring to Louis XIV as Louis XVI, just put an asterisk where it first occurs and a note at the end of your answer or in the margin 'Consistent error. Please read as "XIV"'. Both these conventions are acceptable and you won't lose any marks.

Reminders of the basics

When you're planning a writing assignment, make sure you factor in plenty of time for reviewing and proofreading. You've worked hard on gathering the material and structuring it, so don't spoil it by skimping on this important final stage.

Review and edit on paper. That's the way your marker will probably see it and it's the best way to spot errors and inconsistencies. It's also easier to make notes on it and it lets you see the whole work rather than just a screen-sized segment. You can even spread it out on your desk and get an overview of the whole flow of your argument.

Read it aloud. It's a technique used by professionals and it picks up inconsistencies, repetitions, faulty punctuation and lapses in logic in a way that a silent reading doesn't. (Just don't try it in exams.)

Try mapping your work. By that, we mean take the topic headings from your paragraphs and jot them down in sequence on a separate piece of paper. It'll give you a snapshot of your text and let you check the order, and see whether it flows and whether it's sticking to your original plan. And it makes it easier to move parts of your work around if you feel it's necessary.

brilliant tip

Make sure that you're interpreting the set task in the way it was set. It's very easy to fix on one aspect of a topic and focus on that to the exclusion of other elements. It's like making up a different title and working to that. You'll be marked on how you've responded to the original, not a cherry-picked part of it.

Compare your introduction and conclusion to make sure they complement rather than contradict one another and follow the thread of your argument to see whether it strays off the point anywhere.

Too many words can be just as bad as too few. The main point is that the writing must be clear to your reader. If that means taking longer to explain something, do it. If it means cutting something you've written, cut it, no matter how wonderful you think the sentences you're discarding are. Remember that cutting almost invariably improves a piece of writing.

Create 'white space'. It makes your work look more 'reader friendly'. You can do this by leaving space between paragraphs and around diagrams, tables and other visual material and also between headings, sub-headings and text. And if you justify only on the left side of the page, there's more space on the right.

Neat presentation, punctuation and spelling all help your reader to access the information, ideas and argument of your writing. It may not earn you marks, but it certainly won't lose you any, whereas a messy presentation may make your text – and therefore your argument – harder to decipher.

What next?

Look at an assignment ...

... you've already submitted and go through it using the checklist. Look at just a couple of pages and highlight all flaws, inconsistencies or errors and think about how much these may have cost you in terms of marks. This might help convince you that time spent reviewing and editing is time well spent.

On the same piece of text ...

... practise using the standard proofreading symbols that you've found through the search engine. It'll speed up your proofreading on your next assignment.

Practise condensing ...

... a segment of the text. Look for irrelevant points, wordy phrases, repetitions and over-long examples. Try to reduce it by 10–25 per cent and, when you read it, you'll probably see that you've created a much tighter, easier-to-read, better piece of writing.

 **recap**

The value of reviewing, editing and proofreading.

Choosing a strategy.

A reviewing checklist.

Reminders of the basics.

27 The elements and advantages of good presentation

I't's fair to say that, once you've done the reading, constructed your arguments, written, reviewed and edited your submission, your work's ready to be assessed. But you don't want to risk creating a bad impression with sloppy presentation. The final checks to make before handing it in are on the seemingly trivial but nonetheless important question of how it looks. It's not rocket science to realise that a dog-eared, dirty, coffee-stained bundle of paper won't be viewed in quite the same way as a clean, tidy, professionally prepared document. So it's time for the final pre-submission survey.

Academic conventions of presentation

Most marks for assignments are awarded for content, but some can be won or lost through how it's presented. The way in which you package and deliver it reveals the degree of respect for and pride in what you've written and if you seem to care little for it, it doesn't encourage the marker to anticipate anything very special. We're not just talking about layout and the use of visual elements; we also mean accuracy, consistency and attention to detail. It's part of the proofreading phase, so allow time for it.

Layout

There are so many different types of written submission – essays, reports, summaries, case studies, theses or worked problems – that we can't describe a 'standard' layout. An essay could have a relatively simple structure: cover page, main text, list of references. A lab report might have title page, abstract, introduction, sections on materials and methods, results, discussion/conclusion and references. There'll be variations, too, according to your academic discipline and maybe even your department. You'll have to find out what's expected of you before you get started on your first assignment. Check your course book or ask a tutor.

Cover page

This is the first thing your marker will see, so get it right. If your department has a preferred cover-page design, follow it exactly. It may have been organised that way for a specific administrative purpose, such as making sure that work's marked anonymously or giving markers a standard format for feedback, so stick to the rules.

If there aren't any such rules, write your name and/or matriculation number, the course title and/or code. It's also useful for you to add the name of the tutor. And, of course, in a prominent position, you should put the number and title of the question. The aim is clarity. Don't be tempted to indulge in fancy fonts or graphics: it won't earn you any extra marks.

Main text

Very, very few submissions nowadays are hand written and departments usually expect student assignments to be word processed. As we said earlier, editing is easier on a printout and a good-quality printer gives a more professional result. But if you are writing out your submission by hand, leave yourself plenty of time to copy out your draft neatly and legibly. Write on one side of the paper: it makes it easier to read, and if you make a mistake, you only have to rewrite a single sheet.

brilliant tip

To help you check for 'white space', look critically at your text to make sure you've used paragraphing effectively. If you reduce the 'zoom' function on the 'View' menu to 25 per cent, you'll see lots of your written pages on the screen and get a good idea of how long your paragraphs are and how much 'white space' you've left. You can use this information to make your text more reader friendly.

Font

There are two main choices: serif types have extra little strokes at the end of each letter; sans serif types don't. It'll probably be up to you to choose your preferred font, but serif types with a font size of 11 or 12 are the easiest to read for most people.

Elaborate font types may look attractive or exciting, but they can be distracting and actually get in the way of absorbing the content. The same remark applies to using too many forms of emphasis. Choose *italics* or **bold** and stick with the one you've chosen throughout. If you need to add symbols, use Microsoft Word's 'Insert > Symbol' command.

Margins

A useful convention is for left-hand margins to be 4 cm and the right-hand margins 2.5 cm. This allows space for the marker's comments and ensures that the text can be read if you use a left-hand binding.

Line spacing

It's easier to read text spaced at least at 1.5–2 lines apart. Some markers like to add comments as they read the text and this leaves them space to do so. If you're inserting long quotations, though, you should indent them and make them single-line spaced.

Paragraphs

We've already noted the value of 'white space'. Lay out your paragraphs clearly and consistently. Depending on your department's preferences, you can indent them, which means the first line starts four spaces in from the left-hand margin, or block them, which is when they all begin on the left-hand margin but you separate them by a double-line space. In Microsoft Word you can control your paragraph style using the 'Format > Paragraph' command.

brilliant tip

If you're not used to using computers for writing, note that you don't have to hit 'return' at the end of each line. When you get to the end of a line, the program automatically 'wraps' your writing on to the next line for you.

Quoting numbers in text

The accepted conventions for including numbers in your writing are as follows:

- In general writing, spell out numbers from one to ten but use figures for 11 and above; in formal writing, spell them out from one to a hundred and use figures above that.

- Spell out high numbers that can be written in two words, such as 'six hundred' and when you get into the millions, you can combine figures and spelling. For example: 4,200,000 can also be written as 4.2 million.

- Always use figures for dates, times and currency to give technical details ('5-amp fuse').

- Always spell out numbers that begin sentences, indefinite numbers ('hundreds of soldiers') or fractions ('seven-eighths').

- Numbers and fractions should be hyphenated, as in 'forty-three' or 'two-thirds'.

Figures and tables

If you need to use visual material or data to support your arguments, it's important that you do so in a way that best helps the reader to assimilate the information. Once again, there may be presentational rules that are specific to your subject or department.

Figures

The term figures ('Fig.' for short) includes graphs, diagrams, charts, sketches, pictures and photographs (although sometimes photographs may be labelled as plates). The guidelines for using them are pretty strict, so it pays to know them:

- You must refer in the text to every figure you use. There are 'standard' wordings to use to do so, such as 'Fig. 4 shows that …' or ' … results for one treatment were higher than for the other (see Fig. 2)'. Find what system applies in your area.

- Number the figures in the order in which you refer to them in the text. If you're including the figures themselves within the main body of text (which usually makes things easier for the reader), put them at the next suitable position in the text after the first time you mention them.

- Try to print them at the top or bottom of a page, rather than between blocks of text. It looks neater and makes the text easier to read.

- Each figure should be labelled (the label is called the 'legend'). This'll include the number, a title and some text. The convention is for legends to appear below each figure.

When we were talking about constructing your written arguments, we kept stressing the need for clarity; the same obviously applies here. Make sure, for example, that the different slices of a pie chart or the lines and symbols in a graph are clearly distinguishable from one another. Be consistent by using the same line or shading for the same entity in all your figures. Colour printers are obviously an advantage here, but some departments may still insist on black and white images. If you are using colour, keep it 'tasteful' and remember that certain combinations are difficult for some readers to differentiate.

There are technical reasons why some forms of data should be presented in particular ways (for example, proportional data is easier to read in a pie chart than in a line chart), but your main focus should always be on selecting a type of figure that will make it easiest for the reader to assimilate the information.

brilliant tip

If you use integrated suites of office-type software, you can create graphs with the spreadsheet program and insert them directly into your word-processed text. You can even link the two so that, if you change the spreadsheet data, the change automatically appears in the graph in the text. To find out how this works, consult the manual or 'Help' facility in MS Word. Digital photographs can also be inserted using the 'Insert > Picture > From File' command.

Tables

Tables can summarise large amounts of detailed information, both descriptive and numerical. They generally include a number of columns and rows. Just as with graphs and charts, the convention is to put the categories on the vertical axis (in other words, down the page in the left-hand column) and the variables which are being measured on the horizontal axis (i.e. across the page at the top of the columns). So if we were presenting the data resulting from a survey of attitudes to university teaching, we might have rows for the opinions of students, lecturers, educational experts and the general public, and the columns across the page might be headed 'Positive aspects', 'Negative aspects', 'Value to society', 'Relevance to society'.

brilliant tip

If you have some data which could be presented as either a figure or a table, which should you choose? Well first of all, never do both. The guiding principle should be to select whichever will be more likely to help the reader assimilate the information. If the message depends on visual impact, a figure might be best, but if details and numerical accuracy are important, a table might be more suitable.

brilliant dos and don'ts

DO ...

... insert a single space after full stops, commas, colons, semi-colons, closing inverted commas (double and single), question marks and exclamation marks.

... create one standard line space between paragraphs.

... italicise letters for foreign words and titles of books, journals and papers.

... format headings in the same font size as the text, but in bold.

... use the same figure and table styles that you find in your subject literature.

... check your course handbook for specific presentational requirements.

DON'T ...

... choose flamboyance or ostentation. Go for the safe, standard word-processing layout conventions.

... justify the text on both sides. Left-justified text creates more 'white space'.

... insert a space after apostrophes 'inside' words, e.g. it's, men's, monkey's.

... indent paragraphs. Go for the blocked style, separated by a double return.

... automatically accept the graphical output from spreadsheets and other programs. They may not be in the approved style.

What next?

You may find that you have to ...

... submit written work with only your matriculation mark as an identifier. That's so that work can be marked anonymously. But pages can be lost and it may be difficult for the marker to know whether she has the complete piece of work. So do three basic things:

- staple all the sheets together
- use the View > Header and Footer function to insert your matriculation number in the footer
- add page numbers in the footer too.

Now each page is identifiable as yours and will remain in sequence. If you're not already in the habit of doing this, create an assignment writing template which does these things for you automatically. You can then use it for all your written coursework.

Check out the placing ...

... of tables and figures. Look back at previous assignments to see whether you've been consistent in where and how you locate them. The Table >

Properties command in Word lets you place visual elements to the left, right or centre of a page. Where you put them can affect how your reader perceives the information they're conveying.

 **recap**

The academic conventions of presentation.

Elements of the layout.

Figures and tables.

Dos and don'ts.

PART 5

Developing the
necessary
research and
dissertation
skills

28 Understanding the special approaches needed for dissertations and projects

Dissertations and project reports are more demanding research and writing tasks. They're the sort of exercises that often come later in a degree course or at postgraduate level, but many institutions now make them an earlier part of the learning process. So we need to look at the basics once more because they represent a significant contribution to your marks and, possibly, your overall classification.

A professional approach

Imagine looking at a substantial piece of work on a topic which interests you. It's a bound volume of several thousand words and there, on the cover page, is your name. For many students, it's one of the highlights of their undergraduate academic career. It's taken them a few months to put together, but it's proof that they have the knowledge, understanding and, not least, stamina to make their own choices, follow them through, and show that they've mastered the advanced academic skills of their discipline.

OK, you've imagined it, now how do you set about making it a reality? Well, in broad terms, you'll have to choose your topic, and do lots of research, thinking and writing, and you'll have to present it all in a professional way. And it'll be your unique, original contribution to your subject. You'll get well under the surface of your material and have to push yourself to meet the various challenges it'll present. The skills involved may be close to those that potential employers will be looking for, too. So, in every way, it's clear that you need to treat such tasks with energy, commitment and a determination to show how focused and disciplined you can be.

Getting a good start

All the other types of work we've been discussing so far – essays, lab reports, case studies – have been relatively short-term commitments, with usually a few weeks or even days between the exercise being set and the submission date. But dissertations are long-term affairs and that brings its own problems. With a whole term or more in which to complete the task, it's easy to drift aimlessly at the start and just convince yourself that thinking vaguely about the topic now and then keeps you in touch with it. Students who've written their dissertations often remark that each stage took longer than they expected. So don't be under any illusions: if you don't get organised, the time will rush by and you'll be struggling to meet deadlines.

We spoke earlier in the book of the benefits of good time management – they apply even more critically in this sort of task. Don't fall into the time trap: get yourself organised. As soon as you know what the task is, focus on it, start planning the various elements and make it a part of your routines. The sooner you start, the sooner you'll experience the reality of the job in hand and the more inclined you'll be to commit to something that is exclusively yours. So, do something positive.

- Find out (and make sure you understand) exactly what it is you're supposed to do and how you should do it. Read the course handbook or regulations or talk to your supervisor or, if you don't yet have one, someone who might be your supervisor.

- Start looking at your research area or source material. It'll probably seem vast at first, with jargon that maybe sounds obscure, and you may feel that so many experts have written so much on it that you can't imagine finding anything to add. And yet, in a few months, you'll be handing in a substantial document on it which is all your own work. So get involved in the topic, start reading some background material and start asking questions. The sooner you start, the better.

- Sitting thinking about it is part of the process, but at this stage you should also be active. Start taking focused notes on your background reading, create a plan of action, organise your timetable. In some research projects, you may have to make some early observations or set up a pilot experiment; in others, you may need to source materials and/or textbooks. Whatever initial things your task calls for, get stuck into them.

brilliant tip

Check your motivation. Nearly all of this will be affected by how motivated you are. Your friends, family and tutors may all think you are, but you're the only one who really knows.

- If you are, use the feeling to get yourself energised and tap into it whenever things get difficult.

- If you're not, talk to someone about it. Some supervisors are very good at motivating students, and staff in support services such as counselling and the careers service also have lots of experience of helping in this way.

Work efficiently and effectively

We've stressed the need to organise your timetable. It makes complete sense – you won't lose or waste time worrying about what you should be doing or whether you're on track, and you'll have more time not only for thinking and reading but also for relaxing. So get into the habit of being efficient.

- Plan ahead for each day or part of a day.

- Make sure you know precisely what you're trying to achieve during each day or part of a day.

- Get working as quickly as possible.

- Prioritise tasks.

- Don't get distracted.

- Keep your papers and your workplace well organised.

- Don't overdo it. Take breaks when you need to rest.

As well as being efficient, be effective. That means doing things that actually produce results. Be sure that each thing you do has a point and is contributing in some way to achieving your goal.

- Don't waste time. Get started right away.

- Keep your focus on the end product.

- Cut out unproductive work.

● Watch out for things that are stopping you making progress and find ways to overcome these obstacles.

☼ brilliant tip

Effective working is smart working. For each part of the task you undertake, this SMART goals mnemonic may help you to remember what you need to keep thinking:

● Specific (What exactly are you trying to achieve?)

● Measurable (What achievable targets can you set yourself?)

● Attainable (What can you really achieve in the time available?)

● Realistic (Is the goal you've set achievable?)

● Tangible (Will you be able to see if you've made progress?)

↗ brilliant dos and don'ts

DO ...

... remember you'll need to organise large amounts of information.

... keep records of research sources so you can cite them properly.

... make sure you adopt a professional approach to presenting data.

... allow time for your supervisor to provide feedback and time for you to take it into account and act on it.

... set aside time for your dissertation or report to be typed, or, if you need this service, for graphics to be produced or printed, and for the finished dissertation or report to be bound, if that's what your department requires.

DON'T ...

... underestimate how long it may take to do the research or to actually write the thesis.

... start reading aimlessly just to persuade yourself you're doing something.

... lose sight of the need to maintain your writing skills at a high level.

... plagiarise or infringe copyright. Make it part of your routine to be sure that you don't.

Don't wait – get started right away

When you know you have to write a dissertation or report, get going as soon as you can. Read a basic text to get some background. Start compiling a personal glossary of specialist terms. Ask your supervisor or tutors questions. Start looking at the current research in your area. Look at online databases to begin your literature search. When you organise your timetable, give yourself a good chunk of time for the initial, general reading to get into the feel of it, and make sure you take notes as you go.

brilliant tip

As you get further into your project you'll find that you think about it a lot. Be prepared to have ideas popping into your head at unlikely times. Carry a small notebook around with you so that you can jot them down. Some may turn out to be bad ideas, but lots could be worth pursuing. Don't just assume you'll remember them. You won't always.

Clear the decks. Finish any outstanding tasks, tidy your work area and let your friends know that you may not be socialising quite as much. (Which doesn't mean you should stop. Keep a balance. Remember, 'all work and no play ...' etc.) Start writing, and that includes note-making, because the act of writing is part of the thinking process. Just writing isolated paragraphs on the basis of something you've read or an idea you've had can help to clarify your thoughts and they can be the basis for further development once you've read a bit more. And even if you can't use them, the simple act of writing out some ideas will help you to go further into the topic and understand it better. The more you write, the more you'll develop your own writing 'voice' and the closer you'll get to your particular take on the topic.

> **◆ brilliant tip**
>
> Many projects stall or get abandoned because the person involved is a perfection-ist. If you have that tendency, keep telling yourself that you may be wasting time trying to get a particular thing right when there are lots of other things still to be done. By all means get rid of the major flaws, but don't get hung up over minor things. The important thing is to get the work finished.

Don't let writer's block get in the way. Sometimes the words flow, sometimes they don't. Just accept it. When you're finding that putting the sentences and paragraphs together is a struggle, work through it. Take a break, come back and just start writing anything, even rubbish. The important thing is not to use it as an excuse to stop altogether. It's part of the thinking process.

It won't hurt to review progress each day. Ask yourself:

- What have I achieved?
- What went well?
- What could have gone better?
- Am I keeping up with my timetable?
- What do I need to do next?

What next?

You need to make two important lists ...

... the things you need to do before you can start properly and the things that you can leave until the project's finished. Then be strict with yourself. Focus on working through the first list and don't allow yourself to do anything on the other list – it'll just be a displacement activity.

Make an appointment to meet ...

... your supervisor or a potential supervisor. Have a general chat about the whole process, asking what realistic, achievable goals you might set and what they recommend you get started on.

 recap

Adopting a professional approach.

How to make a good start.

Be efficient and effective.

Don't wait, get started immediately.

29 Deciding what to write about

You're going to spend some significant time on your research topic, and it's going to occupy lots of your thinking, so you need to choose wisely. It's not just a question of looking through a list of options and deciding 'That doesn't look bad. I'll try that.' There are lots of things to consider – personal, departmental and practical. Let's look at the sort of factors that should influence your choice.

Weighing your options

The options open to you will depend on your department's policy. In some, your choice may be limited. Rather than asking you what you want to research, the department will give you a list of possible topics. Or there may be a semi-closed list, where members of staff provide suggestions of broad topics but leave you to select a particular area within one or more of them to investigate. In both these cases, it may be hard to choose and you may feel it's restrictive, especially if you know little about the topics listed. But in each case the idea is to give you as much choice as possible in the areas of expertise of the people who'll be supervising and assessing your work. They'll have thought not only about the topics but also about practical issues surrounding them and the amount of scope they'll give you for developing your own thoughts about them.

If you do have to choose from a list, get moving on it quickly. Some of the topics may be particularly attractive and you'll need to stake your claim early. But don't rush the choice itself. Get all the information you can and allocate time and attention to whatever you need to do to make the right decision. You may want to conduct library or internet searches or discuss aspects of the lists and topics with potential supervisors. Whatever's needed, do it, but get the balance right between a speedy and a considered response.

In some cases, you may not even get a list of options and you'll be expected to choose not only the topic but also the specific research question you'll be trying to consider. Your choice may then have to be approved and you may be asked to write an outline of the question, giving a reasoned argument as to why it's worth investigating and describing the way you'll approach it.

brilliant tip

If you have a specific topic in mind and it's not on a prescribed list of options, try asking a potential supervisor whether it could be considered. But be ready to answer some pretty searching questions about why you think it would make a good research theme.

Whether your system of choosing topics is closed, semi-closed or totally open, there are many things you need to consider to get it right and commit to something which suits you and will produce the best results.

Making it personal

As we keep saying, you'll be spending a lot of time with this topic, so make sure it's something you're interested in, which has scope for exploration and which will be a challenge. If you're bored by or indifferent to it, it'll be all too easy to find reasons to avoid it. You need to feel motivated and use that energy to deal with any problems you encounter.

The fact that you're following a particular course of study indicates that you're already interested in the subject, and your lectures, tutorials and reading will have probably intensified and broadened that interest. But now you're being asked to narrow your focus and look in greater detail and depth at one highly specific aspect of a subject. So how do you weigh up the pluses and minuses of each option? How do you choose?

Survey the field

If it's an open choice, you could brainstorm possible topics and sub-topics, jot down all the possibilities and rank them in order of interest. Start with broader topics and break them down into more closely defined areas for potential research. Think back on lectures, tutorials, seminars or practicals and the discussions you've had about them. Try to recall which aspects of your course sparked your curiosity and interest the most. Use any criteria you think will help to narrow it down to a favourite or at least a short list.

If you're still finding it difficult to identify a theme that appeals to you, try looking at some of the general periodicals in your subject area – such as *Nature, New Scientist, Time, The Economist* or *The Spectator*. They'll have references to emerging issues, new strands of research or possible controversies arising from contemporary developments in your field.

If you have to choose from a list, look properly at each item on offer. Don't allow knee-jerk reactions to make you reject anything until you know more about it. Read some background information first, and look at some of the recommended texts. Consider all the aspects of each option, and then once again rank them in order of attractiveness and potential. As before, this should help you to draw up a realistic short list.

brilliant tip

A simple way of ranking your choices is to give each one a mark out of ten. When you've looked at all of them, set aside the weaker ones and look again at the ones with the higher marks. Try explaining the reasons for your scores to someone else. Expressing your opinions in words forces you to be clear about them to the other person and, more importantly, to yourself.

Some other considerations

But, of course, it's not just a question of choosing what you like; you should also think about how useful the experience and the end product might be. In fact, when you've arrived at your short list, marking each topic on it out of ten for usefulness might be one way of ranking them more precisely. It's just one of many practical aspects you need to consider.

Potential research approaches

As well as choosing a subject, you need to think about how you'll approach it and what your research angle will be. What sort of challenge does it hold? Will you be answering a question, solving a problem, debating an issue? How broad or narrow will your focus be and how will you control it? What sort of research are you actually thinking of doing? These are all things you should consider. Your answers won't restrict you to a single course of action and your approach may change as you progress, but if you form a detailed notion of your intentions, it'll be easier to make your decision. And having a clear idea of the direction you're taking at the start will enable you to get going quickly and increase your chances of success.

brilliant tip

If you're attracted by a research option but not really sure about how practical or relevant it is, ask around. Talk through its possibilities with a potential supervisor or another member of staff. The more people you discuss it with, the more angles you'll get on it.

Time

Yes, we're back to time management again. But it's not just a question of organising your schedules; you need to guard against being over-ambitious. One of the questions to ask about your potential topic is: 'Will I have time to do justice to the work and produce a thorough, satisfactory dissertation at the end of it?' That will include time to read, analyse and present your material, but also the sometimes surprising amount of time it takes just to get hold of the relevant literature. And there's also the possibility that, if the project is taking up too much of your time, it may have a negative impact on your other coursework.

In some cases, your work may have to be approved by an ethics committee. If so, that'll take time, too, and the whole process of actually writing, reviewing and editing a dissertation or a project will probably take longer than you expect. All these considerations should be part of your selection process.

Getting printed resources

This may seem an obvious thing to say but it's important to make sure you can get the information and material you need to do the work. For example, you'll need to refer to the literature to give your work the evidential substance it needs, so you'll require access to printed material. Find out, therefore, whether you can get access to the books and papers you need:

- in your own institution's library
- electronically through your library
- through inter-library loan
- by visiting another library.

 brilliant definitions

Quantitative data – information that can be expressed in numbers, e.g. the number of patients questioned in a survey.

Qualitative data – information that can't be expressed in numbers, e.g. the quality of care provided for patients.

Getting data

When you have to collect data and record and interpret your findings, this needs to be factored into your estimate of the time the project will take. If it's quantitative data which you have to analyse, you may have to learn to use a particular statistical analysis software package and it'll take time. If it's qualitative, you need to discuss with your supervisor the most appropriate methods for gathering and interpreting the information. If it involves devising, distributing, collecting and interpreting questionnaires, you'll need to adapt your timing and your techniques accordingly.

Tracking down sources

Your first stop should be the subject librarians in your library. They'll know most, if not all, of the answers to your questions and tell you about:

- the resources already in your library, including stored materials
- the main ways of getting information, including advanced online searches
- alternative approaches that may not have occurred to you
- less obvious resources and how to access them
- contacts at other institutions who can help
- exclusive databanks held by professional organisations that you might be able to access through your department.

Extent of support and supervision

You're obviously aware that this is a major undertaking for you, but even though the work's all yours, you won't be expected to do it entirely on your own. Your supervisor will guide and help you – you'd better find out at the start, though, just how much you can expect from him. Sometimes it may involve regular meetings between you, and sometimes you'll arrange meetings only when they're needed. Generally, you'll be able to ask questions, seek guidance and discuss key issues. One area you need to clarify is how far and how often he'll be prepared to review your written work and give you feedback on it. He certainly won't proofread it for you – that's your responsibility, and he may not want to read the whole thing until it's submitted for assessment. So find out these things – it's best to know where you stand right from the beginning.

brilliant tip

If you have a choice of supervisor, make it someone you feel comfortable talking to, someone who'll give you support and guidance as well as help you to work hard and complete on time. Ask past students how they've got on with different tutors.

To help you choose ...

Make it an informed choice. Use every available source to explore all the topics you've short listed and the work involved. Discuss them with your course director or assigned supervisor and do some background reading. Make sure you understand all the challenges you may face and, if it seems risky, don't choose it. Speak to students who've already done this kind of study. Get their feelings and reactions about what they felt was important when they were researching and writing.

Look at dissertations and reports from previous years. They'll give you an idea of the style and standard needed. They'll also help you to appreciate the variety of approaches that may be relevant to your discipline. But don't let their professional structure and appearance put you off. Remember that they were written by students who, at the start, felt much the same as you do now. Learn from them: it'll help you make sure you reach your full potential and produce something which looks, feels and is just as good.

Plan one or more dissertations or reports as part of your decision-making process. Sketch out the overall structure, then think about a more detailed plan. If that's the one you eventually choose, you may not stick rigidly to the plan, but the actual business of writing one will help you to sort out the ideas and decide how appealing and manageable they are.

This is a highly personal and very important decision, so get advice, but think for yourself. Try not to be influenced by uninformed opinions or throwaway remarks by others – some of your fellow students may have their own reasons for liking or disliking certain topics or supervisors. By all means listen to what they say, but use your own judgement, not theirs, when you make your final choice.

What next?

The moment you have the necessary information ...

... choose your topic and be prepared to devote time and attention to it right away. As we've said, you'll need to reflect on and dwell over your options, but at the same time you must be aware that you need to get moving on it or others might get there before you.

 **recap**

Considering your options.

Things to help you make your choice.

Sources.

Supervision.

30 How to prepare and submit a proposal

Some universities ask you to write a proposal which identifies the topic and the area you wish to investigate and outlines the scope and research methods you intend to use. This is an administrative exercise, but it'll also help you organise your preliminary thoughts, plan your approach and complete your work on time, so it's worth giving it close attention.

What are proposals?

A proposal can have many consequences. Apart from forcing you to look at your aims in a more considered and structured way, it may help the committee assessing it to decide whether it's a reasonable project and who your supervisor will be. It may also be referred to the appropriate ethics committee in your institution. You'll perhaps get feedback on it and advice on how to tackle it.

> ### brilliant tip
>
> A supervisor may be a lecturer or other member of staff experienced in conducting research and in mentoring students; their input is very valuable. The time they have available for advising dissertation students is precious, so it's important to go to all meetings promptly, prepare for them beforehand and communicate effectively during them. Make a list of questions or issues you want to raise. It'll show your supervisor that you're taking it seriously. And when you get feedback, act on it – it'll almost certainly improve the quality of your work. Remember, too, that your supervisor will be a possible referee when you apply for a job.

The benefits

A proposal will:

- help you to make sure your aims and objectives are achievable in the time allocated

- force you to read and review some of the relevant background material

- make you check that you're being clear and realistic about possible research methods

- make you think about what resources you might need at an early stage

- force you to check that you've considered all the relevant safety and ethical issues which could crop up

- create an outline structure and a viable timetable for your project

- help you to find an appropriate supervisor.

 **definition**

Hypothesis (plural hypotheses) – a theory that can be tested.

How will it be assessed?

In the simplest terms, the committee considering it will expect you to be able to answer 'yes' to the following questions:

- Do you have an up-to-date and accurate view of the research field?

- Have you outlined the focus of your studies (or the theory you intend to test) in sufficient detail?

- Is the scope of your proposed study realistic in the time allocated?

- Is your proposed research sufficiently original?

- Is it sufficiently challenging?

- Will it allow you to demonstrate your academic ability?

- Will it give you the chance to refine your skills?

- Are the proposed methods appropriate, and are you aware of their limitations?
- Are you likely to get access to all the resources you need?
- Are you planning to deal with safety and ethical issues appropriately?
- Are your proposed structure and the underlying research evident?
- Do your proposal's contents conform to the departmental or university regulations?
- Have you carried out appropriate background reading?
- Is your dissertation or project report likely to meet the required standard?

Don't try to cover too 'large' a problem or area of discussion. Highlight your central hypothesis or idea and state it very clearly. That means identifying the core question or topic that you'll be investigating. You aren't expected to suggest an answer or a conclusion because it's not often possible to do such a thing. The important thing is to consider the evidence from all sides of an argument or case, arrive at a clearly stated viewpoint and give your reasons for it. If your topic adopts an unusual perspective on a research area or focuses on the latest developments in its chosen research field, it may be looked on more favourably.

brilliant example

Let's say you're interested in systems of government which have two houses or chambers (i.e. bi-cameral systems). That's too large and vague an area, so you start thinking about how they interact, the checks and balances of such a system, especially when one's elected and the other depends on patronage and selection. So you start thinking about the UK system with its elected and unelected houses and wonder whether that's truly democratic or whether changes might be made to achieve a more equitable balance. This then leads you to want to explore arguments for and against such changes and consider alternative systems. So the topic that's emerging is a consideration of what method might be used to elect the members of the Lords rather than accept birth or patronage as qualifications. In order to explore this properly, you'd need to look at the current composition of the Lords and assess how much a selected group of its members participate in and contribute to the governmental process and compare it with the activities of a sample ▶

of members of the Commons. So, at last, you've dug more deeply and in a more focused way into an area of interest and you can submit a proposal which reads: *Representative Second Chambers: the House of Lords as a case study*.

What should you write?

Your university may have a special proposal form for you to fill in. If it doesn't, find out what length and structure it recommends, if any, and write a neat, concise outline which you can base on the points listed below. Don't be tempted to try to include too much at this point; there'll be plenty of time to expand it later when you get going on the dissertation/ report itself. The members of the committee will have several proposals to consider and they'll need to be able to make a quick decision. If you make yours short and sweet, you'll make their job easier.

Typical elements of a proposal

It's up to you to decide which of the following elements are relevant to your particular field and/or discipline. Some are obvious, others less so, but the list should help you to make your choices.

Component	Content and aspects to consider
Personal details.	So that you can be identified and contacted.
Details of your degree course or programme.	To establish the precise area of study.
Proposed title.	This should be relatively short; a two-part title style can be useful.
Description of the subject area/ summary/background/brief review. Statement of the problem or issue to be addressed.	A brief outline that provides context such as: a synopsis of past work; a description of the 'gap' to be filled or new area to be explored; a summary of current ideas and, where relevant, hypotheses.
Aim of research.	A general description of the overall purpose; a statement of intent.

Component	Content and aspects to consider
Objectives.	A listing of specific things you expect to do to achieve your aim.
Literature to be examined.	Sources you intend to consult during your research.
Research methods or critical approach.	How you propose to carry out your investigation.
Preliminary bibliography.	Details (in the prescribed format) of the key sources you've already consulted.
(Special) resources required.	All the information sources, samples, instruments, people, etc. necessary to carry out your investigation.
Outline plan of the dissertation or project report.	An overview consisting of the likely section or chapter headings and sub-headings.
Names of possible supervisors.	This will depend on your university's system.
Timetable/plan.	A realistic breakdown of the stages of your dissertation, ideally with appropriate milestones.
Statement or declaration that you understand and will comply with safety and/or ethical rules.	This is the committee's guarantee that you've considered these issues. In certain cases, you may be asked to provide details.

As with the writing exercises we've been discussing elsewhere, try not to prepare your proposal in a rush. If possible, write out a draft and leave it for a few days before coming back to it with a critical mind and modifying it if necessary before handing it in.

Pinpointing a central hypothesis or idea will help you to establish a clear focus, whether you're trying to answer a specific question, investigate a particular issue or highlight a precise topic.

Your proposal's important, but it's only a proposal. You don't need to write the complete work at this stage; the intention is simply to prove that you've chosen a reasonable topic and you're likely to succeed in producing a dissertation or project report that meets your course regulations and requirements.

brilliant tip

When you write your proposal, it may be the first time you have to think about a title. The two-part style is quite effective, starting with a short, attention-grabbing statement and adding, after a colon or a dash, a longer secondary title that defines the content more closely. You'll have plenty of chances to change it as you work on the dissertation because your research and evolving attitudes may bring out other aspects which take on greater importance.

brilliant dos and don'ts

DO ...

... get feedback from your peers. Show an early draft to a friend or family member, or swap proposals with a classmate. Ask for comments and respond to them. This kind of feedback is especially valuable to make sure that your proposal's logical and easy to follow and understand.

... use appropriate language. Your proposal should be clear to the non-specialist, but include subject-specific terminology to show that you understand important concepts and jargon.

DON'T

... set yourself unrealistic aims and objectives. You need to be original, but you also need to be able to deliver on time.

What next?

Imagine you're assessing ...

... your own proposal. Write a draft and look back at the list of questions we asked earlier. If there are any that you can't reply to with a 'yes', see if you can improve the relevant wording in the proposal or give more evidence to back up your case.

Make a tentative list ...

... of possible titles and ask your supervisor or fellow students what they think of them. Look at recent dissertations and project reports to get a feel for the modern style in your discipline.

Create a detailed timetable ...

... for your research and writing, including suitable milestones, such as 'finish first draft', and remember to factor in some slippage time.

 **recap**

What are proposals?

How are they assessed?

Typical elements.

Choosing the type of research for your assignment

Broadly speaking, there are two general categories of research – qualitative and quantitative. The first uses investigative approaches that produce information in the form of descriptive textual information; the second usually produces results in the form of numbers. The arts disciplines in general tend to use qualitative research methods whilst quantitative methods are more common in scientific project work, but both can be used for all disciplines and some investigations combine the two methods. There are many variables within each of them and neither can be described as simple. But we'll sketch out their basic principles in broad terms and indicate some of the techniques that characterise them and how you might obtain and interpret the results.

The basics

As we've just suggested, the two aren't mutually exclusive and you can use them in the same investigation. For example, you could conduct a survey which asks people to express opinions about a topic freely and also by means of a questionnaire which asks them whether they agree or disagree with a stated proposition. The first would give you text to analyse, and the second would provide data which you could collate and express as a percentage.

In broad terms, the qualitative approach is for investigating:

● opinions, feelings and values (for example, in political science, social policy and philosophy)

● people's interpretations and responses (for example, in sociology and psychology)

- behavioural patterns (for example, in ethnography, anthropology and geography)

- processes and patterns (for example, in education, economics and accountancy)

- case studies including critical incidents (for example, in nursing and education).

You'd then interpret your results according to your own values and intentions.

The quantitative approach is useful for:

- getting measurements (for example, in biochemistry and physiology)

- estimating error (for example, in physics and engineering)

- comparing information and opinions (for example, in sociology and psychology)

- testing hypotheses (for example, in most investigative science disciplines).

In this case, you should be detached and the results of the study should be objective.

The main features

Qualitative research is generally exploratory. It's especially important in the social sciences, where its aim is often to understand the complexities of human behaviour. It can include:

- case studies ('Student X described her experience on her first day at university as …')

- interviews ('Interviewee A explained that, after seeing the video, his reaction was … This could be interpreted as …')

- focus groups ('One group member stated that her experience of peer marking was …').

Quantitative research is generally conclusive. It's especially important in the sciences, where its aim is often to provide a reliable value for a measurement or test a particular hypothesis. It can include:

- surveys and questionnaires ('Over 45 per cent of respondents agreed with this statement')

- measurements ('The average insect wing length was 3.40 mm with a standard error of 0.14 mm')

- experiments ('Treatment A resulted in a statistically significant increase in weight gain compared with the control').

Qualitative methods

By its very nature, this approach implies a degree of bias, so it's just as important to remain objective in the way you conduct the actual research as it is when you're reporting your findings. Qualitative research generally involves individuals or small, carefully selected samples. These may not be representative of the population as a whole, but that's not necessarily important because the value of this sort of investigation lies in its authentic, case-specific detail. The information you get is potentially richer and deeper than the sort you get from numbers and statistics, and opinions, experiences and feelings can be expressed in many subtle ways. The down side of this is that, while they're complex, subtle and individual, it's less easy to make comparisons between different cases and arrive at generalised conclusions.

 brilliant definitions

Population and sample are terms whose meanings are different from their 'normal' meanings (particularly in quantitative research).

Population – a defined group of items that might be part of a study: for example, all men in the UK; all individuals of a species of bivalve mollusc on a particular beach; all Birmingham householders who use gas as a heating fuel.

Sample – a sub-set of individuals from a specific population: for example, the 28 men whose blood sugar level was measured and compared with that of 34 who had taken drug X; the 50 bivalves collected from Beach A, measured and compared with a similar sample from Beach B; the 45 householders selected for telephone interview about their satisfaction with the service provided by their energy supplier.

Observation and description

This is when you examine an artefact, person or location and describe it. You might also trace developments through time. It's the method you'd use for investigating topics such as:

- primary source material such as that found in an historical document
- a biological habitat
- a patient's symptoms
- a drawing, painting or installation.

Description is sometimes seen as a 'lower-level' academic thought process, but the interpretations and generalisations needed to interpret it further depend on distinctly higher-level skills.

brilliant tip

If you need to compare several sources of information, it's useful to create a grid or matrix where the columns represent the different sources and entries in the rows summarise the specific features of interest. You could adapt this table to include it in a report or dissertation, but it would also be useful when you're summarising the main features of the sources in writing.

Surveys and questionnaires

The main qualitative technique is to ask an 'open' question, for example, 'What do you think about the new property valuation system?' or 'Do you have any further comments?' They can produce answers from a quite complex mini-speech to total silence, but they do provide authentic quotes which illustrate representative and/or opposing points of view and can thus give your work more interest and colour.

When organising your interview questions, make sure you don't lead the respondent by asking some question early on which might put a particular idea or concept in his mind and affect his response to a later question. Try to start with general questions or prompts and move to the specific.

tip

The way you frame your questions will affect how people reply: asking someone 'What do you think of the prime minister?' allows them to express their opinions at great length and in any direction; asking them 'Do you think the prime minister is a) Excellent, b) Good, c) Poor, d) Disastrous?' limits their scope.

If you're conducting a survey, make sure your instructions are clear. If you write 'Do you agree with this statement? Yes/No', some people may circle the answer they agree with, others may score out the one they disagree with (and the scoring out might resemble a tick of approval), and some may make marks which baffle you completely. To iron out problems of that nature, try getting a friend or family member to take the survey before using it on real subjects.

The basic survey rules are:

- Keep it as short as possible. Use the minimum number of questions you need to get the relevant information and ask a question only if you know exactly how you'll use the answer.

- Collect the appropriate demographic information to describe your sample and draw correlations.

- Make sure your questions are unambiguous.

- In deciding the order of questions, try to move from the general to the specific so that there's less chance of early questions influencing responses to later ones.

brilliant definitions

Correlation – the strength and direction of the relationship between two variables.

Variable – a mathematical quantity that can take different values in different cases.

Part of your dissertation or report will consist of a description of how the survey was conducted. This should include the following:

- Sampling methods. How did you contact and choose the respondents? What ethical procedures did you follow?

- Details of respondents. You should provide a summary of demographics (the gender, age and background of those responding). You can get these details from questions, usually at the start of the survey, but it's important to reassure respondents that their privacy and anonymity will be protected.

- Questionnaire design. Discuss the principles and rationale behind it and include a copy in your submission as an appendix.

- Procedure. How did you carry out the survey?

It's normal to correct your respondents' grammar and spelling errors because the important thing is to convey the spirit of what they wrote rather than divert the reader's attention by careless mistakes. Add a note to the 'Material and methods' section to explain that you've done this.

Interview-based case studies

Qualitative research often draws on individuals' experiences of events, processes and systems. These can be reported as case studies. In theory, the best way of carrying out this type of investigation without your preconceptions getting in the way would be to allow the participant to provide a completely unstructured and uninterrupted stream of thought. You'd then draw your conclusions after examining and reflecting on it all. In practice, though, it makes more sense (and it certainly makes your task easier) if you use prior knowledge and experience (your own and that acquired from your reading) to structure an interview by creating a series of prompting questions. If you use a similar structure for each case study, you'll be able to compare results more easily.

Action research

You're sometimes encouraged to undertake studies focusing on local issues, particularly in the 'caring' disciplines such as nursing, social work and teaching. In such instances a popular approach is action research, which involves studying a problem or situation which requires better understanding and, possibly, identifying some change to resolve the problem or improve the situation.

Focus groups

These are small discussion groups (ideally of four to six members), where participants are asked to comment on an issue or, if it's in a commercial context, a product or marketing tool. You can gather several viewpoints at a time and observe the outcomes of open and dynamic discussion among the group members. You need to be careful not to introduce bias by leading the discussion yourself, and also to watch out for any tendency among group members to stick to the middle ground because they're shy about expressing a minority opinion.

brilliant tip

Make sure you have a list of discussion topics or questions which relate to your research interest. Be ready to intervene in discussions to introduce a new topic or bring them back to the point if they start drifting into irrelevant side issues.

Quantitative methods

It's obvious that if you quantify your results they'll be less subjective and it'll be easier to make comparisons between data sets. You must, however, make sure that your approach to data collection is unbiased. Bias can be defined as a partial or one-sided view or description of events and it can be introduced by faulty techniques. It may be that, for some subconscious reason, you select individuals for observation or experiment who don't represent the population, or values or measurements can be distorted, deliberately or accidentally.

Surveys and questionnaires

These are as valuable for gaining quantitative information as they are for a qualitative approach. Respondents can be a representative sample (for example, members of the public chosen at random or using a sampling protocol) or a population (all members of Politics Class P201).

Whereas we looked at the advantages and disadvantages of open questions before, our focus now is on closed questions, which are more useful for delivering data which can be interpreted numerically. The main types are as follows:

- Categorical, which make respondents choose one option, for example: 'Gender: M/F'; or 'Do you agree with the above statement? – Yes/No/ Don't know (delete as appropriate)'.

- Numerical, which ask for a number as an answer, for example: 'What is your age in years?'

- Multiple choice questions (MCQs), which are useful when there are mutually exclusive options and respondents have to 'tick one box'.

- Multiple response questions, which are like MCQs, except that respondents can choose more than one answer, for example: 'Which of the following resources have you used in the past month? (Tick all that apply).

Hard-copy reference books

Electronic encyclopaedia

Textbooks

Lecture handouts

E-journals'

- Ranking (ordinal) questions, which ask respondents to place possible answers in an order, for example: 'Place the items in the following list in order of preference, writing 1 for your most preferred option, 2 for the next and so on, down to 5 for your least preferred option.'

- Likert-scale questions, which are useful for assessing people's opinions or feelings on a five-point scale. Typically, respondents are asked to re-act to a statement. An example would be: 'Which of the following best describes your feelings about the claim that smoking is dangerous for your health? (Circle the appropriate number.)

1 Agree strongly

2 Agree

3 Neither agree nor disagree

4 Disagree

5 Disagree strongly'

Correlation

This is a way of describing the relationship between two measured variables, such as the number of cigarettes smoked per day and life expectancy. A variable is well correlated with another if their values alter together, either in a positive fashion or in a negative fashion, e.g. if life expectancy falls as tobacco consumption rises.

However, it's very important not to assume that correlation implies a direct link between cause and effect. If A is well correlated with B, that doesn't in itself mean that A causes B. The real cause could be something connected with A, or even, due to coincidence, something completely different. If people with high blood pressure are more likely to have heart attacks, this alone doesn't 'prove' that high blood pressure is a cause of heart attacks. The only way to become more certain is to gather more evidence.

Experiments

An experiment is a situation which you create to try to isolate the effects of changing one variable in a system or process. You can then compare the results with the condition where there's been no change. The aim behind many experiments is to show that a change in factor A causes a change in variable B, or maybe to examine in more detail how A causes B. Experiments are at the core of the 'scientific method' which is designed to allow a hypothesis to be accepted or rejected.

Qualitative results

- When you've collected the information you need, the important thing is to organise and present it in a balanced, rational way. Don't be tempted to choose only examples, answers or quotes that support your view. Include the opposing evidence as well, and then conduct a careful analysis of the arguments and literature sources you've consulted to arrive at a conclusion.

- As soon as you can, gather all your sources and scan-read them to get a quick overview before you start describing and comparing them. Always note down more information than you think you'll need. You can always get rid of irrelevant material later, but you can't always go back to find information you missed first time round.

- Choose your interviewees or members of focus groups carefully. Discuss with your tutor what the criteria should be, and then screen participants accordingly. You might, for example, want to interview people involved at all stages in a process (shop-floor, administrative, management, marketing and customer); or a balanced set of students of both sexes and representing different levels of study. You'll need to give the details of the selection criteria in your report.

Quantitative results

- Quantitative research usually gathers information from large, unbiased samples to make sure that the sample is representative of the population as a whole, and to increase the chances of reaching a statistically significant conclusion. But statistics on their own aren't enough. The results of observations, surveys or experiments need to be analysed and it's your analytical and presentational skills that may lift your marks when your work's being assessed.

- Statistical techniques let you compare sets of observations or treatments to test hypotheses and to indicate the probability of your conclusions being right or wrong. They're powerful tools, but just because you can measure something, or compare data sets, that's no guarantee that your conclusions will be certain or relevant. Many scientists accept that there's a 5 per cent chance of their conclusions being wrong. Then again, even if a hypothesis is accepted as correct, the results may apply only to that specific, highly artificial experimental or observational environment. So don't confuse statistical significance with 'importance' or 'value'.

- You must describe your methods fully because one goal of quantitative research is to produce repeatable results from which general conclusions can be drawn. Your 'Materials and methods' section should contain enough information to allow a competent peer to repeat your work.

- Use clear, unambiguous language, and define any qualitative terms you use as precisely as possible. You might, for example, convey the colour of a specimen by referring to a standard colour chart.

What next?

Qualitative

Whether you're writing ...

... a description, conducting a focus group or carrying out a case study, try to find a published study which used a similar technique. Analyse its approach and methods to see whether you can use or adapt them for your own investigation. Study the ways its results have been presented to see if they'd be suitable for you to use.

If you intend using ...

... interviews and focus groups, plan a set of question 'prompts' and possible 'question probes'.

Quantitative

Plan a survey or experiment ...

... or the procedures necessary for a measurement so that the different steps in the process are clear to you. Don't forget to consider things which might restrict your resources, such as how much time you can expect respondents to give you, or, for an experiment, whether test subjects or equipment will be available. Think about and make a list of any potential forms of bias in your research – it'll help you avoid them.

Find out what statistical tests ...

... you can do using the software available to you. Will a spreadsheet program like Excel be enough, or will you need a more sophisticated program? The more initial preparation you do, the easier the actual work will be.

 recap

The basics of each approach.

The main features and methods.

How to produce results.

32 Understanding the need for an ethical approach to your research

The word 'ethics' can extend to cover a wide spectrum of activities and behaviours. In the context of research, it refers to the way you conduct your investigation and implies that you must be careful to treat your subjects, human or otherwise, with respect and consideration. It's a basic requirement in all research that the health and safety of all those involved as participants or researchers should be a priority at all times. If you're in any doubt about your department's or institution's ethical policies and practices, find out about them. We'll just look at the general considerations and highlight the sort of things you should be aware of.

Good research practice

You must get to know the ethical codes that apply in your area and that should be part of the initial discussion you have with your supervisor about how you're going to approach your project. She'll be responsible for making sure that your proposal meets the required standards in all its aspects. If necessary, she'll help you to prepare an application to send to your institution's ethics committee.

Ethical principles

If your research involves human beings, one of its primary imperatives should be that it protects the human rights, dignity, health and safety of participants and researchers. In simple terms, this means that:

- the research should do no harm
- consent should be voluntary
- confidentiality should be respected throughout.

But even if there are no humans involved, there may still be ethical issues to resolve and in widely differing areas. For example, the use of animals, cloning, human embryo research, stem cell research, *in vitro* fertilisation and nuclear research all have clear ethical dimensions and have provoked lots of controversy. In the UK, experiments involving animals are subject to Home Office approval, and any research involving genetic manipulation must comply with the relevant legislation. As with all other aspects of your work, if this is a factor for you, your supervisor will guide you through the relevant procedures.

Ethics committees

The members of these committees are academics from your institution and they monitor research activity at undergraduate and postgraduate levels. Their main functions are to:

- consider and approve applications to conduct research
- hear appeals when approval has not been granted
- give guidance on cases that are unclear
- refer cases of research misconduct to a higher institutional authority.

When the appropriate ethics committee has approved your work, you must follow its approved protocols exactly and if you modify your original proposal in any way, you have to resubmit it to them.

brilliant tip

If any aspect of your work involves risks such as exposure to hazardous chemicals, it'll be covered by policies and procedures set up by your university's safety office and may involve some paperwork on your part. So if you have to fill in forms such as those relating to the Control of Substances Hazardous to Health (COSHH), don't think of it as a chore. In fact, it's an opportunity for you to look at your topic from a different angle and get another perspective on what you're about to take on.

Consent and confidentiality

You may have to inform people who agree to take part in your research about the things it may involve. If so, you'll need to give them a 'participant information sheet'. The information on it should be comprehensive and contain:

- an outline of the purpose of the study
- the invitation to take part and the reason they've been selected
- an acknowledgement that they're taking part voluntarily and that they're free to stop their involvement at any time
- an explanation of what will happen and how long it may take
- an indication of the advantages and disadvantages of participation
- an assurance of confidentiality and anonymity
- information about what will be produced at the end
- information about the funding source
- the names of the lead researcher and all assistants
- information about any sponsorship or affiliation connected to the project
- details of claiming expenses, if applicable.

There are often templates that can be used, but this is sometimes unsatisfactory because the terminology, format and layout may not be clear for non-specialists. All the information you give out should be brief and expressed in ways that can be easily understood by everyone.

After you've told them what's involved, participants usually sign an 'informed consent form'. They may also have to fill in a debriefing form once the data-gathering phase is over.

▶brilliant example

Your research is in medicine and you need to question patients about their treatments. You've gone through the necessary ethical applications and have the committee's approval. But it's still possible for your work to be unethical, even though you don't want or intend it to be. For example, patients are vulnerable and they may feel pressured into taking part but they're afraid to say so because they think they'll get better treatment if they co-operate with you. The research design and consent forms you create must show that you're aware of such possibilities.

You must promise all human participants that their identities won't be revealed verbally or in any printed material that comes out of the research. If you think you might want to quote directly from their responses to questions or in focus groups, you must get their permission in writing to do so and reassure them that they'll be quoted anonymously.

Getting ethical approval

Read the guidance notes from the ethics committee or your department before you start writing your proposal. The format you use for it will depend on your university's preferences. Broadly speaking, you'll need to provide information on:

- the title, purpose and duration of the project, and where it'll take place
- your methodological approach, and information on how data will be stored securely
- the way in which you'll recruit volunteers if they're needed, how old they'll be, their gender and any criteria for including or excluding individuals
- the measures you've taken to cover all ethical dimensions and comply with the appropriate research code of practice in your institution, including confidentiality in reporting results
- the name of any funding body, if appropriate.

brilliant tip

Don't forget, when you're organising your overall research schedule, to allow time for this process of getting ethical approval. Your supervisor may be able to give you an idea of how long it usually takes. While you're waiting, you can get on with some other aspect of the work, such as a literature review.

Data protection

The storage and use of personal information is an ethical issue, too. In the UK, the Data Protection Act outlines what is and isn't allowed. If you plan to store information either in paper files or electronically, check your university's web pages for information and guidance. Even without the pressure of legislation, it's good practice to limit the length of time you'll hold on to data and to tell participants how you'll be storing their data and when you'll delete or destroy it.

What next?

Look at websites ...

... for learned societies in your discipline to get the latest information about ethical issues. Apart from helping you to prepare your application for approval, it may be useful if there's an oral exam on your research project and your external examiner wants to explore its ethics in the wider context of the discipline.

Do some brainstorming ...

... focusing specifically on the ethical dimensions of your research. Write out your title, add major branches for harm, consent and confidentiality, and then elaborate on them and any others that occur to you.

Get to know the ethics guidelines ...

... for research activity in your specialist field. It'll help your personal development and will be part of your professional practice after you graduate.

 **recap**

Ethical principles.

Ethical committees.

Consent and confidentiality.

Getting approval.

Data protection.

33 The forms, features and functions of reports

Writing a report is a slightly different exercise from writing dissertations. The basic principles of gathering and acknowledging materials, structuring them and writing them up coherently with appropriate supporting evidence are the same, but their purpose may be different. And they're certainly different in terms of formatting. Formats may be discipline-specific and the important thing is to know where the information should be placed. We're going to consider common formats which may be suitable for reports on literature survey, science and business.

What is a report?

Reports are designed to convey information, usually on a well-defined topic. There are, in different subjects, some specific conventions that govern structure, style and content. The way in which you've collected and handled the material in terms of scholarship will still be the most important aspect of the work as far as your markers are concerned. The professionalism of your presentation will also be assessed, so you need to know the required format and make sure you stick to it.

It's an important part of your learning at university because its strictness of structure forces you to cover the required ground and organise your findings in a clearly defined presentational style. It also creates a well-organised record of the investigation which can be replicated or used to develop results for future research, and it gives you practice in acquiring and using important professional skills.

The basic features

Preparing and writing a report can take a long time and may involve lots of research in the library, on the internet or in the laboratory, but it's important not to treat the research and writing phases as separate exercises. The style and format of the report may well dictate what sort of information you need to collect and you should be writing as you continue exploring your topic.

There are four general stages to the overall process:

1 'Scoping', where you choose a topic or an aspect of a subject. Sometimes it's chosen for you, but it may be something that comes out of your research. Even if you don't have an exact notion of what you want to do, it helps to have a general idea from the start. You can refine it or change the precise focus later.

2 Research, which is when you find relevant information. You may have to conduct experiments, as in many science subjects, or analyse and evaluate reports, texts and other sources.

3 Writing, which obviously involves communicating your work using appropriate language.

4 Presentation, which is the whole business of organising and delivering your work to a high professional standard. Some of the marks awarded will be earned by good presentation.

brilliant tip

Keep your focus narrow. Don't try to be too ambitious. It's normally better to deal with a limited topic thoroughly than write a shallow report covering a wide area.

Some forms and functions

- Description: reporting your experiments or summarising facts you've gathered.
- Visual summaries: making diagrams, flow charts, graphs or tables to demonstrate your points more clearly.

- Analysis: looking at results or facts and working out statistics to describe/explain them or test a hypothesis.

- Discussion: weighing up the pros and cons of a position.

- Solution(s): explaining different options to solve an issue or problem.

- Evaluation: deciding what's important and why.

- Recommendation: identifying the best solution and giving evidence to support your choice.

- Arriving at a conclusion: stating a position on the basis of your research.

Possible styles

Reports for different purposes and in different subjects follow different designs and include various components, not always in the same order. Let's look first at possible components and what they should contain. We've listed them in alphabetical order, not in the order they'd appear in a report.

Typical components

Abbreviations: a list of any abbreviations for any technical terms you've used, e.g. 'DNA: deoxyribonucleic acid'.

Abstract: a brief summary of your aims, main outcomes and conclusions. It outlines your main findings and what you think they mean, and although you write it last, it's usually placed at the beginning of the report.

Acknowledgements: a list of people who helped you, sometimes briefly saying how.

Appendix (plural **appendices**): a section where you can put items such as a questionnaire template and data or results that would otherwise spoil the flow of the report or make the results section too long.

Bibliography/references/literature cited: an alphabetical list of sources cited in the text, following one of the standard referencing formats.

Discussion (or conclusions) for non-scientific-style reports: a restatement of the problem or issue to be addressed, an outline of the key 'solutions' or responses to it, and an explanation of why one solution is preferred to another with supporting evidence. Sometimes, you may be asked to make recommendations and indicate how they could be implemented.

Discussion (or conclusions) for scientific-style reports: a commentary on the results and an outline of the main conclusions. It could include some or all of the following:

- comments on the methods used
- conclusions from any statistical analysis
- comparison with other findings
- what the result means
- how you might improve the experiment
- how you might implement the findings
- where you would go from here, if you had more time and resources.

Sometimes you might combine the results and discussions sections to explain, for example, why one result led to the next experiment or approach. Remember that lots of marks will be awarded here for originality of thinking.

Executive summary: takes the place of an abstract in a business report. It restates the main points of the report, usually on a single page, starting with a brief statement of the aims of the report and continuing with a summary of the main findings, perhaps as bullet points and then a summary of the main conclusions and/or recommendations. As with an abstract, you'd probably leave writing this until last.

Experimental: a description of the apparatus and method used.

Glossary: a list of terms that might be unfamiliar to the reader, with their definitions.

Introduction for non-scientific-style reports: a description of the context of the study and an outline of the problem or issue to be addressed. You may need to refer here to the literature or other resource material you'll be using.

Introduction for scientific-style reports: an outline of the background to and aims of the experiments and a brief discussion of the techniques you'll use. The idea here is to make it clear to the reader what you're intending to do and why.

Main body of text: your appraisal of the topic. A systematic approach to solutions or issues and an analysis of everything relevant to them. You can sub-divide it into sections to deal with different aspects. In a scientific literature review, it often includes a chronological account of developments in the field, quoting important authors, their ideas and findings.

Materials and methods: a description of what you did. This should be detailed enough to allow a competent person to repeat the work.

Results: a description of your experiments and results, usually presented as tables or in graphic form (but never both for the same data).

Table of contents: a list to help the reader find his way around. It may also include a table of diagrams.

Title page: your full name (with those of any co-authors), the title or code of the module and the date. A business report may also include the company logo, client details and classification (for example, 'confidential').

Common formats

These are examples of the different designs you can use, but you should first check to see if your department has any preferred layouts or guidelines.

- The literature review is relatively simple. It consists of a title page, abstract, introduction, the main body of text, your conclusions and references or the literature you've cited. The main body is the largest section, and it may be sub-divided into sections.

- The general scientific report has more components. There's the title page, abstract, abbreviations, introduction, materials and methods, results, discussion, acknowledgements and references. Its focus is on materials and methods and in some disciplines the components may be in a different order. In chemistry, for example, it'll begin with the title page, abstract, abbreviations and introduction as before, and then move to results, discussion, materials and methods, before ending the same way, with acknowledgements and references.

- An undergraduate lab report will probably be a shorter version of the general scientific format and have a title page, introduction, materials and methods, brief results and discussion/conclusions.

- A non-scientific style of report wouldn't focus on materials and methods, but might have just a title page, introduction, the main body of text dealing with the topic being considered, and a conclusion.

- A typical business report has its conclusions or recommendations as part of the main body and includes an executive summary for quick reading. Often, it also has appendices and a glossary for the non-specialist. So its layout would consist of a title page, executive summary, acknowledgements, table of contents, the main body of text, bibliography/references, appendices and glossary.

Selecting content and shaping your report

If there's no prescribed model in your course handbook, choose one which suits the purposes of your report. You could also copy the format of one you've seen which you feel is well organised. Be ruthless in rejecting irrelevant information. Good reports are short and to the point. It's too easy to think that, just because you've spent ages getting your information or conducting an analysis, it all has to go in. It doesn't. If it's not relevant or if it's repetitious, discard it.

Reports can be dense and hard to read. Go for relatively simple sentences and short paragraphs. Use sub-headings and bullet points to break up the text. It all makes it easier to read and assimilate. If you're using diagrams and graphs, keep them simple. If possible, vary the types you use.

What next?

Use the sample formats we've listed ...

... to help you decide which type best suits your purposes. If you want to include graphs to add variety and impact to your scientific and business reports, check what types are available. The 'Chart Wizard' in Microsoft Excel gives you various options. Enter your data into the spreadsheet and you can use it to get a quick idea of what each would look like.

Remember that you need to use ...

... your higher-level academic thinking skills. Assessments of reports will centre mainly on your analysis and evaluation of a thorough summary of the topic.

 **recap**

What is a report?

The basic features.

Forms and functions.

Typical components and common formats.

34 How to find, list and analyse the literature of your chosen topic

Literature surveys (also called literature reviews) are an essential ingredient of research projects of all sorts. The label suggests a general overview, but they're much more than that; they call for a specific discipline and involve not just describing what others have written about your topic but applying your critical thinking to what they say. Your survey or review should cover all the available publications that relate to your topic. You must list them, note the different approaches within them, identify similar and opposing viewpoints and explore their origins and development. Once again, you're being asked to get beneath the surface and beyond merely describing ideas in order to analyse and evaluate their relevance and meaning.

The review step by step

At the beginning, this process may seem daunting. Academic topics generate lots of literature, from brief articles or notes to thick volumes. The prospect of having to read it all is in itself a challenge, but then to think that, on top of that, you have to understand and summarise it really does seem forbidding. As with all tasks, though, the important thing is to think of it not as a massive undertaking but as something you'll achieve little by little. That's why we're breaking it down into a sequence of smaller tasks.

Choosing a topic

The first task, obviously, is to choose your topic. You may have to pick one from a list, or find it yourself within the broader subject area. Whichever is the case, the first thing to do is read around before you make your final choice. You may already be passionate about a specific aspect of the subject, but just take some time to look at alternatives before you commit.

How do you choose?

There are several criteria you can apply. The more of them a topic satisfies, the more attractive it'll be. So look for one:

- which interests you

- which has a manageable amount of literature – not so small that there's hardly anything to discuss, or so large that it'll take ages to get through it all

- where it's easy to access the literature – for example, one which is well covered by journals available from your library

- which has different views or approaches for you to compare

- which is controversial or topical

- where there's been a recent breakthrough.

When you've got the topic, narrow it down as much as you can and choose a working title. Titles aren't easy because they're short and yet they're trying to indicate a broad, complex study. Think hard about the wording. It's important because it'll tell your readers and markers what to expect. You can alter it as you get further into the topic and it's often useful to add a secondary element to it to refine the exact approach you're taking.

Where do you look for the literature?

These are perhaps obvious, but it's worth noting them. The more varied your types of reference, the greater your scope for analysis and comparison.

- Textbooks are good for getting an overview of a field.

- Monographs are books on a single, often narrow, subject.

- Reviews tend to analyse a research area, usually in more detail than books. They're also more up to date.

- Reference works give you facts, definitions and a concise overview.

- Research papers are very detailed articles published in journals and devoted to specific subject areas.

- Websites aren't always wholly reliable but they may let you compare viewpoints and direct you towards other sources.

- All the different library resources.

brilliant tip

Consult as many different sources as you can. The more you read, the more likely you are to find viewpoints which support or disagree with one another and that makes for a more interesting review.

Building a reference list

Your supervisor may be able to suggest some articles to get you started, or you may get references in handouts. Most of the papers you consult will be in the primary literature. Often, at the start, they seem to be full of jargon, big words and long, impenetrable sentences, but the more you read, the more comfortable you'll feel with the terminology of your subject.

If this is your first real attempt to use library research methods, discuss what's involved with a subject librarian. They'll be able to teach you basic techniques and show you how to access databases and other tools in your search for relevant material. Your library's website may also have tips and provide online links to databases and e-journals.

New academic papers are being written all the time and the primary literature just keeps growing. But if you find one relevant paper, you can use that as a starting point and work backwards from it quite easily. Just read it and note any of the references it gives which are relevant to your specific interest. Check those sources and note their references, too. Each will lead you to others and before long not only will you have a significant list of references of your own but you'll have developed a clearer notion of your specific focus and its wider context.

For obvious reasons, working forwards isn't quite as productive. But in some fields there are citation index journals that tell you which papers have been cited by other people. They let you see if there are any recent mentions of a particular reference. You can also enter key words or authors into a database or search engine and see what turns up or scan current journals for related material.

Keeping track of references

As you read, take notes of important points in a notebook or on index cards. The matrix note-taking format which we described earlier in the book is a convenient way of summarising different aspects of sources and lets you see the whole picture more easily.

You need a filing system which helps you to find notes and papers quickly when you need them. The simplest is to save them alphabetically by author and then by date, as you would in a bibliography. Alternatively, if you think you'll be collecting lots of papers, you can number each one, file them in numerical order, and list the numbers in an index or database. This means you just add papers as you read them and you don't have to mess around leafing through lots of alphabetical entries to find the right place for them.

From the way we keep repeating it, you'll know by now that you must cite your sources in your text and organise a bibliography or reference list. Check your department's guidance notes to find the preferred format or base your style on an example from the discipline literature.

Keep a balance

It's possible, maybe even probable, that you either already have or will soon start developing strong views about your topic and the issues and controversies surrounding it. But it's very important to keep them in check and present all your material in a fair, balanced way. Treat all the conflicting viewpoints with respect, and summarise the reasons for those to which you feel opposed as well as those which support your stance. The impersonal, passive style we stressed earlier helps to keep you, the individual, out of the text.

Nevertheless, you have to try to reach a conclusion. When you do so, make sure you express it reasonably, without emotive or judgemental bias, and give your reasons for preferring that particular angle on it. Don't be afraid of being critical or contradicting 'experts'; if you can back up your position with supporting evidence, you've done what's required.

brilliant tip

Some people like to keep the reference details of their sources on index cards, along with any notes they make about them. This is useful, in two ways:

1   You can put the cards into piles representing different topics, viewpoints or aspects of the issue and then organise each pile into a logical sequence.

2   When you're compiling your bibliography/reference list, you can put them all in alphabetical order and just work through them.

If you're working on a word processor, it's even easier to use such a system by replacing the cards with sub-folders in your files.

The overall approach

It's easy to sit reading a book and convince yourself that you're working. But if you're just letting the words flow in and out of your head passively, you're wasting time. Make your reading useful. Take notes and engage with it. Make sure it's relevant. Start writing as soon as you can.

Your supervisor may not ask to see your drafts, but you'll probably get good advice if you can persuade him to comment on them. Try getting a friend to read them, too, even if she doesn't know your subject. She'll be able to point out bits she doesn't understand, where your explanations are obscure or your writing seems biased.

Organise your references from an early stage. When you get to the end of the review, you'll have gathered material from several different sources and it could take ages searching through them all for details and writing them up in your bibliography. Don't leave it till then; keep them organised and listed as you go along.

Review and edit what you've written. Try to finish writing a week or more before you have to hand it in; then leave it for a day to two and go back to it as a reader, not a writer. You can then look critically at what you've written with fresh eyes and alter it as necessary.

What next?

Make an appointment to have a chat ...

... with your subject librarian. You'll find contact details in the library itself or on its website. Jot down the questions you need to ask beforehand – it'll save time and make things easier for both of you.

Set up your filing systems and databases ...

... on index cards or using a word processor or spreadsheet. There are commercial products for storing details of references, but setting them up takes time and effort (as well as money) and it may not be worth it for a shorter exercise. You'll probably need to set up a file storage system, though, to keep your papers tidy and well organised.

Read some literature reviews and surveys ...

... in your subject area. It'll give you an idea of the writing style and the depth of analysis you should be aiming for.

brilliant recap

The step-by-step approach.

Choosing a topic.

Finding the literature.

Keeping track of references.

Maintaining a balance.

General tips.

35 Making the most of feedback

Feedback comes in many forms: reactions to your contributions in tutorials from tutors and fellow students; discussions and questions about your point of view; and, of course, reactions – verbal and written – to the work you hand in for assessment. When essays are handed back, they usually have a mark on them and some comments. The comments may be in the margins or text and there's usually a general remark at the end. It's all too easy to jump to the grade and not take much notice of the remarks, but they can make a significant difference to your future grades and help to refine your writing and thinking.

Learning from feedback

There are two main types of assessment at university. The first are those where the grade you get doesn't get counted in your end-of-module mark, or counts for very little. They let you know what sort of standard you're reaching and often have a feedback sheet or comments written on them. The second are those which do count towards your final grade.

brilliant tip

Fellow students or members of your family can help by reading your work and commenting. They may not know much (or anything) about the subject, but they'll be able to say how clear your writing is or whether your argument is logical or has gaps.

The simplest form of feedback is the mark itself. If it's good, you'll know you're reaching the required standard; if it's not, you'll know you need to do something to improve. If you're not sure how the grading system works, or what standards are expected, check your course or faculty handbooks. Even very early on, it might be worth trying to find out how your marks, whether they're given as percentages or in some other form, relate to the normal standard degree classes – first, upper second, lower second, third and unclassified.

If you're not sure why you got the mark you did or why the marker made a particular comment, it may be possible to arrange a meeting with him. Normally he'll be happy to explain it for you. But it's not a good idea to try to haggle over your marks. It's OK to point out that they've been added up wrongly, but otherwise, the mark is a genuine response on the part of the tutor to the quality of what you've written. Learn from it.

brilliant tip

Always read your feedback. It's there to point out specific aspects of your work which are being commended or aren't being handled as effectively as they could be. You should use it to make later submissions better, help to develop your structure and style, and deepen your understanding of the topic. If you ignore points that are made, especially those concerned with presentation or structure, you'll keep repeating the mistakes and find yourself penalised for them over and over again.

Feedback comments and what they mean

Although, as we pointed out in an earlier chapter, there's a set of signs which are used when proofreading to indicate various textual problems which need correcting, there isn't an equivalent terminology shared by lecturers and tutors everywhere. If there were, it would imply that both writing and marking are automatic processes with 'right' and 'wrong' answers. Markers may use the proofreading symbols as a sort of shorthand, but their comments will be personal. So you'll need to get used to interpreting the particular ways they express their opinions. Also, if their habit is to scribble notes as they read, their handwriting may be difficult to decipher. Don't hesitate to ask if you can't understand what's being said.

Usually, comments are written in the right-hand margin or between the relevant lines. The words, phrases, sentences or paragraphs to which they refer are underlined, circled or indicated in some other way. All we can do here is give a few examples of commonly used feedback comments and suggest what they mean and how you should react to them to improve your writing.

Comments on content

- **Relevance?, Importance?, Value of example?, So?**
  These suggest that you may have used a quotation that's not right for the context or you maybe haven't explained its relevance. Read your words carefully to test how logical they are and whether the irrelevance is obvious to you. Do you need to explain it further or more clearly? Should you choose a more appropriate example or quote?

- **Detail, Give more information, Example?, Too much detail/ waffle/padding**
  You've either not provided enough detail to make your point or there's too much and your point's getting lost. You may also have realised that your argument's a bit thin so you've tried to make it seem better by putting in lots of description rather than analysis.

- **You could have included …, What about … ? Why didn't you … ?**
  These obviously indicate that something's missing. You should, by reading through it, see where the gap is and what's needed to fill it.

- **Good!, Excellent!, ✓ (which may recur throughout the work)**
  These are the remarks you want – expressions of approval, confirmation that you're on the right track.

- **Poor, Weak, No!, ✗ (which may recur throughout the work)**
  And this is what you don't want to see – expressions of disapproval, indications that there's something wrong with your examples, your quotations, your interpretation of them, etc.

Comments on structure

- **Logic?, *Non sequitur* (which means this doesn't naturally follow what preceded it)**
  Your logic or argument is faulty. It may call for you to make quite radical changes to your approach to and analysis of the topic.

- **Where are you going with this?, Unclear**
  This suggests that you've failed to introduce the topic clearly or that it's gone off course. Check that you do understand the task properly and know what restrictions there are on your response. Then decide how to tackle the subject.

- **Unbalanced discussion, Weak on pros and cons**
  Once again, it suggests a failure in your logic. When you're comparing and/or contrasting in any way, you must give more or less equal coverage to the pros and cons of the argument.

- **So what?, Conclusion?**
  You've failed to conclude the essay clearly. You have to sum up the central features of your writing and shouldn't add any new material at this point. When you do that properly, it shows that you can think critically and define and highlight the main thread of your argument.

- **Watch out for over-quotation, Too many quotations**
  This means exactly what it says. If you include too many direct quotations from your sources, there's a real danger of plagiarism. You need to synthesise the information and reproduce the ideas in your own words to show that you've understood and absorbed it.

- **Move text (alternatively, loops and arrows may indicate the required changes)**
  Suggestions such as this are usually intended to improve the flow or the logic.

Comments on presentation

- **sp. (spelling), ⋏ (insert material here), ⌐ (break paragraph here), ♪ (delete this material), P (punctuation error)**
  These are indications of minor proofing errors and this is where the proofreading symbols may be used.

- **Citations, Reference (required), Ref?, Reference list omitted**
  You've missed out a reference to the original source of an idea, argument or quotation. It's a fault you must correct, otherwise you're once again risking plagiarism. If you provide no reference list, you'll lose marks because it suggests you've done no specialist reading.

- **Illegible!, Untidy, Can't read**
  Again, this is self-evident. (It can also be ironic in that sometimes the marker's own handwriting is very untidy.) You can avoid it by using a word processor.

- **Please follow departmental template for reports, Order!**
  If the department or school provides a template for writing reports, you must use it. If you don't, you may lose marks.

brilliant tip

Don't just use the comments and advice on written coursework to improve your term-time work; think of how you can use it constructively in exams. For example, if you're weak on structure, practise speed-planning answers to make them focused and succinct.

What next?

Look up and understand …

… your department or faculty's marking criteria. They'll help you interpret feedback and understand how to reach the standard you want to achieve.

If your feedback comments …

… are frequently about the same sort of error, concentrate on eliminating it. It may be spelling or grammar; they may suggest you need more examples. Whatever the problem, spend time identifying its exact nature and try to overcome it.

Give yourself feedback …

… which means reading your work as objectively as possible, sensing where the weaknesses are and tackling them. It's the sort of process that should be happening as you review and edit your work and it's an essential academic skill.

Learn from the views of your tutors …

… it's often natural to feel that some feedback's unfair, harsh or has mis-understood your approach. But the fact is that tutors usually have a deeper understanding of the topic than you do and, anyway, the harsh reality is that if you want to do well in a subject, you'd better find out what markers mean by 'good' answers and learn how to produce them.

 recap

Types of feedback.

Feedback comments and what they mean.

Content.

Structure.

Presentation.

PART 6

Developing the necessary examination skills

36 Exams and other assessments

Universities award their own degrees, which are based on how students perform in assessments and exams. This autonomy means that each has its own conventions regarding the style of question asked, exam formats and marking criteria, so while we can give general ideas of the types of exams and assessments you may face, it's essential for you to find out how the system operates in your own institution.

The basic principles

As well as being different in different universities, exam systems and papers vary according to disciplines. You may have a multiple choice component that tests your surface knowledge of a wide range of topics plus an essay section which asks you to go more deeply into some selected topics.

In professional disciplines you may have to show that you're knowledgeable in all areas, but other subjects may require a certain amount of specialisation. Sometimes, your exam may be divided into sections and you'll have to answer one or more questions in each section. It's a way of giving you a degree of choice but at the same time making sure you've covered all major areas in your field of study. As we said, find out what your particular subject asks of you because you really need to know exactly what's expected before you can decide on a strategy for revising for and sitting exams.

Forms of assessment

All modules and courses at university have a set of aims and learning objectives or outcomes. We mentioned these earlier so, just to remind you, they're the knowledge and skills you should have acquired at the end of a specific course or part of that course. Exams and assessments are part of the way the university checks how well you're performing in relation to these aims and objectives.

We've already mentioned two types of testing – those where marks don't count towards your eventual degree and those where they do. To use the 'correct' terminology, these are known respectively as 'formative' and 'summative' assessments.

- Formative assessments are mainly designed to give you feedback on the quality of your answers. They're sometimes called class exams.

- Summative assessments count directly towards your module or degree assessment. Most summative exams are formal tests which you take without any outside help in the presence of an invigilator. These are what are normally called degree exams and, in the honours year, finals. There are usually several of them, perhaps with different papers covering different aspects of the course, and they can be up to two or three hours long.

In some university courses, assessments are based entirely on in-course assignments, which may be essays, projects or solutions to set problems, but normally your overall mark will be made up of a mixture of marks from coursework and invigilated exams. So, for at least a part of your assessment, you'll be performing alone under a certain amount of time pressure.

brilliant tip

There's never any excuse for going into an exam without knowing what format it will have. Check on what to expect. Look at past papers and ask lecturers to confirm that the same system is still operating.

Problem-based learning (PBL)

This is when you're asked to investigate a specific problem, usually related to a real-life professional situation, which may be open-ended. In other words, there's not necessarily a 'right' answer to it. It may be part of a teamwork exercise in which you have to consider the problem, research the underlying theory and practice that might lead to a response, and arrive at a practical solution. The work may be group- and peer-assessed and the focus will be not only on the solution you reach but also on the way you get there. In other words, the process is often at least as important as the product.

Marking criteria

Normally, the person who marks your papers is the one who's given the lectures, tutorials or practical classes on the topics that are being assessed. But classes are getting bigger and there may be alternative systems in place in which the marking:

- is spread out among several tutors
- is automated, especially in multiple choice papers
- may take the form of peer assessment, above all where teamwork is involved.

Your institution will publish details of assessment scales, usually in handbooks and/or on websites, which will often link the marks to degree classifications. These are the same in nearly all universities. The grades are:

- first class (a 'first')
- upper second class (a two-one or 2:1)
- lower second class (a two-two or 2:2)
- third class (a 'third')
- unclassified.

(Note: some universities don't divide the second class into upper and lower bands.)

Sometimes these classifications will take into account all the grades you've been given during your university career; sometimes just those in junior and senior honours years; and for most, only the grades given in the finals. So it's clear that the finals are very important, especially as you get only one shot at them.

These are all reasons why you should follow the advice we keep repeating to find out which system applies in your university, what the different marks 'mean' and how they translate into degree bands.

The marking's rarely in the hands of a single assessor. Universities use several systems to uphold standards and make sure the marking's fair:

- There are explicit marking schemes which give different aspects of your answer a specific proportion of the total.

- Papers may be marked by two or three different people and, if their grades don't coincide, the answer may be scrutinised more closely, possibly by an external examiner.

- Papers are usually marked anonymously, so the marker doesn't know whose answer he's grading.

- An external marker confirms the overall standard and may inspect some papers, especially those which are on the borderline between honours grades or on the pass/fail boundary.

Peer assessment

This is where the members of a study team are asked to mark each other's performance. It's quite a complex process and may look at the effort you've put in, how you've behaved in the team role assigned to you, your contribution to the final outcome and the various social and communication skills you've shown. Marking your peers in this way can be tricky, but you'll get clear guidance on how to go about it.

External examiners and assessors

As their title suggests, external examiners are from other institutions. They oversee marking in specific papers and the idea is that they check that standards are being maintained between universities and that the assessment is fair. They see and comment on the question papers in advance and generally look closely at a selection of written papers and project work. For finals, they may interview students in an oral, to make sure that they do have the level of knowledge that their answers suggest. They may also use orals to assess borderline cases.

External examiners are usually academics who are experts in their field and experienced in examining. Sometimes, though, if the exams are professional qualifications, they may be appointed by an accreditation body.

Modules and progression

There are several reasons why universities are tending more towards modular systems of study:

- They allow greater flexibility when choosing subjects.
- They can cater for students who want to study different degree paths.
- They make it easier for students to transfer between courses and institutions.
- They break up studies into 'bite-sized' elements and allow exams to be spread more evenly over the academic year.

There are disadvantages, however. They can, for example, tend to encourage students to avoid difficult subjects or, once a subject has been assessed, forget all about it. If you're in a modular system, be aware of these dangers.

Assessment can take the form of a blend of formal exams and in-course assessment. If you fail the overall assessment, you may be asked to do a resit or submit new or revised coursework. In some subjects, borderline cases get an extra oral exam. Resits are usually held at the end of the summer break and the result is based solely on your performance in those exams.

At the end of each academic year, and after any resits, you'll have to have met certain progression criteria in order to move to the next level of study – they're normally published in course handbooks. If you don't make it, you may need to resit the whole year or even leave the university. Sometimes you may be asked to study specific modules again in addition to the normal quota for your next year of study.

Length of courses

Depending on entry qualifications and/or experience, students may join university at different levels. There are also several different awards which they may get when they leave – certificates, diplomas and ordinary degrees. Most students, though, enter at first-year level and study for an honours degree. This involves three years of study in England, Wales and Northern Ireland, and four in Scotland. Some universities operate a junior honours year, which means you're accepted into an honours stream at an earlier stage and may have special module options.

brilliant tip

You'll normally get credit for any years of study you carry out abroad or in work placement. Universities have their own schemes for organising this. It includes participation in European Community schemes such as ERASMUS, details of which you can find at http://ec.europa.eu/education/index_en.htm.

Complaints and appeals

There are secure checks and balances to make sure that examination systems are fair. But situations can arise where students feel their assessment is incorrect or unfair, and so every university has a complaints and appeals procedure. It normally starts with an appeal to the course leader; then, if it's unresolved, it goes to the head of the school or department and up through the system. It can go all the way to scrutiny by an external ombudsman. You'll find details of how it works at your university on its website.

There are various reasons why a student's studies may be terminated. Usually it's because he failed to attend the required number of classes or didn't reach the necessary standards for progression. It may also be for disciplinary reasons, for example if he's guilty of plagiarism. But there's still a chance to appeal. He'll have to produce evidence of any extenuating circumstances, such as medical certificates, or notes from support service personnel. He may also ask his tutor to support his application if the tutor is aware of the details of his personal situation.

Getting the information you need

As we said, there's no excuse for going into an exam unprepared and unaware of the format. So make it your business to get a clear idea of what's expected of you. Ask senior students about how it all works. They may pass on some useful tips. Find out where essential information is recorded – maybe in handbooks or web-based resources. And if there's any aspect of the assessment system you don't understand, ask for help.

If you have a disability, tell your institution about it. You may get special concessions in exams, for example using a scribe, being allowed extra time, or having question papers printed in large print. They can all be organised, but they take time, so make sure arrangements are in place well before the exam date. Contact your department and disability support service for guidance.

What next?

We've kept on stressing ...

... the need to get properly informed of what's expected of you. Specifically this means you should find out about:

- the aims of your course and degree
- its learning objectives or outcomes
- the format of assessments and the balance between in-course and final exam elements
- exam dates and times
- assessment or marking criteria
- the grading scheme
- how many marks are given for each of the exam components
- the criteria for progression
- how past exam papers were constructed.

They're all important elements in helping you to decide on your revision or exam strategies.

🔎 brilliant recap

The basic principles.

Forms of assessment.

Marking criteria.

External assessors.

Modules and progression.

Complaints and appeals procedures.

37 Getting your mind and body ready for exams

To perform at your best in exams and assessments, as with anything else, you need to feel and be fit. If you're tired, sluggish or hungover, you're operating at less than your full potential. There's a clear link between a healthy mind and a healthy body, so it's not just your mental ability you need to keep fresh – it's your physical condition, too. Without wishing to turn this book into a fitness manual, we'll nevertheless look at some basic common sense with regard to getting yourself ready for exams.

Getting fit for exams

Most people in most walks of life would like to be fitter than they are and some of them try to do something about it by jogging, swimming, cycling or squeezing into leotards and going to the gym. Students, for the most part, do have youth on their side, but there are factors relating to university life that may not be conducive to maintaining peak fitness.

Well-being, health and nutrition

If you want to be professional when it comes to your exams, you may need to adapt the way you live to eliminate some of the activities and habits that interfere with a healthy lifestyle, such as late nights, fast food, irregular mealtimes and excess of any sort. We're not suggesting you become a health-freak hermit, but think about things that may be having negative effects on you. Try using this checklist:

- Make sure that you're getting enough sleep and that the times you're awake coincide with the times you need to be working, particularly when it comes to exams.

- Cut out or cut down on any chemical stuff which may interfere with your mental capacity. The main one is probably alcohol, which is a known depressant. There's also nicotine, some prescription drugs and most non-prescription drugs.

- The same applies to stimulants, such as caffeine. It's in tea, coffee, Red Bull and Coke-like drinks, and it may give you a temporary boost, but there's a corresponding dip and it may also disturb your sleep pattern.

- Drink plenty of water. If you don't, it'll affect your ability to concentrate and learn.

- Know how and when to relax. By that we mean taking exercise, watching a film, playing games – all the usual things. You can't give them too much time when exams are close, but it's still important to escape into them now and then, to freshen up your perspectives and give you a break from the constant concentration of your studies.

Eat well

Your brain needs a good supply of energy and essential nutrients, so make sure you eat well. Don't miss breakfast (because you went to bed late, had a lie-in and are now late for a lecture). It's good to start the day by taking energy on board. After that, it's better to have frequent, light snacks because large meals slow down your metabolism and mental activity, and you feel sleepy and lethargic. If this is a familiar feeling for you, steer clear of fatty foods; more complex carbohydrates like starch provide sugars which are released more slowly.

If you feel unwell in the run-up to exams, visit your doctor or the university health service. It's not just for a diagnosis and treatment but also, if you perform badly, you'll be able to get the necessary documents to explain why.

↗ brilliant dos and don'ts

DO ...

... keep mentally agile with puzzles, quizzes, sums, examples and reading.

... increase your stamina by working for longer periods.

... get fitter.

... eat well.

... synchronise your body clock with 'exam time'.

... clean away clutter and start with a clear desk.

... sleep well.

... revise actively, not passively, in a way that suits your learning style.

DON'T ...

... abuse alcohol or other drugs that may affect your mental capacity.

... be distracted by less important things such as TV or socialising.

... study so much that it interferes with your sleep.

... avoid important study areas just because you don't like them.

... avoid active forms of revision by simply sitting reading your notes.

... do vague revision that's not in tune with learning objectives.

Physical exercise

Extended exam schedules can be physically as well as mentally exhausting, and regular exercise helps to improve your stamina. Aerobic exercise is a great way to relax mentally, reduce stress and help you sleep better. Non-aerobic and meditation workouts such as yoga, pilates and tai chi can also help you to relax.

There's a more direct benefit as well because your brain needs a surprising amount of oxygen and energy to function well and exercise improves the blood supply to it. So try to do some physical activity on most revision days, even if it's only a walk or swim. It's simple, basic, but it'll help to wake you up.

Mental exercise

You might think that there's no need to exercise your brain for exams because it's already working flat out. In a way you're right. Just as with muscles, the more it works, the better prepared it is for future effort, and revision itself is an excellent workout. But there are also times when it needs to relax and that's when it's useful to think about something completely different.

Physical activities and games can help, since they force you to think about hitting or kicking the ball, teamwork, game strategies and all the other associated mental demands. You also need to relax it properly by establishing a good sleep pattern. Of course, with the stress of exams looming, sleep may not be so easy. If you do have problems getting to sleep, think about how to resolve them. If you get up earlier, for example, you'll be more tired at the end of the evening. If you're lying in bed trying hard to sleep and not succeeding, get up and do something useful until you feel tired, or try focusing on positive things rather than worries and other negatives. And don't eat and drink just before you go to bed.

brilliant tip

Exercise your mind by:

- doing puzzles like crosswords and Sudoku
- playing computer games (but not for hours and hours)
- taking part in TV and pub quizzes
- reading for leisure.

Relax your mind by:

- shutting your eyes and breathing slowly and deeply for two or three minutes
- watching films or TV soaps
- taking a brief walk or swim
- having a bath, jacuzzi or sauna.

Don't overdo these, though. Ideally, you should timetable them into your schedule so that they don't interfere with your revision.

Preparing for revision

To revise effectively, you need to know what exactly you're trying to accomplish, so try dividing revision and sitting the exam into components and look at what you need to achieve at each stage. Basically it's a case of managing information, in other words, the facts and understanding you've gained during your course. There are three main elements in the process:

- information gathering
- information processing
- information retrieval and delivery.

Information gathering

Make sure that you have copies of everything you need close to hand and that it's well organised so that you won't waste time looking for things.

- Have you got all the lecture notes? If not, download or copy them.
- File your notes in sequence.
- Buy or borrow the recommended textbooks, or look them up in your library catalogue and reserve them if they're on limited access.
- Gather together all other materials that might be relevant, such as completed coursework with feedback.
- Bookmark any online resources that you might want to consult.

- Get copies of past papers and model answers.
- Look in your course handbook for guidance notes on the exam and its format.

brilliant tip

Don't let this gathering phase take up too much of your revision time. Like a lot of other things, it can be a displacement activity as you convince yourself you're working.

Information processing

This means analysing and manipulating the material you've gathered with the learning objectives and past exam papers in mind. Don't just read through the written material; do something active to help you to memorise it. At university it's not just a question of collecting information and memorising a bunch of facts from lectures and other source material – you have to be able to use it. So we're back to critical thinking. Yes, you need the facts, but the crucial thing is what you do with them in response to the exam or assessment instruction.

brilliant tip

Get a clear idea of the sorts of question that will be asked and how deeply you'll be expected to deal with the material by studying the learning objectives or outcomes and past exam papers. You can then make your revision active by reducing or distilling your notes and tailoring them to what's required.

Information retrieval and delivery

This is a fancy name for the final phase, which will happen when you sit in the exam hall and use the results of the gathering and processing to answer the specific questions that have been set.

brilliant tip

Use the feedback you got on previous exam and assessment performances to focus on and improve any 'weak' points, especially those which seem to recur quite frequently.

The value of positive thinking

The exams are coming. You're sitting surrounded by reading material, notes, books, mountains of facts, theories and ideas. And you start feeling that there's just too much to do and too little time to do it in. If you give in to that, you're at the start of a negative spiral where you'll begin to think it's not worth trying because you've already failed. It's essential that you resist that. It's positive thinking that gets results. So, if you do feel those negative pulses, try to shake them off:

- Make a start somehow or other. Don't put it off. Once you get into the material, your interest in the subject will take over. Because you've worked at it, you understand it and you're moulding it into the shapes you want.

- Break bigger topics into smaller chunks. It makes it much easier to get the feeling that you're making progress. And you are.

- Mark off what you've completed in your revision timetable. Each tick will feel satisfying and, after a few sessions, you'll have visual proof that you're making good progress.

- Link up with someone else studying the same subject and try to encourage each other. Ask each other questions or work together on things you both find difficult. You'll both begin to feel more in control of the material. And if you still find it hard, you can go together to speak with your lecturer or tutor about it.

- Think about the future, your degree, the type of job you hope to get. Then you'll see how each study session is one small step towards achieving it all.

Just before you go into the exam hall, you need to get yourself totally focused and positive. Yes, it's nice to meet up with fellow students and chat about how you're all feeling and speculate about what questions may crop up. But it'll probably just increase your nervousness. It's best to find somewhere nearby where you can collect your thoughts quietly and think only of the exam.

- Remind yourself of your exam strategy and how you plan to tackle this particular paper.
- Go over how you intend to approach the questions and structure your answers.
- Think about important facts or formulae.
- Maybe plan what you're going to do when all your exams are finished and remind yourself that this particular exam will soon be over.
- Tell yourself how determined you are to succeed and how you aim to squeeze every mark possible out of your brain by working quickly and effectively for every second of the exam and keeping your answers sharp and relevant.

Remember the basics

Eat healthily, with not too many or too few calories and plenty of fruit and vegetables. Make time for pleasure and relaxation. If all you do is study, it won't necessarily mean you get more work done. Listen to music, read a novel, play a game, indulge yourself in a favourite activity – it'll make you feel good, confident and ready. If you're feeling drowsy or finding it hard to concentrate, go for a quick walk. It'll give you a change of scene and wake you up.

What next?

Get rid of …

… all negative thoughts. Forget about past failures or errors; this time things will be different because you've taken on board the feedback they provoked.

Try to become more aware of time ...

... by estimating how long you think has passed in a certain period. What if you think it's 10 minutes but it's actually 20? If your estimation's a long way out, it might influence your time management during the exam.

Practise writing ...

... against the clock. Work out how long you'd have to answer one question in the exam and give yourself exactly that period to write a practice answer. It'll give you a better idea of how much you can write in the time. Also, it will help you to refine your strategies to produce the best answer you can. You might realise, for example, that you need to make your introduction shorter so that you have more time for building your analysis or argument.

 recap

Getting fit for exams.

Eating well.

Physical and mental exercise.

Preparing for revision by gathering and processing information.

Positive thinking.

---

38 Revising and active learning

As exam dates draw near they seem to start rushing towards you and you begin feeling you just don't have time to do all you need to do. The best way to avoid that is to plan well ahead. Get all your activities organised to make sure that you use the time well and walk into the exam having covered all the ground you wanted to.

Getting organised for exam study

Creating a revision timetable has several bonuses. It improves your time management and also helps you to keep a balance between subjects, topics and other activities. It'll help to keep you on track with your studies, but it'll also motivate you and give you a good feeling as you tick off each topic. It'll stop you spending too much time on subjects you like at the expense of those you don't. And it'll factor in some time for relaxation and thereby keep you fresh and able to focus.

Setting up a timetable

Create a blank timetable …

… with the days of the week along the top and the breakdown of each day into segments on the left. The segments might be Morning, Lunch, Afternoon, Evening meal, Evening. You can sub-divide them to create two or more morning, afternoon and/or evening sessions. The way you break it down is up to you, but don't try to cram too many different work sessions into a single slot – it'll be counter-productive. If you make sessions too long, you may get bored with the subject and lose concentration; too short and there won't be time to make decent progress.

Fix your start …

… and end dates, i.e. the date you intend to begin revising and the precise dates of your exams. Print or photocopy enough copies of the blank time-table to cover each week of this period and write in the two dates.

Start filling in …

… the timetable by first of all entering your essential non-study commit-ments – your job, shopping, cooking, travelling, sports and other important social or family duties. Note that we say 'essential' because, during the revision period, you should try to keep them to a minimum. You can make up for it after the exams.

brilliant tip

Filling in a timetable is the perfect opportunity for procrastination. Don't be tempted. Make it quick, functional and straightforward. It's not a work of art – it's a revision tool.

Now decide …

… how many study sessions you want to put in each day and week. Work out what that adds up to in total and decide when they'll be. For example, if you work best early in the day, it might be an idea to get as many of your study periods as possible in your morning slots.

The next stage …

… is to decide which subjects or topics go into which slots. Do this in two stages: first in a broad way by, for example, dividing the total time avail-able by the number of modules you need to cover; then in more detail by dividing the time you've given to each module by the number of individual topics within it.

Think about it …

… and don't just put the resultant topics anywhere. You may want to go into a topic a bit more deeply, so it may need a whole day, or you may want to keep yourself fresh by breaking up a day between different topics to create a bit of variety. As you're doing this, work your way backwards from the exam date – it'll make sure you concentrate on the various subjects just before the date of the paper that's devoted to them.

Keep a balance …

… between topics or subjects. Give more time to 'difficult' ones than to 'easier' ones. Maybe it would be an idea to follow subjects you dislike with ones you like. And when you've done all this, if you don't think there's enough time to do the amount of work you need, maybe you should find some more slots from somewhere and use them.

Be realistic …

… because you can't work continuously if you want to study effectively. If you spend ages revising without taking a break, your concentration will waver and you won't retain what you're reading. The more tired you get, the worse it'll be.

Take plenty of breaks …

… to relax, preferably by doing something physical. If you like, you could organise things so that, when you finish a particular task, you give yourself a reward, such as watching a favourite TV programme or going out with friends. But remember that rewards are what they say they are, i.e. things you get only if you actually achieve your goals.

brilliant tip

As you finish each session, mark it off on the timetable with a highlighter. It'll show you how much you've done and give you a sense of achievement. But note: just sitting with the highlighter poised waiting for the clock to reach the relevant time is *not* making good use of your time.

Leave some of the slots …

… in your timetable empty to allow for unforeseen problems or changes in your plans. Your timetable needs to be flexible. You may lose time at some point because something crops up which you have to deal with; if you've left some slots free, you can use them to catch up.

Near the exam …

… ease back on your revision load if you can. You want to avoid last-minute panics and you want to be fresh for the actual exams.

Studying effectively

This doesn't just mean spending ages doing something. Get yourself organised and use techniques which make the material stick.

Right from the start …

… make sure you've got all the materials you need and they're where you can find them quickly. If you missed a lecture, ask a friend for copies of his notes or download copies of summaries, overheads or slideshows and spend time looking through them to make up for the fact that you weren't at the lecture. If you don't have a particular textbook, go to the library as early as possible to reserve it. But note – this isn't revision, it's preparing for revision, so don't let it take too much time.

Make the timetable …

… your highest priority if other demands start clashing with it. That doesn't mean you're a slave to it but it's obviously an investment in your future so it should be more important than, for example, going out for a drink. And be flexible. If you're really making progress with a topic, stick with it rather than change to another.

Watch out for …

… when you're losing concentration. Take a short break if your mind's wandering or you're reading without taking things in. People who know usually say that 20 minutes is about the limit you can stay fully concentrated.

Take several ...

... short breaks (say five minutes each) during each hour of revision and a longer one every few hours.

Use active learning techniques ...

... to make your revision as interesting as possible. If all you do is sit reading and re-reading your lecture notes and/or notes on books, you're not going to retain it as well and you certainly won't be using your critical thinking skills as you should be.

Keep your revision focused

- If you can work out, or find out, how the exam will be weighted towards different topics, organise your revision time to reflect that bias.

- Use lists to keep track of your progress. As you work, make an inventory of things such as topics you still need to cover or definitions you need to learn. As you complete each job and cross it out, you'll get that familiar sense of achievement and renewed confidence.

- Keep testing yourself. The only way you'll know whether you've absorbed and memorised something is to use techniques such as writing what you think you've learned on a blank sheet of paper. Don't leave it until the exam to find out.

Understanding through active learning

The way to understand and remember things so that you can recall them during exams is to use active learning. That means thinking through concepts, ideas and processes, and using techniques to help you memorise things effectively.

Rote learning

If you've got a photographic memory, you're lucky: you can just read course material and remember it. For the rest of us, just reading is not an efficient or effective way to remember and understand things. Experience and research show that you'll remember things better if you do something with the material. That's active learning. On top of helping you to remember, it sometimes reveals flaws in your understanding that aren't obvious when you're simply reading the material. We'll run through some of the many approaches to active learning for you to choose some that suit you or that you can adapt to fit your needs and circumstances.

Basic approaches

'Distilling' or 'chunking' lecture notes

Try reducing your lecture notes to a series of headings and key points. Go through them a few times and gradually turn pages and pages into a few short sentences or even single words. Another way of doing this is to reorganise them as a grid, with the topics listed down the left-hand side and their various aspects along the top. Both these techniques force you not just to read your notes but to analyse them and select what's important and/or relevant – all of which increases your understanding. And the very act of writing out the material seems to help place it in a 'map' in your brain and makes it easier to remember.

Answering past papers

Looking at past exam papers lets you see what sorts of questions are normally asked. One slight problem is that just looking at them doesn't give you an idea of how deeply you need to go into them. If that isn't obvious, ask your subject tutors. Once you're confident that you understand what's needed, you can try different active approaches:

- The weakest is just thinking through an answer in your head. It makes you focus on the question but doesn't force you to be specific or logical. It's a bit vague.

- Better than that is to write out the plan of your answer. With this you actually have to organise points in sequence and build a coherent structure.

- Best of all is to pretend you're actually sitting an exam. Choose a question, give yourself the same time that you'd have in a real exam and write a full answer. If you can then discuss your answer (or plan) with a subject tutor or fellow students, you'd really be fixing the topic and your technique in your mind.

With all these, though, remember to make them part of your timetabling.

 **tip**

Mock exams help you to practise writing against the clock. They're time-consuming, but they do show you how quickly you have to work and how much you'll need to condense ideas to get them across in the time allowed. They also give you practice in writing quickly and neatly by hand. It's a skill that's being lost because so many people prefer using personal computers.

Preparing to learn and memorise

Understanding concepts, memorising lots of facts, tackling obscure jargon – they're all hard work, especially if it's a subject you don't much like or you find hard. Nonetheless, you need to absorb the material, so make sure you're mentally prepared and that your working environment is set up in the right way.

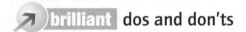 **dos and don'ts**

DO ...

... be ready to learn; set aside all other thoughts which may preoccupy you.

... make sure your desk space allows you to focus on the work in hand. Declutter it. Or, if you need to spread out your papers, take them to a library or a similar place, where there's more space.

... get an overview of what you have to learn. If you see the bigger picture, it's easier to fit the component parts into it.

... visualise and associate to learn. Basically, this involves knowing how many items you need to remember. It could also include recalling a doodle on the page of your notes beside the relevant text. And there are more complex methods, such as associating facts with a familiar journey or place.

DON'T ...

... read material aimlessly in the hope that it'll sink in. Tell yourself that you really want to learn. It'll make your focus more intensive and, if you're intending and expecting to learn, you will.

... try to learn too much. Condense the material into lists or smaller chunks. Split large chunks of information into smaller bits.

... just assume that you've learned the material – keep testing yourself.

brilliant tip

If something's bugging you and spoiling your concentration, try this: write all your problems and issues down on a piece of paper, and then put it to one side. Tell yourself that you'll deal with it all later, but for the moment you'll focus on your studying. It sounds weird, but it works for some. And what have you got to lose?

Make your notes memorable. Use coloured pens and highlighters, but beware of over-use of emphasis or purposeless highlighting – that is, when you highlight almost everything or don't really know why you've high-lighted something. Use concept or mind maps. These help to condense your knowledge of a particular topic. If you include drawings you may find that such image-based notes make recall easier.

Aspects of active learning

● Try talking about your topic to another person rather than writing about it. Talk to yourself if necessary. Explaining something out loud is a good way of checking whether you really understand it.

- Prepare a series of revision sheets. Write details for each topic on a single piece of paper, perhaps as a numbered list. If there's room, use them as wall posters. Pinning them up together may help you visualise the overall subject area. You could use sticky notes in the same way.

- Make up your own exam paper. It's useful to try thinking like an examiner. You can invent your own questions and think about how you'd answer them only if you have a good understanding of the material.

- Memorise definitions. They can be a useful starting point for lots of exam answers.

- Make up lists of key phrases and facts (for example, dates and events) associated with particular topics. Test yourself repeatedly on these, or get a friend to do this.

What next?

Create ...

... your study timetable.

As you finish each section of revision ...

... use questions from past papers to test yourself on how well you've grasped the topic involved. Make it a mock exam. You don't have to write a full answer – an outline plan will do.

Find a study buddy ...

... and compare lecture notes and ideas for questions that might come up in the exams. Together, try out some of the active learning approaches and tips.

Think about ...

... where you usually study. Is it working well for you? Could you improve it? Should you try somewhere else? If so, what's available?

brilliant recap

Setting up an exam timetable.

The various stages.

Active learning.

The basic approaches.

Learning and memorising.

39 Training yourself to remember information

In an exam you don't want to waste time trying to remember facts; it would be better spent using the higher-level skills of analysis, evaluation and critical thinking which we keep on stressing. In other words, your effort should go into using your knowledge rather than trying to recall it. So anything that helps you to improve your memory will pay dividends.

Tools and strategies for remembering information and ideas

Exam questions won't always be what you expected and you may find that you need to apply your knowledge in a way you hadn't anticipated. That's yet another reason for going into an exam feeling confident that you can quickly call up the facts and basics you need to begin building your answer. That confidence will also help to suppress the rush of panic that sometimes occurs when you feel your mind's a blank. Fortunately, there are some tricks which can help you to remember things if you're not one of the lucky few with a photographic memory.

Where memory begins

We called them 'tricks', but these techniques are built on solid foundations and it's important to realise that you need to start working on memorising very early on in your revision. In fact, you need to be able to recognise what it is that you need to remember before you can make the tricks work for you. And that, too, is part of the analytical, learning process.

So the first step is to identify the content of your course, the key themes and concepts of the subject that have been covered in lectures, tutorials, practicals and seminars as well as the topics you've dealt with in assignments. This is what we called earlier 'information gathering'. This is the material you have to synthesise into organised revision notes which carry not only the facts but also your deeper understanding of them – 'information processing'. That gives you all the material you need for revision in a manageable form and you're now ready to use active learning strategies to absorb and retain it ready for 'information retrieval' in the exam.

brilliant tip

In Chapter 7 we discussed different types of learning personality. It would help to remind yourself now of what type of learner you are because different memory techniques suit different personality types:

- Sensory or visual learners normally prefer practical approaches using images.

- Active (extrovert) learners prefer using physical activity such as manipulating materials.

- Intuitive (introvert) learners prefer theoretical and analytical approaches to get at underlying meanings.

- Verbal learners prefer word-based tactics.

Organising notes into memorable formats

As we've said, you need not only the basic material but also the ability to interpret it and show that you understand its deeper significance and can use it in different contexts. So your revision notes mustn't just be bundles of facts; they must also reflect your understanding of the way the course and the subject fit together. Let's look, then, at some of the ways you can organise your notes to achieve this.

Creating lists

The most basic technique of all is to reduce your notes to a series of headings. If you do it in several phases it helps to make the knowledge stick and results in an overview of your subject that gives you both the individual packets of knowledge and the broader context in which they feature. It can help if you number the lists, too. This method works particularly well if your learning preference is verbal–linguistic.

Making time lines

You can use a time line to plot the progress of events, a procedure or a development. As the name suggests, you simply draw a line – horizontal or vertical – and have little boxes along it noting individual events and the sequence in which they occur. Once again, this gives you both events and their overall context. It's especially useful where a significant series of events has been mentioned over the course of several lectures.

Carrying out SWOT analyses

SWOT stands for strengths, weaknesses, opportunities and threats. Under each of the headings you have to list aspects of a situation, argument, case study or whatever the subject involves. You can see how having to decide what notes to put under each heading forces you to get to grips with the material and understand it better. If you arrange the notes in a 2 × 2 grid, with strengths and weaknesses in the top two and opportunities and threats in the bottom two, it'll give you a quick visual idea of the balance of arguments. It's another active learning technique.

Organising complex information in grids

We've seen already how useful grids are for organising notes. They force you to take your haphazard jottings and group them under common headings or in opposing sides of a debate. They're particularly useful for questions where you're asked to compare and contrast aspects of a problem. Put the various possible viewpoints along the top and the interested parties down the side and group the notes accordingly.

Sketching concept maps

Another way of organising chunks of information which we've talked about is variously called a concept map, scatter diagram, spray diagram or mind map. This is useful for exams because if you retain a clear idea of the map, you can reproduce it quickly, almost automatically, and leave more time for the analysis the question requires. The map is made by writing the topic in the centre, and then drawing spokes radiating from it to various different aspects. Each of these aspects then has other lines radiating from it with connected ideas. If you also use highlighters, shadings or shapes to refine it, you can make the image even easier to remember.

Drawing diagrams

Diagrams can be useful for showing hierarchies, processes or relationships. They can take many forms, depending on the topic – they may be a set of linked or opposed ideas, a flow plan or anything which helps people with a visual type of learning preference. You may even want to include them in an answer. If you do, though, be careful to make sure that it makes sense to others, not just to you. You still need to show that you understand how and why all these links and flows work.

Setting up posters or Post-it® notes

Maybe you prefer another technique we've already mentioned – that of creating an area of posters or sticky Post-it® notes on a wall in your hallway, bedroom, kitchen or bathroom to help fix the information in your memory. If your mind goes blank in the exam, you can fill the gap simply by thinking back to the pattern of the notes on the wall.

brilliant tip

Don't underestimate the effectiveness of colour, different types of writing/printing, underlining, bold type, layout, arrows and other symbols. They really can help to group concepts and ideas in a way that makes them easier to recall.

Tricks for recalling your notes

So that's all the preparation done and you've chosen the note-taking methods that suit you; now you need to memorise the material ready for retrieval and processing in the exam. The fact that you've been using active learning to create the notes will already have made it all more familiar to you, but there are tricks which can help. You may need to practise some of them beforehand, but that too will keep up the reinforcement process.

 brilliant definition

Mnemonic – a memory aid involving a sequence of letters or associations. The classic example is 'Richard Of York Goes Battling In Vain' to remember the colour sequence in the spectrum (or rainbow): Red, Orange, Yellow, Green, Blue, Indigo, Violet.

Nonsense words

This is one type of mnemonic. You make up a word by using the initial letters of the list of items you need to remember. It's called an acronym. So, faced with the task of remembering the first line of the periodic table (hydrogen, helium, lithium, beryllium, boron, carbon, nitrogen, oxygen and fluorine), some people choose the unwieldy acronym HHeLiBeBCNOF, while others find it easier to think 'Healthy Herbert Lives Beside Boring Countryside Near Open Fields'.

Rhymes

Once again, an example illustrates the technique best: 'Thirty days hath September, April, June and November ...' You don't have to be a poet to make up your own snatch of doggerel or a lyric you sing to some simple tune.

Spelling tricks

For some of us, there are words we constantly misspell. If these words are important in our particular field, it gives a bad impression of our competence and professionalism. If this is a problem for you, you'll need to design your own tips to help you.

▶ brilliant example

Donnie is an engineer. Among other words which always trip him up, he has trouble separating 'storeys' (the different levels of a building) from 'stories' (tales). So he looks at the words, realises that storeys contains the word store, and pictures department stores with various levels.

Hannah is studying accountancy. She has a blind spot which always makes her confuse 'debit' and 'debt'. In the end she decides that debit rhymes with credit (well, more or less) so she's able to remember which is which.

Journey 'pegs'

This technique uses a fairly long journey with which you're reasonably familiar. First you need to decide how many points you need to remember, and then think of the same number of places as you travel along the route. Relate each of the things you need to remember to one of the staging posts – so your front door is fact one, the bus stop fact two, the supermarket you ride past is fact three and so on. In other words, you've 'pegged' the facts onto your journey.

Special place 'pegs'

In a variation of the journey approach you imagine a familiar room, picture or view and pick items of furniture in the room or features in the picture or view on which to peg your facts. In the exam, you simply see the room, picture or view in your mind's eye and recall the items pegged around it. You can even create a story around the image to bring the various elements together. If we take the example of entering your chosen room, you go in and switch on the lamp (West Germany), and then you switch on the telly (France). You put your mug (Italy) on the coffee table (Belgium), arrange a cushion (the Netherlands) on the sofa (Luxembourg) and sit down. A simple story helps you to recall the six members of the original European Economic Community.

Story 'pegs'

You can extend the story technique further, perhaps by basing it on a familiar tale. 'The three little pigs', for example, might be useful to reflect Napoleon's victorious and ultimately disastrous attempt to colonise Europe – the house of straw (Iberian Peninsula), the house of wood (Italy) and the house of bricks (Russia). You can also create your own and the more ridiculous, violent or colourful they are, the better they work. It's a question of inventing a sequence of events that's meaningful to you and that has all your essential pieces of material pegged to it for easy recall.

brilliant tip

Not everyone is convinced by pegging. It does take time and, in a way, gives you even more to remember (the story and the facts). It's up to you to decide whether it works in your case. If you've tried other things in the past and they haven't worked, this may be the answer.

Numbered lists

Lists are another example of a basic tool and numbering them can be especially helpful, particularly when their contents form a sequence or you know that you have a definite number of items to remember. If you break up larger lists into main points and sub-sections and indent the latter, that also gives visual clues that can help you to recall the image of the page and the list layout.

Practising and reviewing

There's no substitute for going over the material and/or your memory aids again and again and again. So decide which of these strategies suits you and practise them over and over. If it's mnemonics, you should be able to recite them without thinking about it. If it's pegging, make the journey or view the room regularly and make sure you make all the associations.

Part of your practising should also include recalling and writing quickly. In term time you probably don't have to remember things and write them down quickly, but that's a skill you need to have when you're answering questions against the clock in an exam. So don't just dream up your various memory cues, try scribbling them down quickly: it'll help you remember them and it'll improve your writing speed.

Review what you've learned. Don't just assume or hope that the facts and ideas have stuck in your head, check to see whether they have – and do it regularly. If you find they haven't stuck, start again. Repetition reconfirms and reinforces the knowledge. Try the following sequence (you can use it for diagrams as well as lists):

1   As you're reading the material, write it out in list form, focusing fully on each point, trying hard to remember it. Note the number of items on the list.

2   Turn over the list, close your textbook, and hide your lecture notes and any other clues about the material.

3   Immediately, rewrite the list. If you can't remember everything, go back to point (1) and start again until you can rewrite the list completely.

4   Now go and do something else for five minutes, and then try to rewrite the list (again without clues). If you can't remember everything, go back to point (1) again.

5   Then do something else for an hour and try again. If the list's incomplete, go back to point (1).

6   Finally, after 24 hours, try again and, if there are gaps … yes, go back to point (1).

What next?

Start looking over your notes …

… to decide what memory tricks and strategies might suit you. Look for acronyms, mnemonics, rhymes, journeys, stories.

Discuss these strategies ...

... with your friends. They may have developed other forms or variations and you may find a strategy that's particularly apt for your own subject.

 **recap**

Tools and strategies for remembering information and ideas.

How to organise notes into memorable formats.

Tricks for recalling your notes.

Practising and reviewing.

40 Using all the revision resources

I t makes sense to use everything that's provided to make your preparation for exams as thorough as possible. We've spoken at length about lecture notes, books, articles and all the rest, but we've also mentioned past exam papers and other materials. Understanding what those who set the questions are looking for and how they'll be assessing you should be part of your preparation. This chapter suggests the sorts of things that are worth consulting. There may be others in your institution. Find out about all of them and make them part of your revision process.

The resources

Universities publish a great deal of useful information that can help you to improve your exam performance. As well as the direct contents of your courses and modules, there'll be learning outcomes or objectives for each module, marking criteria, past exam papers, model answers and other information on assessments.

Learning outcomes or objectives

You'll probably find these in your module handbook with details of the curriculum. They spell out what you're expected to be able to do as a result of the learning involved in each module. This is what your exams and the other forms of assessment will be testing. In other words, they're fundamental to the whole learning process, so you really should know them in order to be confident that you're doing the right things.

Sometimes, they may be general statements, but they may also be related to individual lectures. The form then might be a statement such as 'After this lecture, you should be able to …' followed by a series of bullet points. As well as outcomes, you may find aims and goals for the entire module. Whatever's provided, use it.

brilliant tip

If you look at past exam papers and match up the questions with the relevant learning outcomes and course material, it's usually easy to see how they relate to each other. But remember that learning outcomes can change over time, so if you're not sure, ask the person who organises the module. The same applies if you don't feel you can achieve a particular learning outcome. You may have misunderstood the topic or the intention behind the outcome; the important thing is to find out and get it clear in your mind.

Marking criteria

Marking or grading criteria tell you the sorts of marks different answers will get when they're assessed using the university's overall marking scheme. They'll be published in faculty or departmental handbooks or websites, because they tend to apply across many modules, but they may also be published in each module handbook.

They'll vary according to subject and discipline but the sorts of things they'll be covering include the following:

- Content: the range of ideas or information discussed and their relevance to the question actually set.
- Depth: the complexity, amount of detail and intellectual insights displayed.
- Writing style: the logic, clarity, quality and readability of the English.
- Presentation: the neatness and possibly also the structure of your work.

- Use of examples: the relevance, accuracy and detail of your examples or supporting quotations.

- Evidence of reading: the use of material from any reading around the subject you may be expected to do.

- Originality: independent thinking (backed by supporting evidence and argument) or a new synthesis of ideas. (Note: this is an area which may well carry extra weighting, especially in later years of study.)

- Analysis: interpretation of raw data or information found in original (primary) sources.

Check your department's marking criteria. If you want high marks, they'll tell you what you have to do to get them.

Using past papers

So you now know what the outcomes are; next, you need to check how they're tested and your best guides to that are past papers or sample questions. They may be on websites or VLEs, or in paper form in the library. If you can't find them, ask staff or senior students for help.

Understanding their structure

As you look at them, ask yourself:

- What form should the answers be in? Essays? Short-answer questions? Multiple choice questions? Others?

- How many questions are there? What types of question are they? How many of each type do you need to answer?

- How many marks are there for each section or each type of question?

- How long have you got?

- Is there any choice involved?

- Do you have to answer on specific topics?

Understanding their style

Once again, ask some questions:

● How much and what type of factual knowledge do you need?

● How deep an understanding of the topic do they expect?

● How much extra reading might you need to do?

● How much or how little freedom will you have to express your opinion or understanding?

● Do lecturers have consistent styles of questions?

You can see how answering all these questions should help you to design your revision and exam strategies and decide on the content of your answers.

brilliant tip

You can make your revision more efficient by linking past papers and outcomes directly. If you photocopy past papers and cut and paste all the questions into separate pages for each topic in the lecture course, it makes it easier to compare these groups of questions with the learning outcomes and what you've been taught. It'll give you a better picture of how you'll be assessed, what types of question might turn up, and what type of revision you need to do.

Model answers

University exams are more about using information to support a reasoned answer than simply regurgitating facts. So, if examples of model answers are given, read them carefully. Look at and think about the question first and jot down some ideas about how you'd answer it. Check which learning outcomes the question relates to and see how the lecturer is using it to assess them. When you've done all that, read the model answer and look at:

● the language and style you should use – the type of introduction, the use of headings and diagrams, the sort of things mentioned in the conclusion

- how deeply you should investigate the topic – the balance between description and analysis, the level of detail in any examples given, such as dates, terminology, citation of authorities and authors

- which of the different facets of the question each part of the answer addresses and how it deals with it.

Set your own questions and exams

Try writing out a few possible questions on your various subjects using the style of the ones you've seen in past papers and ask yourself how you'd set about answering them. Treat them in exactly the same way that you'd treat questions during an exam – make a plan, jot down ideas, decide how you'd link and support them. You never know: some of the questions that actually come up may be close to the ones you invented.

brilliant tip

There's a temptation to try to guess what some of the questions may be. There are several reasons why you should be very careful about doing this:

- Most examiners avoid following identifiable patterns and make sure they don't repeat questions from past papers, and so the chances of your prediction being true are low.

- You may be so confident about your guess that you fail to prepare properly for other topics.

- You may think a question resembles one you've predicted and the temptation would be to answer 'your' question and miss some subtle elements in the wording of the 'real' question.

Sit a 'mock exam'. That's when you try to answer questions or a paper under realistic exam conditions. It can help you to:

- test your knowledge of the subject and give you feedback about what you do and don't know

- get into exam-answering mode so that you can get rid of your rustiness before the proper exams start and, when that does come around, get going and start writing quickly and appropriately

- time your answers so that you don't make the mistake of missing out questions through lack of time

- practise planning and laying out an answer quickly so that you get used to thinking through your answer rapidly and checking how best to present it before you start to write

- reduce the effect of nerves so that you perform better on the day.

What next?

Take some time ...

... to link the stated marking criteria with how you think and how you study. It'll give you an idea of the depth of learning you need to show in your subject and level of study and help you to plan your revision and exam answers.

Set up a mock exam ...

... as part of your revision. It may help to do this with a study buddy doing the same subject.

- Choose a paper that you haven't studied before. (In fact, you could keep one back especially for this.)

- Find a place such as a quiet part of the library where conditions resemble those you'll experience in an actual exam.

- Sit just one question or a few, depending on how you feel.

- Either write a full answer or lay out some answers as plans rather than whole essays.

- Give yourself the appropriate amount of time to answer, whether it's a single question or the whole paper. Make it realistic.

- Afterwards, you could ask a study buddy or subject tutor for their opinion on your answer.

 **recap**

The resources available.

Learning outcomes or objectives.

Marking criteria.

Style and structure of past papers.

Model answers.

Setting your own questions and exams.

How to perform well under pressure

41

On the whole, students aren't always very good at predicting how well or how badly they've performed in an exam. This often results in surprised exclamations (of elation or despair) when they stand at a notice board looking through the results. It's as if the marking and grading was a process that was divorced from what they'd written in the exam. So understanding why some answers are marked down while others score highly is a good starting point for working out how you can improve your results.

Improving your exam performance

How you judge whether your exam performance is poor or good depends on your expectations. If you know you've prepared badly, or suffered an attack of nerves during the exam, or revised the wrong topic, you won't expect to do well and so you won't be surprised to get a lowish mark. Yet, there may be times when you feel OK about the experience but your marks turn out to be lower than you expected. There could be all sorts of reasons for it – you might have misunderstood the question, failed to spot an important part of it, or any number of other slip-ups. What you need to do is plug that gap between expectation and result, and to do that you need to know what things lose you marks.

Finding out what went wrong and how to improve

First, you need to identify your weak points. Look back over past exams – questions and answers – to see if there were obvious areas where things went wrong. Revisit the feedback on your coursework and, if you can get hold of them, read the comments on your exam scripts. If you don't understand them, try to meet with the marker and ask about them.

It's easier to improve if you know exactly where the problems are, so once you've narrowed down the areas where you're making mistakes, think about how to cut them out. We're going to identify some of the basic errors which occur quite frequently. You may spot one or more that apply to you. If you don't, and you still don't understand where you're going wrong or how to correct it, try to arrange a meeting with one or more of your tutors to get their advice and suggestions.

So what, then, are these common errors we've identified? And, if they're familiar to you, how can you stop making them?

- Perhaps the most frequent is that students don't actually answer the exact question as it's set. They may fail to recognise some specialist terms, or do something other than the instruction word requires, or maybe they deal only with some and not all aspects of what's being asked. There are many ways of overcoming these difficulties and we'll deal with them later in the chapter.

- Then there's poor time management, usually through spending too long on one question and not enough on the others. That calls for a better exam strategy.

- Some students don't give the required weight to some parts of the answer and maybe fail to recognise that one part, which may involve more complex ideas, carries more marks than another. This could be solved by creating a better essay plan.

- Perhaps the problem is connected with not providing evidence to support an answer, not giving examples or leaving out basic facts or definitions which seem so 'obvious' they're not worth including. Once again, better essay planning would help here as well as some hard thinking about the importance of providing evidence to back up your arguments.

- If it's the sort of answer that calls for illustrations in the form of diagrams, the diagrams must be relevant and their intentions must be clear.

- Answers can be incomplete or shallow when you don't know enough about the topic or you haven't looked at it in sufficient depth. This needs reflection on how to improve your revision plan and technique or a more thorough understanding of what sort of thinking is required at university.

- If your answer is illogical or badly structured, you need to plan your writing better.

- If the problem is poor English and a failure to express facts and ideas clearly, you need to work on your academic writing skills.

- Factual errors are the result of poor note-taking and inadequate revision. They may also result from poor memory, but the use of memory techniques should help to eliminate at least some of that difficulty.

- Waffling or padding is always obvious in an answer. If you add irrelevant evidence just to fill a space, that's worse than leaving it out. Make a plan and answer the question.

- Sometimes, mistakes are so obvious that students are annoyed they haven't spotted them. The way to avoid that is by reviewing and proofreading the answers conscientiously.

- Illegible handwriting can also be a problem. This is a tricky one, but you really need to try to do something about it. Maybe use a different type of pen, write more slowly and carefully or even change your style of writing.

↗ brilliant dos and don'ts

As we said, the main reason why even well-prepared students lose marks is probably that they don't answer the question. So here's a checklist of what to do and what not to do.

DO ...

... identify the instruction word and obey it.

... consider every aspect of the question.

... plan your work properly.

... explain what you understand by the question.

... keep to the point.

... make sure you answer all the elements of a multi-part question.

▶

DON'T ...

... make value judgements.

... be afraid to include seemingly basic material such as key terms and their definitions, critical dates and names.

... just focus on key phrases of the question in isolation – consider their context.

Review your answers to gain marks

It's perhaps natural to want to get out of the exam room as soon as possible, but resist the urge until you're sure you've squeezed every last mark you can out of the paper. Part of any good exam strategy is to leave enough time to review the answers so that you can pick up simple errors that could mean the difference between a pass or a fail or between degree classifications. So spend the last part of the exam looking at:

- the basics, such as numbering your answers, checking that you've answered the right number of questions, etc.

- spelling, grammar and sense. Read through the answer carefully and critically and correct any obvious errors that strike you. Check that the text makes sense and that sentences and paragraphs flow smoothly

- structure and relevance. Make sure you've really answered the question that was set and followed the instruction(s) in the title. Have you missed anything out? Are the different parts linked together well? Are your arguments consistent?

brilliant tip

If you're getting marked down, check whether you're guilty of:

- not providing enough in-depth information

- being descriptive rather than analytical. In other words, concentrating on listing facts rather than exploring deeper aspects of a topic

- failing to put a problem in context, or show that you have a wider understanding of the topic (but don't overdo this or you may not have time to focus on the topic itself)

- not giving enough evidence of reading around the subject

- looking at only one side of a topic or debate or, if you've looked at both, failing to draw a conclusion.

Discuss your concerns with staff

Exams aren't a battleground. The person who marks your work isn't your enemy. Most lecturers prefer giving good marks, but marking has to be a professional, objective exercise. When tutors see how a simple change of approach could have produced a better mark, they feel frustrated. But even though they know you know better, they can only mark what you hand in. They can't assume knowledge which you don't show them. So make your writing as professional as their marking.

How to improve your performance

Go into the exam well prepared. That doesn't just mean making sure you've memorised facts and concepts. You need to feel good, be in the right frame of mind. You need to have a plan and a positive attitude and be determined to get down to work quickly and effectively.

Do your brainstorming, and then convert it into a plan as quickly as possible. Numbering the headings in the brainstorm in the order you intend to write about them will save time.

Stay relevant all the time. As you plan your answer, keep asking yourself: Am I really answering the question? Have I covered all the necessary material? Is everything I've put in relevant?

Improving performance by study buddying

Talking things over with fellow students in and after tutorials is a valuable aspect of the learning process. Teaming up to help each other as part of a revision strategy extends the value even further. It can help with the actual business of identifying and retaining important materials, but in addition it can be reassuring and contribute to the confidence that's so much a part of good exam preparation.

Revising for exams should be a positive experience. By re-reading and reorganising your notes and books, you deepen your understanding of the subject and start bringing together different elements of your course. If you involve one or more friends who are studying the same or similar subjects, they can add another helpful dimension and perspective to the overall process.

What's the idea?

Study buddying is when two or more students agree to support each other in their learning by having joint study sessions as part of their revision timetable. It can work in many ways. They can:

- meet to work through tutorial questions, compare answers and work out the best approach

- study a chosen topic separately and then meet to quiz each other on it

- speak to each other about a topic and maybe even give a 'mini-lecture' to each other

- share resources, such as missed lecture notes, handouts, and website and textbook information

- share advice about modules that one has passed but the other hasn't

- work together on planning answers to questions on past papers

- provide psychological support and reassurance.

brilliant tip

The obvious contenders for buddying are friends from your class, members of a tutorial group or lab partners. Ask around before or after lectures or put up a request on an online discussion board. It may surprise you to see how many interested responses you get.

The advantages

The study buddy approach works very much on the principle that two or more heads are better than one and that the process of working together to tackle problems, key issues or difficult areas can help everyone involved to learn more effectively.

brilliant dos and don'ts

DO ...

... play to your strengths by helping with areas where you're stronger and learning from others where you're weaker.

... explain your understanding of a topic or aspect to your buddy. It helps to clarify it in your own mind and can help him to hear it explained by a peer rather than a tutor, maybe because the language is less formal and more 'friendly'. It's also easier to ask a friend to repeat an explanation if it's not clear enough.

... try to introduce a fun or competitive element. It can motivate people and it introduces a freshness into what can seem a fairly formal process.

DON'T ...

... spend too much time supporting others and neglecting yourself in the process.

... engage in aimless chat more than you study.

... assume that studying with someone else is an easy option to avoid the hard grind of studying alone. In fact, solo study may be a part of the study buddy process.

Working with others to improve

Arrange meetings

Agree a time, and then find somewhere you can sit and discuss your work without disturbing others. Take with you all the relevant notes, calculators, worked examples and other resources you need, such as dictionaries. There may be areas for group work or study rooms in the library, department, hall of residence or student association. A tutorial or small lecture room with whiteboards and flipcharts might be available. Ask your tutors or the departmental secretary if you can't find anywhere suitable – they may be able to help.

Set the ground rules

Agree some basic rules such as start and stop times and limiting coffee breaks to 15 minutes, and stick to what you've agreed. Working intensively for a shorter time is often better than a prolonged session where people end up chatting about other things. Also, make sure everyone involved knows that if the study buddying isn't working for them, they can walk away without fear of offending the others.

Tackle the revision

Decide on the areas of study for each session and stick to them. Write down a wish list of aims and topics at the beginning of each session and cross them off as you complete them.

Ask for help

If you don't find the answer you're looking for in a particular topic, go to your lecturer or tutor to ask for guidance. They're always pleased to know you're interested enough in their subject to be working on it and are usually happy to answer questions. You may also find it's less embarrassing or daunting to do this as a pair or a group.

brilliant tip

Different partnerships work in different ways, but you can start by trying some of these strategies:

- Work on problems separately for an agreed length of time and then get together to compare methods and answers.

- One of you uses a whiteboard or flipchart to explain a process to the other; you then reverse roles for the next topic.

- Each student makes up a 'bank' of short-answer topics by writing the question on one side of an index card and the answer on the other. Shuffle the cards together and test each other by drawing random cards from the pile.

What next?

Think about ...

... timetabling. If you suspect the main reason for a previous weak performance was lack of organisation, design a more structured revision schedule. And stick to it.

If feedback suggests ...

... that your answers lack depth but you don't fully understand how you could improve, have another look at the critical thinking processes we discussed in Chapter 14. If you're still not sure after you've read it, try to arrange a meeting with a tutor or lecturer to discuss it further. It's a very important part of the whole university experience.

Decide which of your revision topics or exam formats ...

... would suit the study buddy approach. Some material may be best tackled on your own while other topics might be right for a group approach.

↗ brilliant recap

Improving exam performance.

Finding out what went wrong and how to improve.

Review your answers.

Prepare well.

The benefits of study buddying.

How does it work?

The advantages.

How to set it up.

42 How to improve your exam technique

et's assume your revision has gone well, you're confident of the material and your understanding of it, and you're ready for the exam. The only thing left to negotiate now is time and the pressures that'll put on you. If you can come up with a strategy that makes the most effective use of the time available, you're on your way to putting in a good performance.

Devising the right tactics

An exam strategy is a plan for managing time and effort during an exam. If you find yourself rushing your answers or not managing to complete the paper, you've thrown away marks unnecessarily. Apart from that, if you know, as you go into the exam room, that you've got a clear strategy, you'll feel more confident and be able to focus on what's needed rather than worry about whether you can deliver it in time.

The information you need for a strategy

We're not just talking about a one-size-fits-all strategy. Each exam may call for a different approach, so you'll need to research its specific requirements:

- How long have you got?
- How is it sub-divided into sections and questions?
- What sorts of questions are they?
- What proportion of the marks is allocated to each section/answer?
- Are there any restrictions on answering?

You'll get the answers to these questions in course handbooks or from staff. You can also check past papers, but, as we've said, the rules may change, so find out whether the format is still the same.

How to use the information

First, let's assume we have an exam with a set of essays of a similar length or a series of short-answer questions. That's fairly easy to organise:

● Work out how long you have in minutes.

● Set aside a short time (say 5 per cent of the total) to decide which questions to answer and in what order. Allow another 5 per cent for flexibility and subtract these two amounts (10 per cent) from the total time.

● Share the time that's left between the questions to get an 'ideal' time for each answer.

● Now think about how you'll divide the time for each answer into planning, writing and review phases.

● Just before you go into the exam, memorise roughly how long you'll give each section, question and phase.

▶ brilliant example

It's a 2-hour exam (120 minutes) and you have 10 short-answer questions to answer from a list of 20. So you give 6 minutes to reading the paper, choosing questions and reviewing answers. That leaves 114, so for each question you have 11 minutes, and there are 4 minutes left over to deal with the unexpected.

A change to this model would be to review all your answers towards the end of the exam rather than reviewing each one as soon as you finish writing it. In that case, you'd need to subtract 5–10 per cent from the total before working out how much time is left for planning and writing each answer.

More complex papers

If there's a mix of question types, your strategy will have to be more complex. It'll be up to you to estimate how long each type of answer should take. You can maybe use previous experience (in mid-term/semester exams, for example). You should also take into account the proportion of marks awarded for each type of question or section. It'll also be important to decide the order in which you do the different types of question. In a paper with a multiple choice component and an essay section, for example, you may prefer to do a quick sweep through the multiple choice part first, ticking off the easy ones, then write the essays, and finally go back to the MCQs to fill in the harder ones.

brilliant tip

Always try to build a little flexibility into your strategy in case things don't turn out the way you planned them. But don't make major changes to it during the exam unless you're completely confident that it's the right thing to do and you know why you need to do it.

Strategies and people

It's not just the exam itself that dictates the type of strategy to adopt; it may also depend on what sort of person you are. Let's look at a few examples to show what we mean.

Disorganised Dora

Dora jotted down the time and place of her exam on a scrap of paper. But she's lost it. She sort of thinks she remembers when and where the exam is, though, so she goes there to see if any of her classmates are waiting to go in. The trouble is her bus is late and everyone's already inside. She rushes in, sits at a desk and realises that she's forgotten her pen. But that doesn't matter because she hasn't come to the Edwardian history exam she's supposed to be doing anyway – it's a paper on atomic physics.

Next time, Dora:

- check the details the night before
- get an earlier bus – just in case
- use a checklist to make sure you have everything you need
- speak to the invigilator to get the correct information
- get to the right place at the right time.

Nervous Nadeem

Nadeem is a naturally nervous person. On the day of his exam, it's almost unbearable. He needs to visit the toilet immediately beforehand and nearly throws up. He sits at his desk, looks at the paper and can hardly read the words on it. He forces down the panic, reads the first question, doesn't understand it. He reads the rest and doesn't understand them either. They don't seem to relate to any of his coursework. He's got no choice. He stands up and leaves.

Next time, Nadeem:

- think hard about exams well before they come along; try to find out what it is about them that makes you nervous; don't let that spiral of anxiety develop
- try to exploit the rush of nervous energy positively by brainstorming key points as soon as you sit down
- use relaxation techniques in the exam room.

Get me out of here Graham

Graham wants to be anywhere else rather than in an exam room. He speeds through his answers, hands in his paper half an hour before the end and rushes over to the union bar to wait for his friends to come out. As they talk about the exam, he realises that he missed out a chunk of one of his answers and he didn't even try anything in section B.

Next time, Graham:

- find out the format of the paper well before the exam date
- plan your time in the exam so that you use all of it profitably

- use any spare time to check your answers and make sure you've done what you're supposed to.

Patsy the perfectionist

Patsy has spent ages revising and knows the topics inside out. She turns over the exam paper and, lo and behold, there's her ideal question. She smiles and knows for certain that she'll write a perfect answer. One and a half hours later, she's putting the finishing touches to it. Just one problem – there are two more questions to answer and there's just 30 minutes left.

Next time, Patsy:

- plan your time and use it accordingly
- remind yourself that you'll get a higher mark for doing reasonably well in all the questions, rather than extremely well in just one
- practise writing answers against the clock to improve your technique.

Mindblocked Mike

Mike has prepared well for the exam. He feels OK. But when he looks at the question, his mind goes blank. There's nothing there. He can't remember anything to do with the subject material. He just sits there, feeling worse and worse, and simply wants to leave.

Next time, Mike:

- start by brainstorming a topic you know well, jot it down as a mind map, then relate it to the questions
- if you really are totally stuck, ask a departmental representative for a clue; it'll be noted, but it's better than writing nothing and it'll get you started.

Laid-back Lin

Lin's a dreamer. She can't really be bothered with the hassle of exams and all that ridiculous stress that goes with them. But she goes along. She takes ages choosing her first question and even longer thinking up an answer. After a while, she finds herself dreaming of the summer holidays and, suddenly, the exam is over. Lin's just half way through her first answer.

Next time, Lin:

- focus on the exam and how important it is for you
- force yourself to concentrate on the job in hand – it'll soon be over
- think of all that holiday time you'll have to spend revising if you fail.

---

brilliant example

You have a paper with four questions. You really like two of them, so you only answer those, doing your very best to make them perfect. The marker gives you a more than respectable 75 per cent for each. Now let's assume you answer all four, but perhaps not so well (because you gave your favourites less time and you weren't confident about the other two). This time, the marker gives you 60 per cent in two and 40 per cent in the other two.

In the first scenario, you'd get a total percentage of 150 which, divided by 4, gives you an average of 37.5 per cent. In the second, the total is 200, an average of 50 per cent.

In other words, concentrate on the two 'good' questions and you probably fail, but do all four questions and you pass.

Be prepared

There are two main aspects to sitting exams. The most important is to have revised and be in a position to remember and use the information relevant to your course and subject. The other is to have taken care of all the seemingly petty things such as registering and, if necessary, paying to sit the exam. It's this logistical aspect we're going to consider now briefly. If you get that right, you can focus on essentials and feel confident in advance that you're in control.

So, confirm the time, date and place of the exam and how long it'll last. The information will be in the course handbook, on a notice board, website or VLE module. It's your duty to get there at the right time, so make a note of the information, double-check it with someone else, and store it safely. On the day, give yourself plenty of time to get there. As soon as you turn over the paper, double-check the rubric (instruction) at the top, just to confirm you're in the right place and it's the right subject.

Make a checklist of what you need to take with you. Our suggestions are:

- writing kit: pens and pencils (plus replacements), ruler, rubber, highlighter(s), correction fluid
- student matriculation (ID) card
- special equipment: calculators, protractor, compass, Walkman or similar for aural exams (but check beforehand that you can use these aids properly), spare batteries
- texts, where allowed for 'open book' exams
- dictionary, if allowed (you'd arrange this beforehand with your department)
- sweets and a drink, if allowed
- clock or watch for timekeeping
- and, if you think it helps, a lucky charm or mascot.

In the exam room

Make a quick check of the rubric at the top of the paper and make sure that the questions are arranged as you expected. Look carefully at every one, ticking the ones you feel confident about or maybe even marking them out of ten to indicate how well you think you can answer them.

With your strategy in mind and the 'ideal' time for each question established, decide which answers, if any, might need more time, or might get you higher marks if you invested a little more time in them. Also note questions which might need less time. Don't be tempted to give what you think may be a good answer too much extra time. After a while, what you're adding to it will be earning fewer marks than you think, so don't take time away from other questions which might earn you more marks for just basic information.

Answer questions in an order that suits you. It doesn't have to be the order they appear in the question paper. Some people prefer to answer 'fact-based' questions first in case they forget details they memorised just before the exam. Others like to answer their 'best' question first, to get a good start, while some opt to do this second or even later, when they feel 'warmed up'. For a question you don't feel happy about, it's probably best to leave it until last. Ideas about it may occur to you during the exam – jot them down as you go along.

 brilliant timesaver

Keep your answer plans relatively simple. Use spider (pattern) diagrams or mind maps to brainstorm.

If you can, use diagrams and tables in your answer. It saves time you might spend on long, difficult explanations. But make sure they're worthwhile and that you refer to them in the text.

Use standard abbreviations, but explain them the first time you use them. This doesn't apply for standard abbreviations such as e.g. (for example), i.e. (that is) and etc. (et cetera).

You've devoted time and energy to creating a strategy, so stick to it. Always keep your eye on the time. It might help to put your watch where you can see it easily on the desk. You may also find it helpful to work out the end times for each question beforehand.

Think about your writing. You want to write quickly but legibly. Ballpoint and liquid gel pens are probably the fastest, but if they let you write too quickly, are you making your script difficult to interpret?

Don't be tempted to waffle or include facts just because you've learned them. Irrelevant material earns no marks and writing it takes time away from another question.

What next?

Prepare at a very early stage ...

... Even before your thoughts turn to revision, look through the course handbook and other information to make sure you have a good idea of how you're going to be assessed. It'll help you to keep your note-taking and reading strategies in tune with your exam strategy.

Create a strategy ...

... for each of your exams. Discuss it with someone else on the course to see what they think of it and how they intend to handle the exam.

If you're in doubt ...

... about any of the assumptions that may lie behind your strategy, ask a tutor.

 **recap**

The right tactics.

The information you need to prepare a strategy.

Examples of unprepared people.

Be prepared.

What to do when you're in the exam room.

Conclusion: You know where you're going

When we called our introduction 'You are here', we were confident it was a correct piece of information. The veracity of the title we've chosen for our conclusion depends on how useful the book has been for you. Our hope is that, at least in some areas (and preferably all), we've given you some hints and ideas that have helped you or will help you to cope with and make the most of the various new experiences life at university brings.

There are specific points we've hammered at quite often – the need to avoid plagiarism and the associated importance of identifying and citing all your sources, the need to keep your academic style impersonal, the importance of making objective statements which you can support rather than offering value judgements, and many others. All of them, and the frequent 'do this', 'do that' things we've said, contribute to helping you to achieve your academic potential in this very special environment.

But there's one theme which it's worth singling out for special reference – the need for you to exercise your critical thinking. That's the skill that will be most useful to you in everything you do. Life is far more than surfaces – if that's all you see and understand, you're missing subtleties, complexities, meanings that can change your appreciation of people, society, art, music, literature, commerce, politics, even nature itself. So get inside your studies and let them get inside you, look more deeply into the materials you encounter, be intellectually curious. Don't accept all the information with which you're bombarded at its face value – unwrap it, question it, challenge it. Don't be content just to know things – understand them. It's not only productive in terms of results – it's fun.

Fun isn't a word that's occurred very often in these pages, but we hope that you'll experience lots of it during your years as a student. It's often hard work and there are always highs and lows, but it gives you a freedom and a context in which to grow and develop in all sorts of directions. If you're now at the beginning of your undergraduate career (whatever age you are), get everything you can out of the opportunities it opens for you. Before you know it, you'll have moved on and it'll be just a vast store of memories. We hope they all turn out to be good ones.